HUMAN RIGHTS AND COMPARATIVE POLITICS

To the memory of the betrayed people who died for their basic human rights in one of the most savage wars of human kind: The Algerian War
(1 November 1954 - 19 March 1962)

Human Rights and Comparative Politics

YOUCEF BOUANDEL
University of Humberside

Dartmouth

Aldershot • Brookfield USA • Singapore • Sydney

Published by
Dartmouth Publishing Company Limited
Gower House
Croft Road
Aldershot
Hants GU11 3HR
England

Dartmouth Publishing Company
Old Post Road
Brookfield
Vermont 05036
USA

British Library Cataloguing in Publication Data
Bouandel, Youcef
    Human rights and comparative politics
    1.Human rights
    I.Title
    323

Library of Congress Cataloging-in-Publication Data
Bouandel, Youcef.
    Human rights and comparative politics / Youcef Bouandel.
        p.   cm.
    Includes bibliographical references and index.
    ISBN 1-85521-874-7
    1. Human rights. 2. Comparative government. I. Title.
    JC571.B672   1997
    323--dc21   96-39519
                                                                                CIP

ISBN 1 85521 874 7

Printed in Great Britain by the Ipswich Book Company, Suffolk

Contents

List of tables and figures

Acknowledgements

I have incurred many debts in writing this book. Stephen White has been a tireless supervisor whose advice, comments and continuous moral support have been valuable throughout my years of research. Paul Heywood and Derek Urwin both provided useful comments on the original version of this book. Many thanks should also go to Gaele and Olive for their editing skills and to Chris and Fethi for their computing expertise.

I am particularly indebted to the department of politics, the University of Glasgow, for its generous financial support to assist field work in New York, to the Faculty of Social Sciences for the Postgraduate Scholarship for the 1990-91 academic year, without this work would never have been finished and to the Social Sciences Award Committee whose award enabled me to attend a study programme at the United Nations Office in Geneva.

I am also much in debt to M. Staunton, former director of the British Section of Amnesty International, Professor R. Higgins, former member of the Human Rights Committee, Dr. J. Pace, Chief, Research Studies and Prevention of Discrimination, Centre for Human Rights, Geneva and Dr. J. Ryan of Freedom House, New York, for giving up their valuable time to answer my questions. The responsibility of any shortcomings in this work, however, rests entirely with me.

Last, but far from least, I am grateful to my friends Fethi, Greg, Olive and Peter for their constant encouragement and for making my stay enjoyable both in Glasgow and Hull; to my mother and sisters whose endless love, support and sacrifice have made it all possible.

Introduction

Human rights is a central concept in political science, yet it is still poorly understood. It is a concept very much contested not only between East and West but also between developed and developing countries. It has received unprecedented attention since the Second World War. Prior to that, the issue was absent from the political agenda. Almost every country violated human rights: to name just a few, discrimination on racial grounds was common practice in the United States; the maintenance of colonies by France and the United Kingdom and the denial of minority rights under totalitarian dictatorships in Spain and the former Soviet Union. Apart from the recognition of the need to abolish the slave trade - expressed in the Vienna Congress in 1815 and the conclusion of a treaty to abolish it at the Brussels Conference in 1890 - and the humanitarian laws expressed in documents such as the Geneva and the Hague conventions that apply in times of war only, there was no document which restricted states in their behaviour towards their citizens. These treatments - abuse of human rights in this instance - did fall within the domestic jurisdiction of states and any intervention would have been seen as interference in the internal affairs of the country.

However, this state of affairs changed drastically soon after the Second World War ended, and the issue of human rights has since become very significant. It takes an event of some kind for a particular issue to come to the forefront and to raise people's awareness of it, and the Second World War provided the catalyst for human rights. The unspeakable atrocities committed by the *Third Reich* against Jews, communists, and homosexuals, helped by the negative attitudes and appeasement policies adopted by some allied governments towards Hitler and his expansion policies, led to a new vision that some basic rights should be respected. Towards the beginning of the War, when action was still possible, the allies had turned a blind eye to what was happening, and to a certain extent had, indirectly, 'helped' Hitler in his systematic massacre. The United States, for example, not only denied refuge to some of those who fled, but did not enter the war until Pearl Harbour was attacked.

In the aftermath of the War, and after the Allies dealt with those associated with war crimes during the Nuremberg trials, human rights became an issue of international concern. It received a further boost with the establishment of the United Nations whose Charter, in its preamble, states that 'disregard and contempt for human rights have resulted in barbarous acts'. It 'reaffirm[s] faith in fundamental human rights' and according to article 1 encouraged 'respect for human rights and fundamental freedoms for all'. The efforts of the United Nations resulted in the adoption, on 10 December 1948, (celebrated as international human rights day) of the first international document on this subject, the Universal Declaration of Human Rights. It was by no means a binding document, but set a 'common standard of achievement'. Nonetheless, it represented a great leap forward in the politics of human rights, and a solid basis upon which further development was carried out.

Although the end of the War opened the way to discussions on human rights, it also led to a sharp ideological division with the raising of the 'iron curtain' which separated communist countries from liberal democracies; an era known as the 'Cold War'. In addition, the decade which followed saw the emergence of many 'Third World' countries as a result of the disintegration of traditional empires. As a result, Afro-Asian countries became the majority in the United Nations Commission on Human Rights and put forward their interests. Thus, the issue of had become the subject of mutual accusation and vigorously contested between the East and West and developed and developing countries alike. The discussions that took place within the Commission, and most importantly the documents which followed from these discussions, reflected deep divisions between the main actors. While liberal democracies favoured civil and political rights, communist countries stressed economic and social rights, and 'Third World' countries were more concerned with issues of self-determination. When it came to the adoption of binding documents, it was no coincidence that the formerly Western-dominated Commission found it very difficult to come to a compromise. Most of the 1950s and early 1960s were spent searching for a formula which would satisfy everybody. Each party was pressing for the inclusion of a particular set of rights which corresponded to their ideological standpoint. The discussion eventually ended with the adoption, in 1966, of two separate

international covenants: the first on civil and political rights and the second
on economic, social and cultural rights. These were binding documents and
came into force in 1976 when they were ratified by 35 countries. Together
with the Universal Declaration of Human Rights they make the International
Bill of Rights.

While these divisions existed, human rights were systematically
violated by every bloc alike. While the majority of 'third world' countries
were living under military dictatorships, the United States was extremely
active not only in supporting oppressive regimes throughout the world just
because they claimed to be anti-Communist, but was involved in
overthrowing democratically-elected governments: Guatemala in 1954 and
most importantly the democratically elected government of Salvador Allende
in Chile in 1973, provide the most uncontested examples. The United States
has also been active in its mistreatment of dissidents: the treatment of
'communists' during the 1950s. The human rights record of the former
communist countries was anything but exemplary. The former Soviet Union,
for instance, did not hesitate to intervene militarily to crush reformers in
Hungary in 1956 and in the former Czechoslovakia in 1968. It should,
however, be borne in mind that since the mid 1980s, date of the election of
Gorbachev to the post of General-Secretary of the Communist Party of the
former Soviet Union, there has been a relaxation in the attitudes of both the
Eastern and Western blocs. With the collapse of communism and the end of
the 'Cold War', the issue is no longer the subject of mutual accusation, and
instead a spirit of co-operation has emerged.

Since the 1950s the issue of human rights has been consolidated in the
political agenda, and a great number of individuals and institutions have been
concerned with it. Organisations which are concerned with human rights,
such as Amnesty International, Freedom House, and Article 19 have been
mushrooming, though still overwhelmingly concentrated in the West. In
1973, the American Congress recommended that the human rights record of
the receiving countries should be taken into account when economic and
military aid are delivered. Two years later, in 1975, at least on the surface,
this link became mandatory. Different political leaders, for instance Jimmy
Carter in the United States, have championed human rights, and made them
the basis upon which foreign policy should be determined. Other
governments, such as the Netherlands and Norway, have followed suit in
adopting policies of linking aid to human rights.

The central thesis

Research on human rights falls within two camps: the first holds the view that an attempt to measure human rights can be very problematic since there are no valid grounds for measurement, and points to the problems associated with any exercise of this kind. The UN Human Rights Committee, for instance, established under Article 28 of the International Covenant on Civil and Political Rights, abstains from any measurement of this kind and does not produce any ranking of countries in terms of their human rights performance. This neutral stance was criticised and led to calls for more 'objective' measures of assessing human rights practices. Such measures, it has been suggested, may be achieved through 'quantification' of the phenomenon. The call for quantification is championed not only by students and organisations in the field, such as the late Charles Humana and the independent New York-based organisation Freedom House, but also by some Western governments whose foreign policies, especially those of economic and military aids, are at least, on the surface, related to respect for human rights. The US State Department, for instance, has been producing regular assessments of international human rights in the form of the Country Report on Human Rights, published since 1976. The quantification, and therefore the ranking of countries in terms of their human rights performance, becomes a very significant exercise in so far as it influences policy makers at a time when governments have increasingly been using respect for human rights as a condition for their aid policies.

This book provides both an argument and case studies. Its general aim, in the first instance, is to review the literature available on human rights, taking into account the different perceptions. The concepts involved are still poorly understood, although there is a broad measure of agreement that they should be associated with such classic freedoms such as freedom of expression and association. There has still been less agreement about the attempts that have been made to measure democracy and freedom on a cross-national basis. This book, in the ensuing chapters, seeks to answer the following questions: (i) Can human rights be measured? (ii) Still more so, can they be measured on a cross-national basis? (iii) Can countries be ranked on the basis of their performance? (iv) What variables might be employed in a comparative analysis of this kind? (v) Is there agreement about the ranking of countries that emerges from inquiries of this kind?

The structure of the book

Human Rights and Comparative Politics tries to assess the extent to which different inquiries have successfully dealt with the subject. This will make it possible to pinpoint the difficulties that may arise whenever an attempt to measure human rights on a cross-national basis is undertaken. This book is divided into three parts. The definition and content of human rights are not yet universally agreed upon; differences in political ideologies, religions and the variety of historical events have made it difficult to secure general agreement on such issues. Furthermore, the United Nations has increased its list of what can be considered as human rights. Thus, the first part of this book deals with the issues of definition and content. And in order to best cover the significant issues that are involved, this part is divided into three chapters.

The first chapter discusses the concept of human rights in general. It reviews the literature available from the Greek philosophers up to the adoption of the Universal Declaration of Human Rights in 1948, and the Covenant that followed in 1966. This includes different philosophies and religions that have had some impact on the shaping of human rights as they are known today. The second chapter develops the question of rival conceptions of human rights. It will particularly stress the contest between East and West. It is generally agreed that these two groups of states have had two completely different understandings of what human rights are or cover. Such a clash made an agreed definition even more difficult to attain. It should be pointed out, however, that the discrepancy between these rival interpretations has become narrower since the mid and late 1980s, after the different reform programmes introduced in the former Communist countries, and after the collapse of communist rule in the former Soviet Union and Eastern Europe. The third chapter investigates the 'new rights' which have emerged after many 'Third World' countries achieved independence and the changes that the world experienced over the last two decades. These rights are usually referred to as the 'third generation' or as Philip Alston calls them 'rights of solidarity'. This chapter concludes with a brief discussion of relativism versus universalism; a theme particularly contested in any debate on human rights.

After this preliminary, but necessary, discussion, part two of this book examines at length some of the work that monitors human rights or that has attempted to measure human rights and democracy on a cross-national basis.

In this connection the case studies chosen are thought to provide the best possible picture of the difficulties and the limits of any exercise aimed at measuring human rights and democracy on the one hand, and the obstacles one faces when human rights are examined. Thus this part comprises:

Chapter four which examines Amnesty International, one of the most respected non-governmental organisations. Although it adopts a very narrow definition of human rights, its findings are nonetheless very authoritative. It will discuss the organisation and its work, and the extent to which it succeeds in carrying out its mandate. Some of the issues which are relevant to this discussion were raised directly with the staff at the British Section of Amnesty in London. The fifth chapter examines the work of the UN Human Rights Committee set up in 1976 under the provisions of article 18 of the International Covenant on Civil and Political Rights, which tries to help countries enhance their human rights records by providing expertise and advice. Its work, although not comparative in nature, offers a basis of comparison between countries and their efforts to take into account the Committee's remarks and bring their laws within the bounds of the provisions of the International Covenant on Civil and Political Rights. Data relating to the work of the Committee was gathered through interviewing Professor R. Higgins, a former member of this Committee and by watching the Committee at work during several sessions. Chapter six examines the work of the late Charles Humana, a British journalist, who developed a methodology whereby human rights can, at least in principle, be measured. Although his work appeared in 1983 and in its second edition in 1986, it has become a matter of public controversy since the publication of the Human Freedom Index by the United Nations Development Program in June 1991. Chapter seven concentrates on two studies which have attempted to measure democracy: this includes the work of both Robert Dahl and Kenneth Bollen. The cross-national study of democracy is bound to create some controversy concerning the variables chosen and the methods applied. In chapter eight a lengthy discussion focuses on the work of another organisation which is concerned with human freedoms: the independent New York-based organisation Freedom House. The chapter scrutinises the Survey it publishes and the different ranking of countries that the Survey contains. Some of its data was gathered through a direct interview of Dr Joseph Ryan, the Survey's Director.

This book concludes, in part three, with a discussion of the extent to which political scientists and the organisations considered have successfully conceptualised the problem of human rights, and whether the task of comparing human rights on a cross-national basis is possible. It also indicates some of the elements that might form part of the agenda of the comparative study of human rights in the future.

Breaking new grounds

This book, through a combination of theoretical and empirical research tries to advance beyond the available literature on, and approaches to, the subject. Its main focus is measuring human rights and how political systems can be compared based on the extent to which they violate human rights. Human rights, as a subject of study, falls within the disciplines of law and international relations. The reasons for this are easily discernible. To begin with, conventions and treaties which regulate how governments treat their citizens are studied from a legal point of view. Similarly, committees and commissions, and most importantly, bodies which attempt to remedy any abuse of human rights, such as the European Court for Human Rights, involve the practice of law. In International relations, the issue becomes relevant whenever relations between countries are discussed. Abuse or respect for human rights may determine a government's action vis-à-vis another. Applications to join the European Union, for example, are carefully scrutinised and can be rejected on, among others, human rights grounds. Turkey, for instance, provides a good example of a country whose human rights record has been used to reject its application. In the field of politics, research on human rights has been largely dominated by political theorists, and many academics have devoted their research to definitions, content, origins and foundations of human rights. Comparativists, on the other hand, in general have been reluctant to devote their research to this particular area. This book endeavours to present a theoretical as well as an empirical contribution to the cross-national measurement of human rights and democracy.

This book is the only attempt, as far as the author in aware, to look at the major attempts to measure human rights on a cross-national basis. While it looks at these particular case studies, it does not overlook the other side of the argument which stipulates that human rights are not necessarily measurable. This book should be of interest to a number of audiences. It should make a contribution to the on going debate about human rights and be of particular interest to students of comparative politics, law and international relations since it overlaps these disciplines. Finally, it should also be of interest to activists in the field.

Part One: The philosophy of human rights

[T]he more the fight for human rights gains popularity, the more it loses any concrete content, becoming a kind of universal stance for everyone towards anything, a kind of energy that turns all human desire into rights. The world has become man's right and everything in it has become a right: the desire for love a right to love, the desire for rest a right to rest, the desire for friendship a right to friendship, the desire to exceed the speed limit the right to exceed the speed limit, the desire for happiness the right to happiness, the desire to publish a book the right to publish a book, the desire to shout in the street in the middle of the night the right to shout in the street (Kundera, 1991, 153).

While it is impossible for any single book to cover the different aspects of human rights, the first part of this book attempts to map the general debate on the subject and provides an overview of the developments in this area. It is divided into three chapters. In chapter one I look at the historical background to human rights and examine it on three separate headings: origins, definitions and contents and briefly comment on their strengths and weaknesses. In Chapter two, which follows from the theoretical discussion in the first, I look at how human rights have been contested between East and West, and I chronicle the different changes that took place, in Eastern Europe, after the arrival of Gorbachev to power in the former Soviet Union. The period after 1985 saw a 'rapprochement' between the two blocs when the former communist countries took particular steps in the area of political rights and civil liberties. Chapter three I look at what is generally referred to as the 'third generation' of human rights or as Philip Alston calls them 'the rights of solidarity'. They are a different set of rights in that they are not individual rights and cannot necessarily be invoked against a particular government. The part concludes with the two theoretical challenges to the whole approach to human rights, namely, universalism and cultural relativism.

1 Human rights: a historical background

[T]he best reason for asserting so bluntly that there are no such rights is indeed of precisely the same type as the best reason we possess for asserting that there are no witches, and the best reason which we possess for asserting that there are no unicorns; every attempt to give good reasons for believing that there are such rights has failed (MacIntyre, 1981, 67). ⟩ Implying that there are no rights,

none of the so-called rights of man goes beyond egoistic man, man as he is in civil society, namely withdrawn behind his private interests and whims and separated from the community. (Marx, in Waldren (ed.), 1987, 147).

The idea of human rights as it is known to us today is a product of a process that can be traced back as far as the Greek and the Roman philosophers. Different religions, cultures, philosophies and circumstances have made significant contributions towards the understanding and the broadening of such a concept. 'In international politics', Rosenbaum argues that 'differences of culture, national traditions, and political interest must be counted for their impact on the conception of human rights' (1980, 7). This made the definition as well as the origins of the idea quite a wide issue upon which consensus and agreement among scholars has yet to be reached.

In this chapter an attempt will be made to clarify different issues surrounding the concept of human rights. Having said that, it does not automatically mean that there will be no disagreements on the issue after this work. The aim is to show the reader that human rights is one of the most fiercely contested issues in politics. Many scholars have tried to define human rights in terms of their content on the one hand, and their origins and universal character on the other. Furthermore, I shall look at the philosophies that have had a strong influence on existing definitions of human rights.

Considering these facts the approach in this chapter will be historical; mainly to review available literature on the subject and highlight disagreements among scholars. In the course of doing so, the concept of human rights, as will be seen later, keeps 'stretching' to include different rights that were not known at certain historical points in the evolution of society. For example when declarations of the rights of man were adopted by the French, they meant men and not women; (a point very much criticised by feminists and in French reference is still made to *'les droits de l'homme'* - *men's* rights - when reference is made to *human* rights); economic and social rights, apart from that of property were not known at all; voting was based on property and class and was only extended to women after the turn of this century. Therefore, it is proposed that human rights should be looked at as a gradual and an evolutionary process. Although the concept of human rights is relatively new, the idea however, according to Paine, can be 'traced back to the creation of man itself' (Morsink, 1984, 311-12), and most scholars trace it back to the Greek and Roman philosophers. Weston argues that: '[M]ost students of human rights trace the historical origins of the concept to ancient Greece and Rome, where it was closely tied to the premodern natural law doctrine of Greek stoicism' (Weston, 1984, 258).

My main argument here is not to state which of the theories is true and which is not, as much as to state that some forms of human rights were known to man very early in his development. Greek philosophers spoke of many freedoms that are essential today, and Roman cities witnessed some practices which are at the heart of today's ideas of human rights. Freedom of movement, for example, was known to the Romans and, 'at the time of the empire', Cranston states that 'persons from foreign extractions made up almost ninety per cent of the population of Rome itself' (Cranston, 1973, 33). However, practices of slavery and serfdom were found to be legitimate.

The origins of human rights

It is difficult to come to a general agreement concerning the origins and justification of human rights. No theory of human rights will ever achieve acceptance, as different philosophers 'within one nation, much less in multicultural world society, have never agreed on where rights come from and what are rights properly speaking' (Forsythe, 1989b, 160). The situation is made even worse by the fact that many theories, as the quotes at the beginning of this chapter suggest, actually reject the idea and the existence of human rights. Gewirth, for instance, states that: 'Kant, Kierkegaard, Nietzsche, Mill and Marx, who hold, respectively, that the criteria for having rights consist in or are determined by reason, religion, power, utility and economic class or history' (Gewirth, 1982, 42).

Human rights are held by many writers to ground the source, and therefore justification, of religion. Christianity, Judaism and Islam, the major religions in the world, have some aspects of human rights. Rozier, for example, argues the Catholic sources for human rights (1989, 53-66). Akroun, on the other hand, stresses that what is important is to 'demonstrate that Islam, as a religion, is not only open to proclaiming and defending human rights, but the 'Quran' words of God, defined these rights at the beginning of the Seventh Century, well before the revolutions in the West' (1989, 25). (For an account of the Jewish origins of human rights see Kaplan, 1989, 15-24.)

These claims, however, were much criticised. What religions have brought are not rights but 'mere duties'. Donnelly, for instance, stresses that there are no human rights, as they are now understood, in Islam. He states that '[T]hese alleged human rights, however prove to be only duties to rulers and individuals not held by anyone' (1989, 51). Most of the 'rights' proclaimed in Islam, or even in the ten commandments, were originally perceived as duties. The right to life, and of freedom of expression, are mere duties not to kill and to speak the truth. However, what is important, is that religions played a significant role in the shaping of the concept of human rights. Although these 'rights' did not satisfy many who advocate that what religions brought were only duties, they helped to safeguard some of the 'rights' and the human dignity that human rights seek to secure. Furthermore, by rejecting these 'rights' on the grounds that they are mere duties, Donnelly seems to be contradicting himself. He states that '[R]ights and duties are two facets of the same picture. Whoever demands a right to liberty has to respect a similar right in others which circumscribes his right to personal liberty very considerably' (1985, 77). Thus, if rights and duties are basically two different names for the same relation, or are two sides to the same coin, then it would be safe to conclude that what religions really brought were rights? If A (the duty bearer) has a duty to B (the agent who benefits from this duty) as regards Y (the object of the duty), then an argument that B has a right to Y would make sense. Therefore, what is one's duty can be somebody's right, and vice versa.

Following from this, human rights are also depicted as a new version of natural right, and are seen as God-given (Weston, 1984, 257). In other words, the concept clearly specifies that human rights find their source in nature, rights held by humans by the mere fact of being human. Macfarlane, for instance, argues that '[T]he concept of human rights emerged out of the much earlier conception of natural right, which initially was no more than a derivative element in the medieval Christian doctrine of natural law' (1985, 5). In his view, natural rights were the moral expectations men had and should behave towards others.

The natural theory was developed first by John Locke, who is seen as the source of the doctrine of human rights. He stressed that men have natural rights to life, liberty and property. A century later, Thomas Jefferson rejected the right to property and stressed that of the pursuit of happiness. Men, in Locke's society, are rational and capable of action. In other words, they pursue happiness and look for self-preservation. Such natural rights are enjoyed by everybody and because they find their origin in nature entail respect by others. However, when man entered a civil society, the need for a new structure for society was created. Thus, man entered into a 'social contract' with the state. Weston argues that:

> Humankind surrendered to the state only the right to enforce these natural rights, not the rights themselves; and that the state's failure to secure these reserved rights (the state itself being under social contract to safeguard the interests of its members) gives rise to a right to responsible popular revolution (1984, 258).

Thus, Locke used his individualistic theory to challenge the divine right of the kings, and to argue the supremacy of the parliament. The idea behind the social contract is that the two parties should fulfil what they have agreed upon. Each party has undertaken some obligations that should be respected. The state is a result of a social contract which would create the conditions for these natural rights to be realised. And because these rights find their origins in nature and not in the state, the latter cannot take them away. In other words, the legitimacy of the state depends of the extent to which it is able to defend and enforce these rights. When it fails to protect such rights, then a popular, responsible revolution is legitimised.

However, if man has a natural right to do anything, then it follows that nobody has the duty or the responsibility of respecting others' natural rights. This point was made by Hobbes, who argued that 'the right of all men to all things, is in effect no better than if no man had right to do anything. For there is a little use of benefit of the right of man hath, when another as strong or stronger than himself, hath right to the same' (Macpherson, quoted in Raphael, 1967, 3). In such a state of natural rights, in the Hobbesian sense, rights would hardly be respected, and any attempt to enforce their respect would be self-driven.

Obviously, although they both derive from natural law, the two theories differ. Locke sees men as sociable and rational; their rights are effective and everybody in society respects them. Hobbes, however, sees society as a jungle where the strongest dictates his will. By nature man tends to transfer some power of the others to himself. By the same token, whenever two interests are in conflict one always tends to resist such a transfer. His model was an irrational individual, with the strongest keeping the rest in order. In effect, he was advocating total monarchy or statism.

Both Hobbes's absolute theory and Locke's limited one are rooted in the theory of natural rights. Their main concern was the individual. This individualism influenced the different events and philosophies in the Eighteenth Century. The English, French and American Revolutions undoubtedly laid the foundations for the emergence of the concept of human rights. Moreover, it is customary to group human rights into three categories in accordance with the slogans proclaimed by French Revolution: *Liberte*, *Egalite*, *Fraternite*. The influence of the natural rights theory could perhaps be seen in the American Declaration of Independence (1776), which states that 'all men are created equal, that they are endowed by their Creator with certain inalienable rights, that among those are life, liberty and the pursuit of happiness' (Weston, 1984, 260).

The natural right theory was not immune from criticism, and was challenged as a source for human rights. Philosophers such as Burke,

Bentham and Marx, among others, simply rejected it. Everybody who is concerned with human rights or political theory is familiar with Bentham's savage attack on natural law. He argues that '[R]ight is the child of law, from real law come real right, but from imaginary laws, from "law of nature", come imaginary rights. Natural rights is simple nonsense; natural and imprescriptible rights (an American phrase) rhetorical nonsense, nonsense upon stilts' (Weston, 1984, 261). Green, on the other hand, gave three justifications for rejecting the natural rights theory: the assumption that individuals have rights which derived from nature and not from society; that these rights can be held against society; and its detachment of rights from the corresponding duties individuals owe their society (Freeden, 1991, 20).

Apart from religions and the natural law theory, the rapid changes brought by with the industrial revolution, leads Donnelly to suggest that the concept of human rights can be traced back to the emergence of capitalist markets and modern society in Western Europe. He asks 'why there were no human rights in traditional non-western and Western societies?' and believes that '[B]ecause prior to the creation of capitalist market economies and modern states, the problems that human rights seek to address, the particular violations of human dignity that they seek to prevent, either did not exist or was widely perceived to be central social problems' (1989, 64).

The criticism of socialist thinkers such as Engels and Marx is particularly important to the development of human rights. Undoubtedly the clash between the two main doctrines had a great impact on the understanding of human rights and their codification by the United Nations in international documents. Rosenbaum rightly argues that the 'main contribution to human rights theory in the nineteenth century, and practically to the idea of freedom and equality, must be appraised with respect to the clash between (liberal) individualism and (socialist) collectivism. Whereas the liberal critique was largely directed toward social change within capitalist framework, the Marxist critique advocated the abolition of capitalism in favour of economic collectivism' (1980, 20).

I shall not go far in highlighting the differences between the two approaches, as this will be dealt with in more detail in the next chapter. However, the point that needs to be stressed is that such a clash added a new dimension to the understanding of human rights. Socialists stressed the need to suppress a number of individual rights to achieve higher rights for mankind as a whole. To Marx, individual rights were nothing but abstract, bourgeois rights. He recognised that civil and political rights are meaningless unless economic and social rights are provided. As a result of the provision of economic and social rights people will be able to take advantage of civil and political rights. The unit of analysis should be moved from the individual to the collective or the community.

According to the Marxist view, what people really want are concrete rights, which can only be achieved under socialism. According to the dialectics of change in society, socialism is a further step forward in the development of mankind, a superior stage to capitalism. Such a transformation will eventually lead to a classless society: Communism. Therefore, a new structure for the society is needed and a break from actual socio-economic conditions is of paramount importance for this transformation. The abolition of private property, collective ownership of the means of production and the centrally planned economy, in the Marxist view, are able to safeguard such ideals that human rights try to protect. By removing class conflict, there will be no other obstacles for the development of mankind. Given the socio-economic conditions of a classless society, human rights would no longer be addressed. According to Marx, human rights are determined by historical events and social class. Since society is divided into two classes, a state of imperfection which justifies the constant class struggle, any talk of equal, inalienable and universal rights is meaningless. The individual's place in the society's class structure determines what rights he enjoys. The realisation of these rights would have to await the achievement of communism (Mochan, 1975, 41). The individual would enjoy rights as a member of the society or the collective.

There is no doubt about the impact of Marxist thought and its criticism of liberalism, on the issue of human rights. The adoption of such an ideology by different countries in the Twentieth Century has opened up the debate, once more, not only about the origins of human rights, but about what they really are. The debate which preceded the adoption of the first international instrument on human rights, the Universal Declaration of Human Rights, provides the best example of the differences in opinions and on what should be included. As a result, a compromise was reached and unlike any previous declarations, the Universal Declaration included provisions for economic, social and cultural rights. A close look at its articles show that the first twenty one deal with civil and political rights, and Articles 22 to 29 deal with economic, social and cultural ones.

Such an inclusion undoubtedly reflected the views of those who believed in these latter, more 'concrete' rights. There were long debates in the

United Nations' Third Committee to agree on the final draft of the Declaration. When it came to its adoption, it is interesting to note that both the former Soviet Union and Saudi Arabia were among the countries which abstained from voting. The delegate of the former Soviet Union, for instance, Lazreg notes, 'considered that the draft did not satisfy the three conditions which were indispensable to the completion of the Declaration, namely; a guarantee of basic freedoms for all, with due regard to the sovereignty of states; a guarantee that human rights could be exercised with due regard to the particular economic, social and national circumstances prevailing in each country; and a definition of the duties of the citizens to their country, their people and their state' (quoted in Pollis and Schwab, 1979, 36). The Saudis, on the other hand, believed that the provisions of the Declaration have been known to them, because of their religion, for over fourteen centuries. They also argued that the Declaration seeks to apply a Western model in a very different social and cultural environment.

However, when it came to the adoption of a legally binding instrument for human rights, it was soon realised that a single instrument could not be achieved. The ideological divide between liberal democracies and the former communist countries was impossible to bridge. Each was pressing for the inclusion of a specific set of rights. The divide can be clearly seen in the adoption of two different covenants in 1966: one on civil and political rights, the other on social, economic and cultural rights. They both came into force a decade later (1976) after thirty five states had ratified each of them. Moreover, the period after the War saw the membership of the United Nations increase as a result of movements of independence in the 'Third World' which led to different demands. As a result, a series of international human rights instruments were adopted, whereby the issue of human rights came to represent more than civil and political rights and social and economic rights.

Definition of human rights

Having discussed the historical setting of the development of the concept of human rights, a definition should be attempted. Like many concepts in politics, such as freedom and democracy, human rights is very difficult to define. I shall try to give different definitions and will develop them further in the sections that follow.

Most scholars (Cranston, 1962; Donnelly, 1985), suggest that the term human rights is generally taken to mean a twentieth-century name for natural rights. Donnelly goes on to state that 'Human rights are those held simply by virtue of being a person. To have a human right one need not be or do anything special, other than to be born a human being' (1985, 8). However, this definition seems to be inadequate for two reasons: firstly, not every right held by a human being is automatically a human right: contractual rights, to give just one example. Donnelly himself acknowledges this fact (ibid.). Second, it seems that the definition above excludes any action. In the sense that right is a claim. Human rights, as they are known today, are a result of claims or revendications against governments of a group of people. This definition excludes the claim element which presuppose the implementation of these claims and protection of these rights. Levine, for instance, rightly argues that 'in its original sense, a right is a claim advanced by an individual or group enforceable by law' (Quoted in Rosenbaum, 1980, 137).

Having established the fact that a right, as a human right, is a claim in itself, the concept as a whole has become clearer. While the definition implies that human right are both 'human' and 'rights', none of the concepts are easy to define. The word 'rights', according to Donnelly, 'encompasses at least two concepts of great political and moral significance. On the one hand, 'right' refers to moral righteousness, as in 'it is just not the right thing to do'! On the other hand 'right' may refer to entitlements, as in the claim 'I have a right to'. This second sense of entitlement distinguishes rights, as human or otherwise (1985, 3).

Such a distinction between these two kinds of rights helps to identify where human rights stand. In this division, Donnelly suggests that human rights are rights in the political sense of the concept. They are entitlements for everybody. The sentence 'I have the right' is certainly stronger than the moral version of, for instance, 'what you did was right'. Rights in the moral sense cannot be seen as human rights according to Donnelly's distinction. Let us try to imagine a situation where someone has just helped a hungry man by giving him enough money to buy his food, or donated blood to save a dying patient at a hospital bed. From a moral point of view, what the person did was 'right', nonetheless, does the hungry man or the dying person have the 'right' to the person's money or blood? From a moral viewpoint, the hungry man had a moral right to the person's money. Nonetheless, the claim is even stronger in the case of the patient. It might be argued that depriving the patient of that blood is actually killing him, or deliberately letting the person die.

While Donnelly distinguished between political and moral rights and concluded that human rights are political ones, Cranston, on the other hand claims that they are moral rights. He distinguishes two types of rights: legal and moral rights (in Raphael, 1967, 47-9). Within the category of legal rights, he identifies five types: (a) general positive rights, (b) traditional right and liberties, (c) nominal 'legal' rights, positive rights, (d) liberties, and immunities of a limited class of person and (e) positive rights, liberties, and immunities of a single person. To him, none of the above types of rights can be said to constitute human rights since they are limited in scope; either they deal with a person and a privileged group or with people under a given jurisdiction. In the second type, i.e., moral rights, the types identified are: (a) moral rights of one person only, (b) moral rights of anyone in a particular situation, and (c) moral rights of all people in all situations. Since the definition is that they are rights by the mere fact of being human, it is no surprise to see that human rights in Cranston's division fall within the last category. He concludes that 'The place which human rights occupy in my classification is readily understood. Human rights are a form of moral rights, and they differ from other moral rights in being the rights of all people at all times and in all situations' (ibid., 49). Because they are universal, we should expect them to be few in number and generalised in their formulation.

The two scholars differ in their classification of human rights: the former sees them as political, the latter as moral. If the second classification, which seems fairly adequate, is taken into account, more questions need to be asked. If human rights are the moral rights of all people in all situations, then are they rights in the sense of claims or entitlements, or are they duties and obligations? If they are moral, as Cranston suggests, how can we speak about the universality of morals? It is common knowledge that religions, circumstances and traditions play a significant role in the shaping of the morals and the conduct of people in a particular country. Universality based on morals is accordingly a difficult proposition to argue convincingly.

Professor Raphael also distinguishes two types of rights; of recipience and of action, and concludes that human rights are rights of recipience (1967, 65-9). To him, a human right is a positive right: it must mean receiving something, and is a right in relation to others.

However, all these definitions and classifications do not so far speak about the implementation and protection of human rights. Freeden claims that: '... a human right is a conceptual device, expressed in linguistic form, that assigns priority to certain human or social attributes regarded as essential to the adequate functioning of human being; that is intended to serve as a protective capsule for those attributes; and that appeals for a deliberate action to ensure such a protection' (1991, 7).

Once again this definition does not satisfy the questions asked at the beginning of this chapter. Here one is faced with a question of choices and priorities as a protective measure towards the proper functioning of a human being. This definition seems to suggest more questions than it provides answers. Although it provides the reader with a new element in the definition of human rights, it opens up the possibility that human rights are not rights enjoyed by everybody by the mere fact of being human. The choice among 'certain human or social attributes' is a vague one, and does not automatically lead to the same demands. This definition suggests that human rights depend on the circumstances and the choices made and the priorities assigned at one particular period of time in a given country.

What is quite clear from the discussion above is that there is no precise and universally agreed definition of the concept of human rights. In a multicultural world, with differences in beliefs, traditions and in economic conditions, what seems to be a human right for someone does not seem to be so for someone else. Mochan rightly concludes that 'more recent human rights theorists have argued that they must be defined in terms of some desired ideal of what human communities should be. Here again in the ideal terms of which the rights are to be defined emerges from human desires, preference, or choice and cannot be identified as true or correct. For as long as their source is a desire or choice without a standard of right and wrong, these rights are not objective but arbitrary, even if widely accepted' (1975, 42). This can be best understood by considering the content of human rights.

The content of human rights

It was suggested elsewhere in this chapter that the most fruitful approach to human rights is an historical one and that rights should be regarded as an evolutionary process. Different philosophies and circumstances have added new rights to the original list which most scholars refer to as the 'first generation' of human rights, i.e., civil and political rights. Economic, social and cultural rights, which have come to be known as the 'second generation', have emerged out of the writings of socialist thinkers such as Saint-Simon, Marx and Engels. For the time being I shall limit myself to these two types of rights only. It must be borne in mind that there is another category or generation of human rights, which will be the focus of the third chapter.

Whenever human rights are discussed, it is common that economic and social rights take second place. It is civil and political rights that first come to mind. When a government is criticised for its human rights record, be it by another country or by an organisation like Amnesty International for instance, it is because it failed to safeguard political rights and civil liberties. Whether human rights should include both generations or just the first is a question which has created a lot of controversy. Rosenbaum argues that '[P]hilosophers generally agree that civil and political rights must be counted as human rights. However, there is a basic controversy about whether socio-economic rights, or, as they sometimes called, welfare rights, are to account as human rights' (1980, 30). Scholars, including Cranston, have argued that the second generation cannot possibly be accepted as human rights and its inclusion hinders the protection of the traditional human rights (1973, 65). As such there can be no definitive conclusion as to whether or not economic, social and cultural rights are human rights. The situation is made more difficult by the debate on the universality of human rights. Moreover, the enjoyment of economic and social rights depends very much on how prosperous a country is. In other words, the enjoyment of the second generation of human rights depends on the wealth of a country, and how able it is to provide for such 'rights'.

Such arguments assign civil and political rights to the category of human rights whereas economic, social and cultural rights do not qualify. The latter's scope is narrower since they deal with nationals of a particular state only. In other words, they are not human rights, but citizens' rights. People have to qualify to enjoy them. Cranston argues that 'if we may continue to call these social and economic rights which Babeuf and Tom Paine were claiming the droits du citoyens, it may help to make clear that these droits du citoyens (in a rather special sense) belong to a logical category which is distinct from that of the droits de l'homme, or natural rights, or human rights traditionally (and, as I maintain correctly) understood as "political and civil rights"' (quoted in Raphael, 1967, 98).

Apart from this objection to the inclusion of the second generation into the category of human rights, Cranston has developed a three-fold test upon which the authenticity of human rights is judged (1963, 40-42). According to him, a right has to be tested for three characteristics in order to judge whether the right in question is a human right or not. These tests are:

Practicability

Cranston sees that it is absurd to claim something as a right if it cannot actually be exercised. Can governments be asked to provide something they are unable to? This analysis leads directly to the material question, discussed above, concerning how wealthy a country is. It is practically impossible for certain 'rights' to be secured for everybody in less prosperous societies.

Securing civil and political rights can be done by simply establishing judicial guarantees which would eventually safeguard these rights. The rights to life, freedom of movement and of thought, for instance, depend on governments' will, whereas economic, social and cultural rights are for certain categories of people only and depend very much on the material conditions of every country. The most popular argument against the inclusion of economic and social rights is 'the right to rest and leisure, including reasonable limitation of working hours and periodic holidays with pay' provided for by Article 24 of the Universal Declaration of Human Rights. This example suggests that such rights are only limited to working people. These rights do not embrace the population as a whole and therefore cannot be considered as human rights. Apart from the fact that their achievement is dependent on the material resources of the country, it might be argued further that these rights are only enjoyed by certain members of a society, i.e., nationals, or peoples within one category such as workers. The enjoyment of these rights does not extend beyond the borders of the state to include everybody.

Up till now, there is not much ground for disagreement with Cranston. Obviously, he had made a significant impact on judging the authenticity of human rights. However, his first test is clearly inadequate for two reasons based on a close scrutiny of the Universal Declaration.

Firstly, Article 22 of the Universal Declaration reads as follows: 'Everyone, as a member of society, has the right to social security and is entitled to realisation, through national effort and international co-operation and in accordance with the organisation and resources of each state, of the economic, social and cultural rights indispensable for his dignity and the free development of his personality.' This Article suggests that the Declaration has taken into account that social and economic rights have to be in 'accordance with the organisation and resources of each state', which seems to be one disagreement upon which Cranston had based his judgement. Furthermore, the Declaration calls for international co-operation in the realisation of these rights and stresses that these rights are undoubtedly significant but inadequate in providing for the dignity of the human person. There is enough food to feed the poor and there enough resources to overcome poverty. However, without any international co-operation to overcome these problems, this status quo will prevail for sometime to come. The wording of these Articles suggest that these are not rights, but something which governments aspire to achieve. They are goals which can be achieved through a more equitable distribution of not only national resources, but international resources also. Thus, it goes without saying that not many governments are very keen on the idea.

Secondly, paragraph (1) of Article 21 of the Declaration provides that: 'Everyone has the right to take part in the government of his country, directly or through freely chosen representatives.' It is common knowledge that taking part in government is a political right, nonetheless, this right has the peculiarity of being limited in its scope. Every civil and political right included in the Declaration addresses 'everyone', however, the right in Article 21 addresses 'everyone in his country'. This suggests that a person has to qualify to enjoy such a right. This provision of this Article suggests that right is not a *human* right but a *citizen* right: someone has to qualify to enjoy it. It would be absurd to think that a person from an African country, for instance, had the right to take part in the government of Japan or Sweden. This is practically impossible. Macfarlane rightly concludes that: '[P]racticability is an issue with all human rights, not just economic and social rights, since resources are always required either for their realisation or protection' (1985, 10).

Because civil and political rights need only the will of governments, and economic, social and cultural rights need material resources for their implementation, they have come to be known as 'negative' and 'positive' rights respectively. This division is based on the fact that violating the first category causes harm, whereas any violation of the second category is merely a failure to meet demands or provide assistance. There are many objections to such a division and, as Macfarlane has suggested above, both sets need resources for their implementation. It goes without saying, as pointed out earlier, that the enjoyment of social and economic rights depends on the resources of a country. Nonetheless, any violations of these rights would certainly result in causing harm. If harm is the barometer whereby the authenticity of rights is judged, then failure to provide food, medical care and shelter will cause harm, even more than violating freedom of speech and of association. Further, the enjoyment of civil and political rights requires qualified judges, the training of the police and the military forces, for which resources are needed. Such programmes require the positive action of government and as a result civil and political rights may be thought of as positive rights.

It would perhaps make more sense to imagine the practicability of social, economic and cultural rights in the long run, bearing in mind the resources of each state, and the international co-operation the Universal Declaration seeks, rather than concentrating on the problems of nationals from one state taking part in the government of another sovereign state.

Genuinely universal

The second test Cranston suggests is that the right should be genuinely universal. It overlaps with the previous one in many instances; however, I shall try to avoid repeating points that have already been considered.

Human rights, according to Cranston, are moral rights for everybody wherever they are. Any right which excludes any people, or requires any qualification to enjoy it, cannot possibly be considered a human right. Furthermore, if one takes Tom Paine's suggestion that 'there could be no rights without duties' (Cranston in Raphael, 1967, 96), to impose on men a 'duty which they cannot perform', Cranston argues, 'is as absurd in its way, though perhaps not cruel, as bestowing on them a "right" which they cannot possibly enjoy' (ibid.).

This test undoubtedly disqualifies social, economic and cultural rights from the category of human rights for the reason discussed earlier. Such rights are meant for specific categories of people. Furthermore, they impose a burden on states which cannot be overcome. However, the right to take part in the government, for instance, is restricted to nationals of any given country as is the case with social, economic and cultural rights. Furthermore, it may be limited and excludes certain people within the country. Depending on the constitution of countries, people may be restricted from enjoying such a right for different reasons such as age, health or criminal record. So, if one has to speak of a right being genuinely universal, one has to define what is meant by that first. Genuinely universal, as one understands it, means that a right should be enjoyed by everyone, everywhere, regardless of sex, race, religion, etc. This, it follows, confirms that not only the right to life and liberty, for instance, are universal but that different economic rights are as well. The right to food, subsistence, shelter and medical care are indeed universal. They are needed by everybody wherever they are to preserve the right to life itself and protect the dignity of the human person. Further, if this test is taken seriously, then, apart from the rights discussed above, another set of rights qualifies also. The 'third generation', discussed in chapter three, such as the rights to peace and to a healthy and ecologically balanced environment, to name just a few, can be considered to be truly universal. On the right to a healthy environment, Doyal and Gough, for instance, state that 'DDT, for example, is just as bad for an Islamic Mullah as it is for the Pope and for precisely the same biological reasons' (1991, 200).

Paramount importance

This is the third and last test and the one which raises most difficulties. It would be very difficult, if not impossible, to judge whether one set of rights is of paramount importance, or more important than the other. Furthermore, even within the same set of rights, if a more pragmatic approach is taken, it can be said that some rights are more important than others. Within civil and political rights, for instance, the right to life and freedom from torture and other cruel and inhuman treatment is clearly of paramount importance: more important than the denial of freedom of speech or of movement. Charles Humana, for instance, in his second attempt (1986) to measure human rights on a cross-national basis, selected seven rights, based on the degree of endurance and pain, among his list of forty, which he thought were of paramount importance. His work will be explored further in chapter six. This would result, it seems, in the fact that not all civil and political rights are human rights if the test is to be applied. The aim behind this test, and others, is to make a selection of what could be considered as human rights. Whichever 'right' fails to pass cannot be considered as a human right.

Now, I turn to contrast the two sets of rights. The rights are weighted to achieve their importance. Nonetheless, this is very much a matter of who the person is and where he happens to be. The importance of something can be very flexible. It may mean different things to different people. It goes without saying that the prevention of murder, or equality before the law, are more important than, for instance, holidays with pay. Nonetheless, the degrees of importance may vary from one country to another, and that does not always lead to the conclusion that civil and political rights are more important than economic, social and cultural rights. Dominguez, for instance, argues that: '[A]t the top of the hierarchy, I would place concern for any identifiable government action that reduces a people's right to life and health. Attention would be focused not only on political massacres, arbitrary action by the government, but also on governments whose identifiable actions aggravate famines and epidemics' (1979, 23). To the poor, the underfed and the ill, undoubtedly food, shelter and medical care are more important than freedom of movement or expression. Isaiah Berlin further stresses that 'it is true that to offer political rights, or safeguards against intervention by the state to men who are half naked, illiterate, underfed and diseased is to mock their condition; they need medical help or education before they can understand, or make use of, any increase in their freedom' (quoted in Pollis and Schwab, 1979, 61). The former set of rights in this case will not only enhance the human personality, but may preserve the right to life itself.

It can be asserted that although such tests are important, they do not offer a clear cut distinction between the two sets of rights. This conclusion is also reached by Professor Raphael who states that: 'I agree with Mr Cranston that there are appropriate tests, but they do not in fact draw a clear line between the earlier and the later concepts of human rights' (1967, 63). The example given above will further confirm this claim. It seems that Cranston has based his tests on the 'right to holidays with pay', which he mentioned as the example in his tests to prove their validity. For a test to be successful, it should not only concentrate on one right only, but it should also include the different rights included in the Declaration (Alston and Quinn, 1987).

Therefore, in the light of the above discussion, it may be safe to conclude that agreement among scholars has yet to be reached on what human rights are, and where they come from. Some scholars, among them Cranston, have taken them to mean just civil and political rights. Others have selected a comprehensive set of rights which includes both sets. Falk states that:

Fouad Ajami emphasises four set off concerns that embody the maximum feasible consensus at the time:

1 - The right to survive; hence the concern with the war system and nuclear weaponry.

2 - The right not to be subject to torture.

3 - The condemnation of Apartheid; it is accepted that other societies violate social equality but that South Africa's blatant, officially sanctioned and codified racism is practically intolerable.

4 - The right to food (1979, 22).

If one looks at Ajami's selection of rights, one sees that it includes different rights that are not included in the Universal Declaration. While the right to food, not to be subjected to torture, and the right to survive are familiar ones, it is not the case for the condemnation of apartheid. It should be pointed out that the right to survive, in the sense that it is concerned with the war system and nuclear weaponry, can be understood to mean the right to peace. This right, and to some extent, the condemnation of apartheid, are rights of the third generation, which will be discussed in more detail in chapter three. The differences in this perception undoubtedly have a significant impact on the policies taken by different countries, and how they provide for what they think are human rights. This, in turn, will influence what can be labelled as a violation of such a right. The traditional clash between the liberal and socialist viewpoints is the best example, and it will be discussed further in the next chapter.

2 Human rights East and West: a comparison

In any measure, it is evident that the former communist countries have witnessed dramatic changes since March 1985 when Mikhail Gorbachev came to power. The changes ranged from the end of communist rule to the total disappearance of these nations (East Germany, the Soviet Union and Yugoslavia). To provide the historical context for a discussion of these changes, this chapter looks at the state of human rights before the changes took place, which have dominated the political agenda of both Eastern and Western countries for a number of years. Ideological differences between East and West manifested, as we have seen in the previous chapter, in their perception of human rights, which led to mutual disagreement and accusations. Such accusations reached their peak during what was known as the 'Cold War'.

In their criticism of capitalist societies, communist theorists regarded individual rights as abstract and argue that people should be concerned not with the form of human rights, but with their content. While world opinion condemned the communist countries' record on human rights, their spokespersons always claimed that human rights were better provided for under their systems. In their interpretations, 'the rights available in socialist societies were "qualitatively superior" to those existing under capitalism, in which "only those who own the capital (had) the full range of rights"' (Bouandel and White, 1993, 17). Their different perceptions of human rights and therefore disputes can be summarised as follows:

Firstly, capitalist countries believed in the supremacy of the individual, while communists focused on the community and the unconditional priorities of class interest. Hence, the individual benefited from these group rights, as his/her rights were better provided for within the community.

Secondly, within the debate on human rights there had always been a conflict between the Western assertion of the primacy of civil and political rights and the socialists insistence on the superiority of economic and social rights. Communists gave priority to what they regarded as the content of human rights, that is, economic, social and cultural rights, and insisted that they could not be separated from the class character of society in which they existed. By contrast, in capitalist countries the stress was on the traditional civil and political rights and these contrasting stances were the central issues between the two ideologies. The Western media, over the years, had extensive coverage of refugees fleeing oppression in communist countries and seeking 'freedom' in the West.

Finally, as regards the international supervision or monitoring of human rights practices, while some Western countries called for international mechanisms for the monitoring of human rights records, communist countries always rejected any supervision and traditionally saw this practice as interference in their internal affairs. This attitude resulted in former communist countries overemphasising the principle of states' sovereignty. In China, for instance, Edwards et al argue that 'any inquiry into the Chinese rights situation by a foreign government or international organisation is regarded as intervention in Chinese domestic affairs and, consequently, a violation of international law' (1985, 52-3).

Less than a decade ago, this was the general situation. Because of such priorities and commitments from both sides, each progressed very well on the priorities undertaken. Communist countries in general, at least up to the 1970s, achieved significant advances in the fields of social and economic rights. The provision of jobs, housing, medical care and education, among others, were the pride of communist countries and the indicators upon which they compared themselves with the West (Marcham, 1992, 26). However, their ideological stance led them to ignore or fail to secure the traditional rights, as to them the concept of human rights meant something completely different from that accepted in the West. This point was best illustrated, at an international human rights conference held in Canada in 1985, by an American delegate who stated that: 'We talk about human [i.e., political and civil] rights and they [the Soviets] talk about unemployment and racism' (Goldstein in Claude and Jabine, 1992, 38). Furthermore, they had always resisted international monitoring systems and did not co-operate with international or regional bodies.

Before going into in depth, the discussion of the changes in Eastern Europe, I shall present a comparative study of human rights between East and West, before the changes took place. I shall concentrate on the priorities assigned to the two sets of rights by each party to stress the differences between them. However, it is beyond the scope of this study to cover every aspect of the two sets of rights in countries in both the Western and Eastern worlds. Thus, I shall limit myself to some aspects of each set and apply them to a few countries where appropriate. Freedom of movement and of expression, as samples for civil and political rights are the subject of the first section. In the second, I look at economic and social rights and how they are provided for in different countries, paying particular attention to the rights to work and to medical care. The chapter concludes with an account of the recent developments that have occurred in the countries of Eastern Europe. The improvement that has taken place in different aspects of civil and political rights, and how economic and social rights have been affected, is of particular interest.

Civil and political rights

Civil and political rights lie at the heart of human rights. Some take them as the principal measurement to judge whether a government respects human rights or not. Because of their commitment to the content of human rights, communist countries have generally tended to ignore this category of rights. Moreover, since the traditional perception of human rights encompasses only this dimension, communist countries have always been criticised for not securing such rights. In the following, I shall look at two aspects of the question; how were they provided for in communist countries? And are they absolute in the West or not? The aspects considered are:

Freedom of expression

Freedom of expression means freedom of speech, to hold any opinion and express it freely without any interference from anybody. It is the subject of Article 19 of both the Universal Declaration on Human Rights and the Covenant on Civil and Political Rights.

It is seen as one of the most important rights. Because humans are thinking and rational, then they have the right to free expression and thought. It represents one form of democracy by which civilised governments are ruled or ought to be ruled. By securing this right, a government brings its citizens into political life, makes them more active in political matters, and helps them to feel that they have a say in the running of their country. As a result, different countries, either in theory or practice, claim to respect this right. However, even though constitutions do provide for this right, it should not be taken at face value and the practices of those particular governments should be scrutinised. Freedom of expression is generally restricted either by laws, in matters of states' security, or by moral obstacles, so as not to do any harm to anybody. In other words, one person's freedom finishes when another's begins. Such a right is widely believed to be secured in Western countries. However, the situation was completely different in the former communist-ruled nations.

In the former Soviet Union, for instance, freedom of expression was guaranteed by the 1977 Constitution. Article 50 stated that: 'In accordance with the interests of people and in order to strengthen and develop the socialist system, citizens of the USSR are guaranteed freedom of speech, ... Exercise of these political freedoms is ensured ... by the opportunity to use the press, television, and radio.'

While freedom of speech was secured by the Soviet Constitution, (Article 28 of the Chinese 1982 Constitution guaranteed this right also), there was a gap between what was printed and what was happening in reality. It was connected to the interests of the people, on the one hand, and the strength and development of the communist system on the other. This implicitly implied that any speech which did not satisfy these conditions may be punished by law. Furthermore, it was linked to the means of communication controlled by the state apparatus such as the press, television and radio. In this connection, the formerly leading role of the Communist Party of the Soviet Union, and the system through which certain posts had to be approved by this party is of a particular interest when, as Milne argues, it 'is the duty of the communist citizen loyally to follow the directives of the Communist Party in all political matters. To challenge the political leadership of the Party is to proclaim oneself an enemy of Communism' (in Dowrick, 1979, 35). In addition to this, the reliance on a heavy system of censorship, a common practice in the former communist countries, under which all information had to be subject to a very close scrutiny, which controlled what could be said. More importantly, when a government thinks that any knowledge by the outside world of its human rights, among other aspects, may jeopardise its interests, it may use its resources and ability to control any flow of information or distort it. The former Soviet Union, for instance, ceased to publish 'crime rate data in 1935 by Stalin's order, when the rate increased', and did the same with 'infant mortality data in the 1970s ... [when] it began to increase' (Samuelson and Spirer, in Claude and Jabine, 1992, 63).

Under such circumstances, it is very difficult to speak about freedom of speech? How could the Soviet citizen use such means, i.e., the press, television and the radio, which were controlled by the state, to express his opinion if he was criticising the system? The Soviet writer Anatolii Kuznetsov explained when he left his country that: 'life is like some constant unbroken theatrical production. You never say out loud what you really think, only what you ought to say. Insofar as we have to live in that theatre, every person has a sort of collection of phrases which he speaks and says publicly, and a corresponding collection of actions. For a normal human being, it is extremely difficult to lead such a double life' (quoted in Dallin, and Breslauer, 1970, 126-7).

The former Yugoslavia, to some extent, represented the exception to communist countries. In comparison to other countries in Eastern Europe, it can be argued that the situation there was slightly better. 'One simple measure of the difference between Yugoslavia and the Communist regimes was to compare the newspapers. The Belgrade daily *Politika* was no longer entirely taken up with success stories about production in Yugoslavia... It has begun to carry again informative surveys of international politics' (Wilson, 1979, 76). This was perhaps due to the fact that it had more contact with the West. Different Western newspapers, for instance, could be easily found in the former Yugoslavia; and movement across international borders was largely unrestricted. However, having said that does not automatically mean that in this country citizens were free to express themselves. There were some restrictions; the political leadership, for instance, could not be criticised; different trials and harassment took place such as in the case of Milovan Djilas and the Praxis group.

Freedom of movement

One of the major issues upon which former communist governments, and in particular the former Soviet, was criticised was freedom of movement. In sharp contrast to Article 13 of the Universal Declaration, and especially the provision of the International Covenant on Civil and Political Rights, this right was not guaranteed. The Chinese Constitution does guarantee it, and according to Edwards et al, Freedom of movement of the individual within China is restricted by the policy of banning any move from the place of registration, except on assignment' (Edwards et al, 1986, 55). Similarly, the 1977 Constitution of the former Soviet Union did not provide for this right, despite the ratification by that government of the International Covenant (See Chapter five). However, although not recognised as a right, practices had shown that a substantial number of people, mainly Soviet Jews, Soviet Americans, and Soviet Germans had been granted exit visas to emigrate (Edwards, 1985, 634).

Furthermore, foreigners visiting these countries did not easily obtain entry visas. They had to be subjected to a very intensive administrative process. There were some variations among the former communist countries such as in the case of the former Yugoslavia. There had been a relaxation of its borders, tourists could go to Yugoslavia without the need for any formal or diplomatic invitation. Former Yugoslav citizens could travel abroad, especially workers who were sent to Germany because of unemployment prevailing in the country.

The attitude of the former Yugoslav government could be ascribed to the economic situation in the country. Yugoslavia had one of the worst economic performances among the communist countries; an increasing level of unemployment and a very high level of inflation. Thus, there was a tendency towards encouraging tourism and sending its workers abroad as a source of hard currency.

The attitudes of former communist countries towards civil and political rights were not very different, such as freedom of assembly, of religion etc. ... However, the point that needs to be stressed here is that it would be a mistake to conclude that in the West, these human rights are provided for ideally. According to Novosti Press Agency, in the United Kingdom, for instance, 'Citizens' freedom of movement was restricted during the strike (miners' general strike, March 19, 1984, March 13, 1985). Police would often stop people on the road to investigate them, turn them back or arrest them. In the first 27 weeks of the strike, 164,508 alleged participants in pickets were denied entry into the County of Nottingham alone' (1987, 39). Capital punishment, for instance, exists in the United States; not only this, in common with the former communist countries, it is inflicted on minors as well. According to the Novosti Press Agency, 'in 31 of the states [of the United Sates] which practice capital punishment, the age limit is still lower or is not specified at all. Both black and white citizens from the poorest sections of society are as a rule sentenced to death if their supposed victim is white' (ibid., 56).

Economic, social and cultural rights

Despite the claims that these are not human rights, former communist countries have achieved significant advances in the area. Economic and social rights were the rights upon which they compared very favourably with capitalist countries. Former communist countries have been concerned with the enhancement of the standards of living of their population; providing jobs and housing, free education and medical care. Indeed it might be argued that, according to statistics up to the 1970s, they have achieved very high levels of literacy, provision of jobs, cheap housing (the rent did not increase since 1928), medical care, and free education.

These regimes' obsession with this set of rights is seen as an attempt to increase their legitimacy and popular support. Tokes suggests that 'because of the Eastern European regimes' chronic difficulties in gaining genuine popular support on ideological grounds these processes have compelled the communist party-states to shift the foundations of their legitimacy from political-ideological justification of domination to economic performance and satisfaction of popular expectations for increasing living standards, accelerated delivery of social services and other tangible material benefits' (1979, 3).

Whatever arguments were used against or in support of the provision of economic and social rights, in what follows I shall concentrate on some aspects of this set of rights and attempt comparison with capitalist ones. The aspects are:

The right to work

In general terms, this right has been secured in the communist countries. Work, as defined in Article 23 (1) of the Universal Declaration, was not only a right but a duty. Hence, former communist countries tried to embody it in their constitutions and legal codes. Article 40 of the Constitution of the former Soviet Union, for instance, promised everyone a job, in contrast to

Western countries where unemployment was seen as unavoidable. According to the Novosti Press Agency; 'In the developed capitalist countries, when their economies are experiencing a degree of recovery, there are 28 million people who are fully unemployed. According to official data; 8.5 million Americans, 3.2 British, 2.3 French, and 2.2 million residents of the Federal Republic of Germany' (1986, 28-9).

Unemployment has been seen as one of the major sources of social problems such as delinquency, prostitution and different kinds of crimes. By securing the right to work, communist governments tried to avoid the emergence of these phenomena while encouraging everybody to help in the development of the society. According to the UN Economic and Social Council's report on the world social situation in 1985, 'in the socialist countries guaranteed employment is a basic principle, the citizens having the right and the duty to participate in society through work' (ibid., 30).

In addition, the right to work in the communist countries was linked to different social values; 'it is a duty', 'an honour', and as result had to be fulfilled by everybody in the society who was able to do so. Szymanski argues that:

> Not only a job is considered to be a workers' right but, also working is considered to be a social duty. Soviet law stipulates that no one can live from rents, speculation, profit or black marketing, as such activities are considered to be living off the labour of another - social parasitism (1984, 139).

Moreover, the law provided for the punishment of those who did not work. Article 209 of the former Russian Soviet Federation Socialist Republics Criminal Code, as interpreted by the Presidium of the R.S.F.S.R. Supreme Soviet in 1975, provided for 'social parasites'. Macfarlane notes that 'persons living on unearned income with avoidance of socially useful work for more than four months in succession or for periods adding up to one year, along with systematic vagrants and beggars, to be punished by imprisonment or corrective labour for up to one year' (1985, 113).

Nevertheless, the overall situation could be considered to be better than cases in the USA or in the UK where 'no guarantee of a job can be given as the demand for jobs in the private sector will be determined by market forces' (ibid.). There is equality between men and women in recruitment for jobs on the one hand and in equality of pay on the other, in contrast to the West where women 'are paid 32 per cent less than men against the background of the widespread sex segregation of the work force. According to the May 19, 1984 issue of the San Francisco Examiner 49,000,000 American females are regularly victims of wage discrimination' (Novosti Press, Agency, 1987, 39-40).

However, unemployment in the former communist countries did exist under different forms such as 'disguised unemployment', 'political employment' or 'underemployment'. This means that if the capacity of a company is 60,000 workers for instance, it may employ a higher number than that to absorb the unemployed work force since its aim was not to make profits. Furthermore, there was no competition among companies since they were all owned by the state.

In the former Yugoslavia, however, unemployment represented a heavy burden on the government's shoulders. It was not able to cope with the different economic problems, if not crisis, the country faced over the years. It was one of the countries which realised the lowest economic growth among the communist states.

There were some variations among communist countries in providing jobs for their citizens, but, what was generally achieved was the right of workers to participate in the management of their companies. Article 8 of the 1977 Soviet Constitution speaks about the 'right of workers to participate in decision-making process of their collective'. This was widely followed in Yugoslavia through a system known as 'self-management'.

The right to health care

One measure upon which one can judge how developed a country is through the ratio of doctors and hospital beds to the population, life expectancy and the percentage of infant mortality. Health care received special attention in the former communist countries, and in general these countries have made significant leaps forward in the area of health.

When the communists came to power in 1917, levels of disease and life expectancy were low (life expectancy, for example, was just 30 years in 1900, compared to 47 in the US) and infant mortality was very high. Since, there have been enormous efforts and huge investment by the former Soviet Union (for instance, it was the first country to introduce free medical services) to bring about changes and to improve medical service. According to Szymanski:

In the 1969-78 period, the USSR increased the share of GNP spent on health, as well as its spending per capita. In 1969 2.3% of its GNP was spent on health (and 13.6% on military activities); in 1978 2.4% was spent on health (and 12.2% on military activities). This corresponded to a 59% increase in absolute resources allocated to health (1984, 136).

The efforts resulted in tremendous changes in the Soviet society, and indeed challenged the most developed capitalist countries when it came to the ratio of qualified doctors per population and the availability of hospital beds as indicated in the table below, which is based on 1977 statistics:

Table (2) 1: The ratio of doctors and hospital beds to the population in the former USSR, USA and the UK

Country	Doctors per 10,000 population	Hospital beds per 10,000 population
USSR	34.6	121.3
USA	17.6	63.0
UK	15.3	89.4
Source: Szymanski, 1977, 136		

Furthermore, in a more recent publication (1986), the Novosti Press Agency in Moscow stated that: 'According to the World Health Organisation the optimal proportion is 280 doctors for 100,000 of the population. In the USSR this proportion has been exceeded - there are 412 doctors for every 100,000 of the population. The USA has 233, the Federal Republic of Germany 299, France 208 and Great Britain 183' (1986, 34).

If one does not argue about the quality of medical care, then there is no doubt that the former Soviet Union had higher standards compared to western countries. Only the former West Germany exceeded the optimal proportion of doctors put forward by the World Health Organisation. Moreover, what matters more is that in the communist countries treatment was free and available for all. This is in contrast with the practice in the United States. The provision of medical care in particular and economic and social rights in general seems to refute the idea that providing for economic and social rights is a matter for economic resources. The United States, Macfarlane argues 'provides a shameful example. The bottom black neighborhood area in Detroit, for example, had in the early seventies an infant mortality rate as high as San Salvador and over three times the United States average' (1985, 122).

The table provided by White et al, gives general information relating to indicators on social welfare and offers the possibility of a comparison between the communist and the western countries examined.

Table (2) 2: Comparison of some communist and non-communist countries on selected social indicators

	1	2	3	4	5	6
UK	43	18.2	9	75	3256	112
USA	60	25.7	10	75	3645	257
India	n.a.	n.a.	99	58	2238	58
USSR	78	43.3	25	69	3399	177
China	n.a.	13.6	32	69	2630	18
GDR	66	31.9	9	73	3814	79
1	Housing units completed per 10.000 population, 1988.					
2	Doctors per 10,000 population, c. 1987.					
3	Infant mortality rate per 1000 births, 1988.					
4	Life expectancy at birth, 1987.					
5	Daily calorie supply, 1986					
6	Students in education per 10,000 population, 1988.					
Source: White et al, 1990, 327.						

What should be borne in mind when one makes such comparisons and concludes for instance, that communist countries were ahead of capitalist countries in terms of economic and social rights, is that generalisations do not allow for analysis of the exception. One may find some capitalist countries provide better social and economic rights than socialist ones as in the cases of the United Kingdom, for instance, as compared to the former Yugoslavia.

Changes and new developments

The election of Gorbachev marked the beginning of the end of communism in its traditional sense, not only in the former Soviet Union but also in eastern Europe. He embarked on a series of dramatic political and economic reforms, with far-reaching consequences, which were unimaginable even a decade ago. Therefore, it is imperative to stress the role and the impact of the Soviet leadership in explaining the new political map and the transformation of some regimes from authoritarianism to 'rights-protective' regimes. Had Gorbachev not come to power and, most importantly, the former Soviet Union maintained support for local communist elites and suppressed any uprising in its former satellite countries, Hungary in 1956 and the former Czechoslovakia in 1968 for instance, very few people would doubt that communist regimes would perhaps have lasted. In addition, because of Gorbachev's reforms, the study, promotion and measurement of human rights has received further attention in East-West relations following the collapse of communism in eastern Europe in the late 1980s. Different studies have been undertaken to look at the changes these countries have experienced and their evolving characters, not in the manner of ideological confrontations and mutual accusations which previously characterised their relations, but in a spirit of co-operation and mutual respect (Juviler et al, 1993; Forsythe, 1994).

When formulating his new thinking and vision for the future, Gorbachev, perhaps because he was a lawyer by training, stressed the importance of law as a major pre-requisite if his new policies were to stand any chance of succeeding. He wrote: 'There can be no observance of law without democracy. At the same time, democracy cannot exist and develop without the rule of the law, because law is designed to protect society from abuses of powers and guarantee citizens and their organisations and work collectives their rights and freedoms' (Gorbachev, 1987, 105).

Hence, in the light of this stance, the direction of Gorbachev's reforms was not surprising. First of all, reforms of the judicial system to establish the rule of law upon which any future reform would depend, and secondly, the establishment of democratic practices by reforming the electoral law to give people more choice of candidates and parties and by guaranteeing freedom of expression without which any talk of democratic practices would hardly make sense. The discussion that follows concentrates on these reforms more closely and examines their implications for human rights in this part of the world.

As the rule of law was central to Gorbachev's policies, reforms of the judicial system is of particular interest. To a certain extent, communist regimes had in common their heavy reliance on a secret police; a constricted flow of information; and a certain ambiguity in their laws. Consequently no one knows the exact number of people tortured, exiled into labour camps, killed or interned in psychiatric hospitals. The latter practice was generally the fate of dissidents who openly spoke out against the system. While these practices were taking place, the authorities did their best to hide the reality. The Soviet people, a representative of the government told the Human Rights Committee 'were proud of their achievements in human rights and had nothing to hide from world public opinion in that field' (UN Doc. CCPR/C/1/Add. 22 par. 3). In China, for instance, according to Fang Lizhi, '[T]he true record of human rights ... has been hidden: the Chinese authorities have blocked any communication about it. Some have been misled to believing that China has been free of human rights violations' (1992, 2).

It is significant then that under Gorbachev the recognition that there were some shortcomings within the Soviet laws and the realisation that without a proper legal system and independence of the judiciary from any interference, there would be no guarantees of citizens' enjoyment of their rights and freedoms. Veniamin Yakovlev, for instance, the Deputy Head of Public Commission on Humanitarian Questions and Human Rights, told a press conference on 4 February, 1988 in Venice that: 'The RSFSR criminal code is being reviewed and the infamous article 70 [a vaguely worded article which dealt with anti-Soviet agitation and propaganda] may be eliminated or changed' (Trehub, 1988, 4). This was eventually ended by the adoption of the new Fundamentals of Criminal Law, 1991. Furthermore, almost two years later, during the discussion of the former Soviet Union's third report to that body, the Soviet representative told the UN Human Rights Committee that the Soviet government realised that there had been some shortcomings in the area of human rights and that different draft laws had been adopted or were waiting to be approved to put an end to that situation (UN Doc. CCPR/C/SR 928, par. 6). He also publicly acknowledged that 'a matter of major concern to his [the Soviet] government was the lack of effective machinery for the full realisation of civil and political rights' (ibid., par. 8). Another measure that had been taken in the field of judicial reforms, which has marked a significant break from past practices, was 'the legislation on the courts, introduced in 1989, established for the first time the principle of presumption of innocence of the accused' (White, 1992, 43).

The use of psychiatric hospitals against dissidents, once a common practice in the former Soviet Union but never publicly admitted, was reduced, if not completely abolished. It has also been reported that 'the cases of people who were detained in China have been reconsidered, and different reports of the specialised agencies suggest that there has been improvement on this front' (Baehr, in Hill and Zielonka, 1992, 192). Gorbachev had publicly acknowledged its widespread use and called for the practice to be stopped and for those interned to be released (*The Times*, 12 September, 1988). As a result of this, and in recognition of the efforts deployed by the authorities in the former Soviet Union, the 'World Psychiatric Association decided in October 1989 to readmit the Soviet organisation, along with those of Czechoslovakia and Bulgaria. In 1983 the Soviet Psychiatrists Association resigned from the World Psychiatric Association rather than face expulsion as a result of a report on the use of mental hospitals to imprison dissidents' (ibid.).

Elections in the former communist countries did not amount to anything more than citizens confirming the candidates already chosen by the party. There was no choice between candidates, let alone between parties. Therefore, electoral law reforms are at the heart of the democratic revolution that has been taking place in those nations. Some of these countries experienced their first genuine elections in the late 1980s, where citizens had, for the first time, the opportunity to choose between more than one candidate for each seat contested. This resulted in non-communists being elected to government, while, at the other end of the spectrum, some countries saw the end of communist rule. In the former Soviet Union, for instance, Gorbachev first flirted with the idea of electoral reform in early 1986 at the 27th Party Congress when he suggested the need for its 'perfection' and to develop its 'democratic principles' (White, in White et al, 1993, 21). According to the new electoral law, adopted on 1 December 1988, citizens would be given a choice of candidates at all levels of government. The elections of March 1989 to the Congress of People's Deputies saw the spectacular application of this new law and presented the authorities with a real challenge to their reforms. The results of these elections showed that even senior communist Party and Government officials failed to secure election (White, 1991; Lentini, 1991).

Similar elections took place in Hungary, the former Czechoslovakia and Poland. In Poland, for instance, general elections were held in June 1989, and Solidarity, the once banned trade union, was free to contest emerging as the victor. Solidarity won 99 of the 100 seats contested in the upper house of parliament. However, since the Polish Law reserved two-thirds of the lower house to the Communist Party and other groups,

Solidarity was only allowed to contest the remaining one-third of the seats, all of which it won and resulted in an end to a forty year power monopoly by the Communist Party (Addo, 1990, 90). Similarly Hungary, according to Racz, 'passed as important milestone in the Spring of 1990. The elections which brought the democratic forces into power completed an unprecedented peaceful systematic change from Marxist-Leninist one-party rule to a plural system of governance' (1991, 84). Likewise, the Communist government in Prague saw the end of communist rule as well in December 1989, and a non-communist being elected to the post of president.

In addition, freedom of expression considerably increased, for example, banned materials found their ways to libraries and book shops. Newspapers were no longer concerned with the achievements of socialist society, but were more concerned with current national and international issues, and tackled aspects that they were not allowed to consider before. Some even went further and openly criticised the assumed achievements of the former Soviet Union. Elena Bonner, Sakharov's widow, for example, argued that not even social and economic rights were provided for in the former Soviet Union, as it had 'the worst medical care and in child and infant mortality is in fifty-third place in the world' (in Juviler et al, 1993, 19). More critical pieces appeared in the press and censorship was actually abolished by the 1990 media law. For example, Khrushev's famous speech to the 20th Congress of the Communist Party in 1956, in which Stalin's atrocities were condemned, was published in 1989.

Gorbachev's new thinking and reforms laid the basic foundations for a democratic revolution. This in turn led to the critical examination of the perception of human rights traditionally held by many socialists. Lukasheva, a member of the Soviet delegation to the 45th session of the UN Commission on Human Rights, suggested that unconditional priorities of class interests, traditionally central to the socialist conception of human rights, inevitably pushed the interests of the individual to the background. Such was the extent of this new thinking which shook the conceptions traditionally held by many that she and Kudryavtev, vice-president of the Russian Academy of Sciences, suggested that '[t]otalitarian theories nurtured lawlessness instead of the rule of law, rejecting the legal principles and mechanisms without which any concept of democracy and human rights is meaningless' (Kudryavtev and Lukasheva in Juviler et al, 1993, 98). Lukasheva even went further to suggest that '[p]roletarian dictatorship is essentially incompatible with human rights and individual freedoms' (ibid., 57). The situation was such that even those who, in the past, had always prided themselves on the achievements of the former Soviet Union and vigorously defended them, had by 1993 come to conclude that their own writing was 'not representing reality in any way whatsoever' and had realised 'how hypocritical many laws turned out to be' (Chkhivadze, in ibid., 17).

Apart from the changes discussed above, and in the new spirit of openness that has characterised the period since the 1980s, the former communist countries co-operate with international monitoring agencies, and less use is being made of national sovereignty as an excuse of non-compliance with their obligations. In the case of the former Soviet Union, for instance, former Deputy Minister of Foreign Affairs, Vladimir Petrovsky, stated that 'compliance with international human rights standards is a Soviet priority' (Current Digest of the Soviet Press, 1990, 20). By February 1992, Andrei Kozyrev, Russia's former Foreign Minister, was able to claim that the delegation of his country 'advocated to the 48th session of the UN Commission on Human Rights more effective mechanisms for the introduction of democratic human rights standards into the international political life of individual states' and that it was 'important to increase the effectiveness of international supervision of human rights' (1992, 290).

In their perception of human rights, in general the East shifted more towards the West, and civil and political rights were given greater attention than ever before. The collapse of communism and the end of the 'Cold War' meant that arguments over differing concepts of human rights were no longer a subject of mutual accusation and a spirit of co-operation has evolved. Without any suggestion that the conceptual basis of their earlier disagreement has disappeared, there is more acceptance of the traditional rights by the former communist countries and this has meant in turn that there is a broad agreement on how the phenomenon is perceived. The Soviets claim that they are not 'abandoning [their] ideological convictions [and they] are not thrusting them upon [their] partners as the only acceptable convictions ... the dialogue on human rights is now gradually leading to a convergence of [their] positions and the West's on what had seemed a completely hopeless question' (Current Digest of the Soviet Press, 1989, 17). This, however, has been achieved, to a certain extent, at the expense of social and economic rights. The results and effects of market reforms on human rights have included emerging inequalities in wealth and living conditions, including high levels of unemployment and inflation. The former communist states had always taken pride in their achievements and claimed that human rights were better provided for in their countries; the changes brought about since the end of communist rule suggest that they no longer provided the best human rights in those terms.

While the traditional rivalry between East and West was on the increase, the 1960s and 1970s saw 'Third World' countries entering the debate on human rights, and stressing a new set of rights. At the same time, as a result of the changes that have been occurring around the world, new claims emerged. I shall discuss this point in the next chapter.

3 The third generation of human rights

It has been suggested in the previous chapters that human rights may be divided into three distinct categories on the basis of the slogans put forward by the French Revolution in 1789. The first refers to civil and political rights, and the second to economic, social and cultural rights. The international community embarked, Vasak argues, 'upon a third generation of human rights which may be called 'rights of solidarity' (1979, 29). This 'third generation', is the result of many 'Third World' countries achieving independence, and the challenges that the world has witnessed over the past three decades is also referred to as rights of solidarity.

It should be pointed out from the beginning that a clear-cut definition of what the 'Third World' means is yet to be achieved. This, in turn, makes a homogeneous stand towards the question of human rights difficult if not impossible. Nonetheless, since the majority are newly independent countries suffering from poverty, illiteracy and neo-colonialism coupled with their new role within the United Nations, they have tended to press the debate on human rights to embrace different new aspects apart from ones already acknowledged. 'The enlargement of the Commission' [on human rights], Robertson and Merrills argue, 'was intended to encourage the participation of new members who were particularly concerned with such problems as racial discrimination and apartheid, colonialism and underdevelopment' (1992, 74). These countries felt that, initially, they did not have any say in the formulation of human rights, and that the time has come for them to express their concern.

In this chapter, I shall attempt to address these 'new generation' rights and consider how valid they are. The reader should bear in mind, however, that the discussion will be brief, mainly to highlight the fact that new elements have emerged in the human rights debate. A deep reflection on the subject is certainly beyond the scope of this work. Furthermore, the rights that have emerged are not only a result of many 'Third World' countries achieving independence, but a result of many threats to mankind as well. Therefore, this chapter begins with a discussion of these new rights, and then moves on to discuss their authenticity. In other words, are they generally accepted as human rights? And finally, can they be measured and applied on a cross-national basis?

What are these rights?

Karel Vasak identifies the 'third generation' of human rights to include four rights. He argues that

> Such rights include the right to development, the right to a healthy and ecologically balanced environment, the right to peace, and the right to ownership of the common heritage of mankind (1979, 29).

The rights included in the above list could be divided into two broad categories: the first includes the right to development and to the ownership of the common heritage of mankind. The second includes the right to a healthy and ecologically balanced environment and the right to peace. The former category could be identified with the demands of 'Third World', while the latter are of a general character and of a genuine importance to everybody and to every country no matter what its level of development may be. It is perhaps not by chance that the first three 'rights' (development, peace and environment) in the quotation above have been the subject of articles 22, 23 and 24 respectively of the African Charter on Human and Peoples' Rights of 1981.

However, before going in depth into the analysis of the above rights, it may perhaps be appropriate to discuss, at least briefly, a significant right associated with 'Third World' countries: the right to self-determination and their constant search for a better deal in the international economic system usually referred to as the New International Economic Order.

The right to self-determination

This right was the subject of the first articles of both the international Covenants (1966) and Article 20 of the African Charter. It is of a different nature from those considered in the previous chapters. Jenks argues that it [the right to self determination] 'is of a wholly different nature from civil liberties in that it cannot be made effective by legal process, and also from economic and social rights in that it is not a guiding principle of national policy to be made effective progressively by legislation and administration (in Joyes, 1978, 156).

However, the applicability of this right is also different. It could be applied not only to countries which are under foreign domination, but to different peoples within independent states such as, for instance, the Kurds in Turkey and Iraq. Nonetheless, for present purposes, reference will be made only to how 'Third World' countries are concerned since they see self-determination as a form of decolonisation.

With the majority of these countries achieving their independence and entering the debate on human rights, the stress has grown within the United Nations on different situations where people are still suffering external domination. According to the preamble of the Declaration of Teheran (1968), the denial of human rights in a number of countries is mainly due, among other things, to such people being denied the right to self-determination and racist policies such as apartheid (United Nations, 1971, 538-40). This linkage between self-determination and colonial moves was stressed further at Algiers in 1976, and particularly in United Nations Resolution 32/1977. Principle "e" of this Resolution reads:

> In approaching human rights questions within the United Nations system, the international community should accord, or continue to accord, priority to the search for solutions to the mass and flagrant violations of human rights of peoples and persons affected by situations such as those resulting from apartheid, from all forms of racial discrimination, from colonialism, from foreign domination and occupation and threats against sovereignty, national unity and territorial integrity, as well as to recognise the fundamental rights of peoples to self-determination and every nation to the exercise of sovereignty and national resources (Marks, 1981, 440).

There is no doubt about the influence of foreign domination on the observance of human rights. Being subjected to such a domination hinders, if it does not eliminate, any chances the people might have in choosing their form of government. Therefore, this right is a pre-requisite for any attempt to observe human rights. The reader should bear in mind, however, that self-determination or independence does not automatically lead to a better human rights record. It offers, at least in principle, a favourable environment in which individuals or peoples can freely choose their political status and economic policies. So this right represents a call on colonial powers to take every step to ensure that peoples are free to pursue their choices. It should also be stated that self-determination and sovereignty do not mean political freedom or independence only, but the economic aspects of the right too. Resolution 2581 (XXI) of 25 November, 1966, for instance, '[R]eaffirms the inalienable right of all countries to exercise permanent sovereignty over their natural resources' (United Nations, 1971, 334).

Apart from the denials of human rights being linked to the issues of self-determination and armed conflict, in accordance with resolution 32/130 of 16 February, 1977 (United Nations, 1980, 734-5), 'Third World' countries further stress the interdependence and indivisibility of civil and political rights on the one hand, and economic, social and cultural rights on the other. They have 'been pressing vigorously for concerted new measures to redress the existing inequalities between the richer and poorer nations, and for this purpose have adopted as its slogan the concept of a "new international economic order". It has been claimed that the establishment of the new economic order is a pre-condition of respect for human rights in many countries' (Robertson and Merrills, 1992, 256-7).

The right to development

After a full discussion within the United Nations (it was first proclaimed by the Commission on Human Rights in 1977), the General Assembly of the United Nations eventually adopted on 4 December, 1986 Resolution 41/128 in which it confirmed the right to development as an inalienable human right. The first article reads:

> The right to development is an inalienable human right by virtue of which every human person and all peoples are entitled to participate in, contribute to, and enjoy economic, social, cultural and political

development, in which all human rights and fundamental freedoms can be fully realised (United Nations, 1990, 717).

'Third World' countries, in general, have stressed that the denial of human rights in their part has been a result of historical reasons. Such reasons include being subjected to foreign domination and the increased gap between the developed and developing countries. A former President of the United Nations Commission on Human Rights, Mr Keba M'baye of Senegal, for instance, 'recognises that in many African countries governments are struggling to combat famine, illness and ignorance and tend to overlook the classic liberties. He deduces a "right to development" as a necessary corollary of other fundamental rights recognised in international texts' (Robertson and Merrills, 1992, 13). However, although they stress the indivisibility of human rights as suggested earlier, they believe that civil and political rights depend on economic and social rights. These countries, according to Grosespiell, 'affirm that the solving of the essential problems of food, health, housing, clothing and education holds priority over the question of 'formal' rights, which are an unknown factor and are practically without interest to the ignorant and hungry masses which inhabit many of these countries' (in Ramcharan, 1979, 64).

This has polarised the debate on human rights between what has come to be known as the 'North' and 'South'. The 'South' refers to developing countries, and the 'North' to developed ones; the Eastern bloc did not enter the debate because it claimed it was not responsible for the situation in 'Third World' countries. Most of the criticism to which 'Third World' states are subjected involves the claim that they fail to provide for the freedoms most treasured in the West, which in turns, fails, according to 'Third World' viewpoint, to take account of their internal situations. This has led to a two-way argument: the North argues that the South uses underdevelopment as a pretext for not providing for civil and political rights, while the South insists that the North's stress on civil and political rights hampers the indivisibility of rights and hinders the chances of any help to improve their situation.

It is an undeniable fact that human rights do not function in a vacuum. The political, economic, social and cultural context, or situation in which they develop, are key factors in their explanation. Given the appalling conditions and problems that 'Third World' countries face, it would be difficult to imagine a proper respect for human rights. However, 'Third

World' states, in general, have tended to over state the importance of economic and social rights to the total observance of human rights. Certainly there may be priorities regarding the provision of rights, but abuses of human rights that some of these countries have been experiencing have nothing to do with their economic and social conditions. The fact that country A, for instance, sets its sights on providing social and economic rights does not explain torture, detention without trial and large-scale killing. It would be absurd to try to justify these acts in terms of economic circumstances. The argument is not whether development policies generate respect for human rights or not (Forsythe, 1989a), as much as it is for an international co-operation in the field of human rights. 'The achievement of the right to development requires a concentrated national and international effort to eliminate economic deprivation, hunger and disease in all parts of the world without discrimination' (United Nations, 1990, 721).

The right to development is linked to different rights, particularly the right to self-determination and full sovereignty over natural wealth and resources. Keba M'baye sees it 'as the natural consequence of the right to self-determination and the rights of all peoples to freely dispose of their national wealth, and resources - rights which are proclaimed in both the UN Covenants' (Robertson and Merrills, 1992, 13). It is also linked to the other rights of the third generation such as the right to peace, and the right to a healthy and ecologically balanced environment. The United Nations have stressed the need for a sustainable development: development policies which should take into account their effects on the environment and the needs of the future generations. I shall return to this point later.

The right to a healthy and ecologically balanced environment

Perhaps one of, if not the most challenging threats to humankind, is the achievement of a healthy and sound environment. There has been growing awareness of the fact that there has been a population explosion coupled with an increase in the use of resources and its different effects on climate change. The increase in the already high levels of water and air pollution and the steady decrease of forests are in fact alarming signals to the international community. The arms race and the huge stocks of weapons of mass destruction add to these difficulties. This led the late Willy Brandt, in his report, to insist that 'the quality of life is meaningless without health, which depends on proper nutrition and a healthy environment' (1980, 16). Such a healthy environment is not only the responsibility of each state but of the international community also. In this context, the United Nations Social and Economic Council adopted a resolution on 30 July, 1968 in which it:

> took note of the continuing impairment of the quality of the human environment caused by such factors as air and water pollution, erosion and the forms of soil deterioration, secondary effects of biocides, wastes and noise. Concerned with the consequent effect thereof on the condition of man, his physical and mental well being, his dignity and his enjoyment of basic human rights in developing as well as developed countries, the Council was convinced of the urgent need for intensified national and international action to meet the situation (United Nations, 1971, 473).

Each epoch has had its challenges; this amongst others to ensure a successful transition from the age of wasteful consumerism to that of a sustainable world in which human beings enjoy a sound environment. The United Nations and other organisations have recognised the difficulties towards which the planet is heading. The United Nations Conference on Human Environment held in Stockholm in 1972, the Brundtland Report (1988) and the Earth Summit which took place in June 1992 in Rio are examples of the importance of the issue. The Stockholm Conference played a significant role not only in increasing the popular awareness of the dangers that humankind faced, but marked the date when 'the right to a healthy environment' was recognised in the work of the United Nations. The Conference's Secretary-general stated that 'the Conference was launching a new liberation movement to free men from the threat of their thraldom to environment perils of their own making' (United Nations, 1975, 319). Principle I of the Declaration reads:

> Man had the fundamental right to freedom, equality and adequate conditions of life, in an environment of a quality that permitted a life of dignity and well-being, and he bore a solemn responsibility to protect and improve the environment for present and future generations (ibid.).

The right to a healthy environment is not only of a general character but is also a result of the special circumstances of every country. Its general character lies in that everybody in every country may be affected by it. A need for urgent and co-ordinated action at the local, regional and international levels is of paramount importance. Falk sees that the 'grounds for concerted action seem clearest when the causation is clear. If country X impairs health, destroys life, or harms the environment in country Y and Z, or more widely, in a region, the oceans, or the globe as a whole, then it is obviously at fault. If evidence mounts that cancer arises from increased radiation and a particular government engages in radiation-producing activities, then it is "ecological aggression"' (in Dominguez et al, 1979, 243). It is also a result of the special circumstances that a particular country, whether developed or developing, may be experiencing. Environmental problems are a result of both underdevelopment and development (United Nations, 1975, 319). The advanced levels of technology developed countries have achieved certainly did not come at a low cost. The intolerably high levels of air and water pollution, the increase in the number of cars, factories and technological accidents undoubtedly led to more damage. Developing countries, in general, lack the means whereby to tackle these problems. Thus, it should be looked at from a general viewpoint. Developed countries, at best, ought to help in the transfer of environmentally sound technology and update the infrastructure of 'Third World' countries to meet these new challenges. Failing to do, at least they should abstain from expanding their industries to countries with low environmental standards.

It should be borne in mind that environmental and ecological problems should not be looked at in isolation of other factors. They are very much linked to issues of development and the arms race. 'Environmental impact assessment' Brandt argues 'should be undertaken whenever investments or development activities may have adverse environmental consequences whether with national territory concerned for the environment of neighbouring countries or for the global commons' (1980, 115). Such measures have been adopted, but there is still a need for international unified ones as some countries have tended to set lower standards to attract investment and create jobs (ibid., 114). It is further linked to the issue of the arms race as the use of these weapons could have fatal consequences on the environment and humankind in general. As a result, it is not a surprise that a great deal of attention has been paid to this issue both at the regional (an interparliamentary conference on the environment held in Bonn in 1971 resolved that mankind has a right to a healthy environment (Marks, 1981,

443), and the international level. The importance of the environment led some to suggest that it should be given still more weight. Falk, for instance, argues that 'environmentalists and NGOs (non-governmental organisations) can build a greater understanding of environmental rights as a key sector of human rights, and generate pressures to translate this understanding into a revised Universal Declaration of Human Rights and a new Covenant on Environmental and Ecological Rights' (in Dominguez, 1979, 244).

The right to peace

Peace offers the best opportunity under which respect for and realisation of human rights and fundamental freedoms can be achieved. Most human rights violations occur during times of war. They are a threat to the basic right of life, without which other rights are meaningless. However, it should be borne in mind that the right to peace does not only involve refraining from wars - although a very important factor - but the solving of other serious problems such as poverty and hunger. Brandt argues that this issue 'not only raises the traditional questions of peace and war, but how to overcome world hunger, mass misery and alarming disparities between the living conditions of rich and poor' (1980, 13). In his introduction to the Medium-Term Plan of the UNESCO, its then Director-General stated that:

> Peace is more than simply a matter of refraining from war; there can be no lasting peace if individuals are deprived of their rights and liberties, if people are oppressed by other peoples, if populations are beset by poverty and suffering from malnutrition or sickness (quoted in Marks, 1980, 341).

Although there is an apparent danger to the right to peace, because of the violations of human rights discussed in the quotation above, wars, however, remain the most significant ones. After the Second World War, the world embarked on a rapid and massive arms race, encouraged in that by the peak of the Cold War in the 1950s and 1960s. Weapons of mass destruction became the biggest threat to the existence of humanity as a whole. The creation of troublesome areas around the world has meant that this industry has grown more than ever before. Different issues such as national security and territorial integrity have come to play significant roles in the decisions made. Although the right to peace was first suggested by the Commission on

Human Rights in February 1977, the issue itself has had a long history. The General Conference of the Agency for the Prohibition of Nuclear Weapons in Latin America, for instance, proclaimed 'the right to peace as a human right in a resolution adopted on April 27, 1979' (Marks, 1981, 446). The non-proliferation Treaty signed in 1968 and the consideration by the 'Commission of Human Rights in March 1971 whether *conscientious objection to military service* could be declared officially a human right' (Joyce, 1979, 233), are examples of such efforts. Further, on 15 December 1978, the General Assembly of the United Nations adopted Resolution 33/73 in which it 'reaffirmed the rights of individuals, states and all mankind to life in peace'. Principle 1 of the Resolution reminds us that 'every nation and every human being, regardless of race, conscience, language or sex, has the inherent right to life in peace. Respect of that right, as well as for the other human rights, is in the common interest of all mankind and an indispensable condition of advancement of all nations, large and small, in all fields' (Osmanczyk, 1985, 610). Hence, the elimination of the threats inherent in the arms race is the basic instrument towards the maintenance of peace. However, to ensure a long lasting peace, people should have their civil and political liberties and their social and economic needs met. Military expenditure, both in developed and developing countries, could certainly overcome many of the problems that planet earth is facing today. Diseases, inadequate housing and environmental problems could be more readily tackled if this military expenditure was diverted towards these issues.

The right to the common heritage of mankind

This right was suggested to be part of the third generation of human rights. It was first applied to the sea-bed in a declaration by the United Nations' General Assembly on 17 December 1970 which proclaimed that 'the sea-bed beyond the limits of national jurisdiction is part of the common heritage of mankind' (Marks, 1981, 447). Its scope has widened to include different areas such as the oceans, space, the Antarctic and different cultural monuments.

Are they human rights?

Having identified the rights of the third generation, the most fundamental question remains: can they be accepted as human rights? There is little doubt that the emergence of such rights has added to the already controversial question of what human rights really are. It was pointed out in the first chapter that economic, social and cultural rights have not been accepted, at least by some scholars, as human rights, and the stress has always been on the traditional set of rights. The inclusion of such new rights has added to these difficulties.

It was suggested in the first chapter that the approach to human rights, in this book, would be evolutionary and dynamic. While the two sets of rights discussed above are the products of the French, American and Russian revolutions, the rights of solidarity are prompted by the experience of 'Third World' countries and the new challenges mankind is facing. In a word, these new challenges have certainly opened the debate on the possibility of considering additional human rights. Thus the scope of these rights is different, and their achievement requires the efforts of everybody. In this respect, Karel Vasak, in his inaugural lecture to the Tenth Session of the International Institute of Human Rights, Strasbourg, July 1979, stated that they:

> are [the third generation of human rights] new in the aspirations they express, are new from the point of view of human rights in that they seek to infuse the human dimension into areas where it has all too often been missing, having been left to the State or States... [T]hey are new in that they may be invoked against the State and demanded of it; but above all (and herein lies their essential characteristic) they can be realised only through the concentrated efforts of all actors on the social sense: the individual, the state, public and private bodies and the international community (quoted in Marks, 1981, 441).

Not only these rights are new, in terms that they address new dimensions, but their reference is very vague as well. The beneficiaries of these rights and against whom the claims can be made are quite difficult to determine. While civil and political rights deal with the integrity of the person, not to be tortured and/or detained without a trial to name just a few, social and economic rights refer to the satisfaction of goods and needs. The rights of solidarity refer to something vague and sometimes ambiguous. This is especially true when it comes to 'the right to the common heritage of mankind'. It also seems that with 'Third World' countries entering the debate on human rights, these rights more or less benefit them and may be invoked as a reason for their poor human rights record. It is borne in mind that the rights to a clean environment and to peace are for humankind as a whole. 'Rights of solidarity' seem to represent the rights of 'Third World' countries on the developed world. Self-determination, in the sense of independence and development are a call on colonial powers to end their domination and to take steps towards developing this part of the world. Likewise the rights to a healthy and ecologically balanced environment and to peace, although they are for the good of the planet, are a call on the developed world, which has the technology and the know-how to deal with environmental problems and help 'Third World' countries overcoming them.

However, to what extent can we conclude that a person is denied human rights if that person is denied the right to development or is living in an imbalanced environment, in the same sense that he is tortured or denied the right to take part in the government? As far as the author is aware, only the right to development was recognised as an inalienable human right by the United Nations in December 1986. There is enough ground upon which an argument can be made that the right to peace and the right to a healthy and ecologically balanced environment could be considered inalienable human rights. The United Nations is aware of the importance of these factors and many steps have been taken, as discussed above, to reduce the threats to the environment and of wars and to set standards for achievement. If the reader recalls the definition of human rights Donnelly suggested in the first chapter, that 'they are rights one has by the mere fact of being a human being', and the conclusion Cranston reached that they are 'the moral rights of all people in all situations', then it becomes apparent that the rights to peace and to a healthy environment fall within this category. 'If advocates of the "new human rights"', Alston argues, 'assert that we have a moral right to peace, to the environment, and so on, then many will be inclined to agree' (1984, 259). From a moral point of view, it makes little, if any, difference if a human being is killed or being exposed to radiation or other diseases that may result from an unhealthy environment. Life itself is endangered under such circumstances. These rights, contrary to the ones discussed before, are not contested from a universal versus relative view-point. They are universal, and for biological reasons, affect everybody to the same extent regardless of other considerations. However, against whom these rights are invoked remains the most difficult question to answer.

As far as the first two generations are concerned, governments are responsible for the denial of such rights. Although it depends on how wealthy a country is, in the case of economic and social rights, still the responsibility of failing to provide for these rights is much easier to determine. In the case of the 'third generation', however, the task is difficult, if not impossible. A need for international co-operation is urgent and the relationship between these rights is greater. Van Boven reminds us that it 'is absolutely important that in an era of explosive population growth, exhaustion of natural resources, immense stockpiling of weapons of mass destruction and so-called conventional weapons, international co-operation in such areas as disarmament, development, ecology and human rights is a *sine-qua non* for survival' (in Forsythe, 1989, 133-4). In this respect, the United Nations has been organising different programmes to respond to the challenges of the major current issues. The 29th Graduate Study Programme held in Geneva, July 1991 entitled 'United Nations: International Response to Global Issues', which the author attended, held development, disarmament, environment and human rights as the major issues under discussion.

Undoubtedly, the rights of the 'third generation' have created more ambiguity surrounding the concept of human rights and have widened its scope. It goes without saying that, from a moral point of view, they can be claimed as human rights, but they are too vague in scope and application. Marks stresses that it 'is frequently said that the rights of the new generation are too vague to be justifiable and are no more than slogans, at best for advancing laudable goals of the UN, at worst useful for the propaganda of certain countries' (1981, 451).

Whether they are slogans for propaganda, or they are used to advance debate within the United Nations, their challenges and threats to the human person cannot be denied. Humankind is faced more than ever before with the prospect of self-extinction. The time has come for human rights to be looked at from a global point of view, and efforts should be joined together to face up to these challenges. That is what the rights of the 'third generation' try to address. However, until the process of law-making, of turning these 'rights' into internationally binding documents is set in motion, talk of a third generation of human rights, on the same scale as the first and second generation remains in a world of speculation.

The third generation of human rights on a cross-national basis

Before any comparative study of human rights on a cross-national basis, which includes the rights of the third generations, is attempted, it would be more appropriate to consider their quantification. Can the rights of the third generation be measured at all? How can these measures be applied on a cross-national basis? Have they been used, especially in connection with the case studies undertaken in the next part of this book, in the comparative study of human rights?

The rights of the 'third generation' are relatively easy to quantify. An exception must be made for the right to the common heritage of mankind, and to a lesser extent the right to development. There are scientific methods whereby precise statistics about the levels of air and water pollution can be obtained. This leads to the setting up of minimum standards of achievement below which no country is permitted to fall. In other words, it provides a benchmark against which the performance of countries in this area is judged. It leaves no room for argument that historical circumstances or religious reasons, for instance, as is the case with the previous set of rights, play a significant role in determining these rights. It does not take a lot of effort to convince anybody that particular levels of pollution are intolerable and that the health of the people is at stake. Thus, in principle, it makes a comparative study of human rights on a cross-national basis a relatively easy task. Whichever country is less polluted, the healthier and ecologically more balanced its environment is, the better its human rights are. Nevertheless, the question is not as simple as might be seen for several reasons. Firstly, some countries may set lower standards than others to attract investment. As long as the minimum standard is achieved, they may not look far beyond that. Secondly, environmental problems that industrialised countries face are simply due to the levels of technology they have reached; developing countries simply do not have the means to decrease the danger. Further, protection of the environment requires a well-informed population aware that every action has its consequences on the environment. This awareness is yet to reach the agenda of many 'Third World' countries where poverty, illiteracy and hunger still prevail. Finally, and perhaps the most important of all, pollution of some countries may not be the fault of their own. It may be a result of natural disasters, or the actions of their neighbours. Switzerland provides the best example of this, where pollution, it claims, is caused by neighbouring countries.

Given these circumstances, although it is possible to imagine a ranking of countries on such grounds, it is doubtful if it could yield genuine and convincing results. Why should country A, for instance, be ranked below Y or Z at a time when the latter had high levels of pollution for reasons beyond their control? Further, a country lacking the technology to recycle and preserve the environment is bound to be near the bottom of the ladder. The same measures could be applied to the right to peace. Is it fair to suggest that the more a country produces arms, the less it observes human rights? There is no doubt about the relationship between armament and the right to peace. Nonetheless, this would leave many 'Third World' countries outside the scope of comparison, and as a result they would benefit from such an exercise. It goes without saying that every country violates human rights in terms of polluting the environment and producing arms. Nevertheless, in the case of the latter, only a handful of countries are capable of producing weapons of mass destruction. Upon what scale can we judge these countries? Would not every country produce the same weapons if it had the means? While the most important question remains: is there enough information on this delicate issue to carry out a valid comparative study?

. The aim of the foregoing discussion is not to deny how important such issues are in terms of human rights. Whether they are inalienable human rights or not is still a debatable question. What is certain is that they constitute very significant moral claims to be considered as such. However, applying them on a cross-national basis poses a lot of difficulties. How does one obtain a ranking of countries? And upon what basis should the ranking of these countries take place?

It is relatively easy to compare countries on the dimensions discussed above. The right to the common heritage of mankind poses some problems. However, these rights have yet to be combined and used to compare countries in terms of human rights. As far as the present author is aware, some of these have indeed been used, explicitly or implicitly, in different attempts to quantify human rights on a cross-national basis. I shall particularly look at this in connection with the different attempts discussed in the next part of this work.

Universalism, relativism and human rights

As pointed out earlier, it has been the general practice among scholars of human rights to group them into three competing perceptions: those of western, socialist and 'Third World' countries. Each perception is associated with one of the three generations of human rights. It is also usually argued that the idea of human rights is derived from the Western liberal democratic heritage which has little, if any, relevance to other parts of the world. Others suggest that human rights should be applicable anywhere regardless of place or time.

There are two major competing schools of thought in the ongoing debate on human rights: universalist and relativist (Donoho, 1991; Renteln, 1990; Donnelly 1984, 1993). The former emphasise the universality of human rights and their applicability everywhere, whereas the later stress diversity and difference. The discussion that follows will compare and contrast these two differing views, their impact on human rights, and will set the theoretical background of the arguments contained in this work.

For rights to be universal, they should be enjoyed by everybody regardless of any other considerations. Thus, universal human rights cannot be based on some conditions which have to be met. They cannot be earned, in the sense that one has to qualify to enjoy them, and cannot be renounced. They are held by everybody by the mere fact of being human and their basis is moral rather than political. On the universality of rights, there is an emerging widespread consensus regarding definitions of human rights. This can be partly explained by the findings of anthropologists which will suggest that some values can travel cross-culturally. Some practices such as torture and killings are condemned almost everywhere. Moreover, the Universal Declaration of Human Rights (1948) has come to be accepted universally, and the rights it embodies should be respected. Article 1 of this Declaration clearly epitomises this universal view:

> All human beings are born free and equal in dignity and rights. They are endowed with reason and conscience and should act towards one another in a spirit of brotherhood.

Furthermore, the fact that the two International Covenants (1966) have been ratified by a growing number of countries suggests that the universality of human rights is an actuality. The preambles to these documents cite 'the inherent dignity and the equal and inalienable rights of all members of the human family' as the basis for human rights. In addition to these, the 'socialist' concept of human rights, discussed in the second chapter, had begun, even before the end of communist rule, to incorporate much of the 'liberal' definition. With the collapse of communism, they have come to accept the Western perception of human rights and steps have been taken to ensure the respect of many of the civil and political rights formerly denied. This, undoubtedly, leads to a greater consensus on human rights and a more universal view. The end of the 'Cold War' has particularly helped the universal argument. Donnelly (1993), for instance, suggests that the traditional division of rights into categories is no longer relevant. Economic and Social rights have been highly valued in many Western countries. The British welfare state and the Scandinavian countries provide the best example. Similarly, political rights and civil liberties have come to the forefront of the political agenda of former communist countries in the late 1980s. Their experiences, and those of some 'Third World' countries suggest that these rights are valued by the people regardless of what their governments may say.

The other theoretical approach is that of relativism. Relativist theorists (Renteln, 1990), argue that human rights are a social and historical phenomenon and therefore cannot be explained outside their specific environment. If one recalls Cranston's test to judge the authenticity of human rights, he stresses that they should be universal, and concludes that 'human rights are moral rights of all people in every situation' (in Raphael, 1967, 47-49), or a universalist's view that the basis of human rights are moral not political, then the universality approach can no longer stand. Morality is a practice that can be accepted, explained and justified in a given culture or society, which does not necessarily mean acceptance in another. Ruth Benedict, an American anthropologist, rightly concluded, after observing the diversity of customs, that 'morality differs in every society and is a convenient term for socially approved habits' (Rentlen, 1990, 66). Anthropologists have long shown that some practices which cannot be accepted in some societies are followed in others. The diversity of cultural and political traditions between societies results in a diversity of values and positions vis-à-vis particular social practices. It goes without saying that some of the practices carried out in an Islamic state, for example, might be seen as barbaric in another country even though they are accepted in the society in which they occur. 'Relativists suggest that the specific content depends upon the cultural, political and social characteristics of each country' (Donoho, 1991, 368). Marxists, for instance, support this claim. Human nature, according to them, is neither universal nor fixed. It depends on material conditions. Moreover, the wording of the International Covenant on Economic, Social and Cultural Rights, as a matter of fact, suggests the relativist idea of human rights. The Covenant addresses states party (for further details see chapter five) with reference to their national economy, which may influence the extent to which they would guarantee the rights recognised in the Covenant. Moreover, the fact that the International Covenant on Civil and Political Rights has provided, in Article 4, for the states party to the Covenant to 'take measures derogating from their obligations' is another argument in favour of the relativity of human rights. Thus, as a matter of fact, considerable diversity does exist and continues to exist. Institutions, social and political, have varied and evolved in time and space. However, does this mean that human rights should be seen as culture specific and the search for universality should be abandoned?

There is no easy answer to this question. In any case, it is very difficult to take either side of the debate, as each approach has its strong arguments. What is clear, however, is that most, if not all, countries in the 'third world' have come to take the relativist approach to human rights. It must be acknowledged, however, that sometimes this approach has been taken as an excuse to violate these rights. The difficult economic and social conditions of these countries have a bearing on their economic records. One may sympathise with these countries that because of practical difficulties some of the human rights are not provided for. However, poverty does not justify torture or extra-judicial killings. On the other hand, by arguing that mankind is one and taking the universalist approach one is bound to overlook the social, economic, religious and cultural factors which shape the conduct and morals of peoples in a given society.

Human rights involve disputes about their proper uses and contents. It is an 'essentially contested concept' (for a general discussion on this see Connolly, 1983, 9-45). It is commonly used for rhetorical and legitimisation purposes, but still poorly understood. It can mean different things to different people, although it is very much associated with particular freedoms and needs. It does not describe something in particular, but refers to certain norms and values. In the next part of this book, I shall conceive of the concept of human rights in normative terms. However, even though there are some values shared by different cultures, the approach leans more towards relativism than universalism.

Part Two: Case studies

After a general discussion of the definitions and development of human rights, this part deals with some of the attempts that have been made to measure human rights, freedom and democracy on a cross-national basis. It should be pointed out from the beginning that two of these case studies have refrained from such a directly comparative exercise: Amnesty International and the United Nations Human Rights Committee. For them this phenomenon cannot be measured and they accordingly abstain from any attempt to do so. Amnesty's role is to publicise cases and pressurise governments to treat their citizens fairly. The Human Rights Committee, on the other hand, deals only with states which are party to the Covenant on Civil and Political Rights, under which the Committee was established. These states have accepted the rights of the Committee to examine their reports on compliance with the provisions of the Covenant, and to seek expert advice whenever it is needed.

Others, despite difficulties which will be discussed at a later stage, have developed frameworks within which the measurement and therefore ranking of countries in terms of human rights, democracy and freedom on a cross-national, and sometimes continuous basis can be achieved. These include the works of Charles Humana, Robert Dahl, Kenneth Bollen, and Freedom House, each of which will be discussed in the second part of this book.

The choice of these particular case studies has been made on several grounds: first of all they serve the purpose of this work - to assess the different attempts to measure human rights. Secondly, they are among the leading authorities on the subject: for instance, Amnesty's reputation for impartiality is second to none, and Humana had, before his recent death, become an international authority on human rights whose work was adopted for its own purposes by the United Nations Development Program. Thirdly, they have different approaches to the subject: while some studies produce tables of rankings, others just publicise cases or help countries to comply with internationally binding documents. This is turn, enables them to establish the most effective way in which the human rights situation in the world can be improved. Fourthly, the availability of information and especially primary material, and access to people involved with these case studies such as Professor Rosalyn Higgins, a member of the Human Rights Committee at the London School of Economics and Political Science or the Director of the British Section of Amnesty International, dictated the selection of these cases rather than others.

Within these case studies I look at a number of countries: different countries in each case study. One may object to this and prefer the inclusion of the same countries in each case to assess the extent of differences, if any, within these case studies when dealing with the same country. This is a possible option, however, the choice of different countries in each case study has been made for practical reasons. First, some countries, the United States of America to name just one, have not ratified the International Covenant on Civil and Political Rights and therefore cannot be included when looking at the work of the Human Rights Committee. Moreover, the first (1983) and the second (1986) edition of Charles Humana's study dealt with only 75 and 89 countries respectively, and the choice of countries can only be taken from the countries he considered. Thirdly, the countries in question were chosen to redress the shortcomings from which any individual case study may suffer.

By taking these case studies and the different countries included in each, it is aimed to demonstrate the limits attendant upon any exercise seeking to measure human rights on a cross-national basis. The differences in the approaches taken in the case studies help to establish the most effective way to achieve an overall improvement in the realisation of human rights, and finally, to draw attention to the lessons that can be learned from each of the case studies for future research on the comparative study of human rights.

4 Amnesty International

In this chapter an attempt will be made to evaluate the work of Amnesty International and its usefulness to comparative politics. In other words, does Amnesty International offer a broad basis upon which it is possible to compare political systems in terms of human rights on a cross-national basis? And if it does not, how can one make the best use of the information provided by Amnesty International to compare political systems?

To answer these questions this chapter will be divided into four main sections. The first section examines the origins of Amnesty International as well as its structure, with a view to determining whether the organisation is really as independent as it claims. Then, the mandate or the basis upon which its work is carried out will be discussed and the difficulties that may arise are considered. This mandate should help to establish whether Amnesty's work is widely applicable when looking at particular countries. China, Nicaragua and the Middle East are examples of countries which offer a real challenge to the work of Amnesty. The chapter concludes with an overview of the discussion from the perspective of comparative politics, difficulties that will face the comparativist in conducting research and how the best possible use can be made of Amnesty's work.

The origins and structure of Amnesty International

The origins of Amnesty International

Amnesty International, winner of the Nobel Peace Prize in 1977, is a world-wide, non-governmental organisation aiming to defend human rights. It arose under its original name of 'Appeal for Amnesty 1961', the year which marked 'the centenary of the freeing of the slaves in the United States and the Serfs in Russia' (Power, 1983, 10). When it was launched there was not a single treaty, apart from the Geneva Conventions which are applied in times of war and which curtailed or prohibited governments from carrying out such barbarous acts (A I. Report 1986, 1). People were imprisoned, tortured or killed simply because they held different opinions from those of the state.

An incident that took place in Portugal, during the days of Salazar's dictatorship, inspired Benenson to launch his appeal. Two students were arrested and sentenced to seven years' imprisonment solely for raising their glasses for freedom. Such incidents were, and are indeed, very common in many countries. Benenson protested outside the Portuguese Embassy in London and decided to launch a campaign aimed at bringing attention to injustices occurring in the world. With the help of friends, 'Appeal for amnesty 1961' was launched, after an article was published in *The Observer* in May 1961 entitled 'The Forgotten Prisoners'. In this article, Benenson highlighted the cases of eight people from different countries who had been imprisoned because of their political opinions.

Nevertheless, what began as a one year campaign to put an end to such practices and publicise them wherever they occurred, soon developed into an organisation after the general international concern and attention it received. Soon different Amnesty International sections had spread throughout Europe, beginning in what was then West Germany. Moreover, after only eight weeks since its official birth, delegates from Britain, France, Belgium, Ireland, Switzerland and the United States of America met in Luxembourg to decide about the future of their movement. They realised that the movement should not be limited to a one year campaign, but had to develop into a permanent organisation, bringing injustices to the attention of people and working on behalf of those wrongly imprisoned. Moreover, it had to change its name to Amnesty International in order to reflect its status (Amnesty International, 1976b, 2). By the end of that year, there were Amnesty sections in different countries with their headquarters in London.

The organisation went through different crises and tensions in the mid 1960s which could have had dire consequences for its future. For example, the black African leader Nelson Mandela was imprisoned in 1962 and adopted by Amnesty as a 'prisoner of conscience'. However, two years later, when he was charged with sabotage, Amnesty decided against adopting him in order to safeguard the concept of 'prisoner of conscience'. Mandela advocated violence and, according to Amnesty standards, did not have the right of adoption. However, it had to make sure that he would have a fair trial. Further, the discovery of the involvement of the British government in helping the organisation financially could have killed the movement. Benenson became very suspicious of his friends, thinking they were part of British Intelligence who were infiltrating the organisation (Power, 1983, 16-17). At the same time there was tension in the relations between Amnesty and the Foreign Office over Amnesty's report on Aden, a former British colony. This had negative effects on the work of Amnesty as its leadership split.

Nevertheless, the organisation survived these challenges, grew and expanded, especially in the mid 1970s as a result of the civil protest associated with the Vietnam War. The ill-treatment reported in different countries made thousands of people believe in the goals of Amnesty and joined its campaign. This, in turn, led to the expansion of countries investigated, such as China or Nicaragua, where the first missions and reports were carried out in the mid 1970s (Interview 2).

What began as a small movement became an organisation of more than 1.2 million members, subscribers and supporters in almost every country. This number increased over time because of the efforts made by the organisation in raising peoples' consciousness about their rights. The International Rock Tour 'Human Rights Now!' which began on 2 September, 1988 in London and comprised different countries from the four corners of the world, was instrumental in raising many peoples' consciousness and winning them over to Amnesty's side. At each concert, the text of the Universal Declaration of Human Rights was read and distributed. Moreover, the organisation established sections and local groups throughout the world. In May 1991, for instance, Amnesty was authorised to open an office in Moscow (Benn, 1992, 30). The groups work on behalf of prisoners from different ideological and geographical backgrounds. Amnesty does not recognise any boundaries while carrying out its work. 'It rejects charges that such action is 'interference in the international affairs of that state in question' (Garling, 1979, 8).

The structure of Amnesty International

Amnesty International's sections and groups are the bottom of the structural hierarchy of the organisation which are recognised by the International

Executive Committee. However, it should be pointed out that there are some local groups even in countries where there are no sections. These groups can be set up by either the Amnesty International section or from the International Secretariat in London. There are more than 6000 Amnesty groups in more than 70 countries (Garling, 1979, 8). They usually consist of 10 to 15 members whose main task is to work on behalf of individual prisoners. Their organisations differ from one group to another in a manner which they think will achieve better results, as long as the statutes and the goals of Amnesty International are observed.

Sections, however, are of great importance to the work of Amnesty. They publicise its goals, increase peoples' awareness and engage in fund-raising. Their size depends on the country in which they operate. They might have a central headquarters and different regional offices, or just a few members. In carrying out their work, they can appoint either one person or a group to act as country co-ordinators or co-ordination groups. Their main task is to co-ordinate efforts of the work in one specific country or one special part of the world. In other words, they play a key role between the Research Department in the International Secretariat in London, and different sections throughout the world to produce high quality and accurate reports about the countries that are chosen for investigation. Thus, co-ordination is viewed as one of the major tasks of Amnesty's work. Nevertheless, it should be pointed out that these sections 'work on behalf of up to three political prisoners - always selected from contrasting backgrounds and never from the group's own country' (Garling, 1979, 9). In this way, Amnesty attempts to make its work more 'objective'. Moreover, professional groups such as doctors and lawyers may help these sections in working on behalf of different individual cases. Furthermore, these sections send delegates to the International Council.

The International Council used to meet every year. However, from 1983 onwards it decided to meet every two years. About two to three hundred delegates or representatives of all the national sections attend the International Council, which is a democratically elected governing body and the only body which has the authority to decide the movement's future policy. It reviews the activities of the past two years, sets the plans for what is to be done for the next ones and approves the budget, and also elects eight members, including a treasurer, to the International Executive Committee.

The International Executive Committee consists of nine elected persons, seven representing different Amnesty sections or countries, a treasurer, and a further member representing the staff of the International Secretariat. Apart from the latter who is only eligible for two years, all the others are eligible for two years renewable up to three mandates. The Committee is the main governing body between two council meetings. It meets four times a year. It is responsible for implementing decisions taken by the International Council, and for discussing missions, publications and how to approach governments. Among its members, it elects its senior staff. Therefore, elections have been seen as one of the major tools through which Amnesty tries to safeguard its independence and impartiality (Interview 2). A sample of these elections could be seen in those who hold the post of General-Secretary. Up to 1981 there were: Irish, German, Swede, Chilean. Moreover, since the mid 1960s, all Amnesty finances are carefully controlled and scrutinised to avoid any governmental involvement. 'No government donations can be accepted by any part of the movement, nor can government money be sought for international budget. The International Executive Committee must be notified for all the donations to sections that amount to more than five per cent of their annual income' (Amnesty International, 1983, 34). Its budget is controlled either by the International Council or the International Executive Committee, and the treasurer is responsible for its expenditure. The records are always kept and are available for public inquiry. It can set up international specialist advisory committees to help it in carrying out its work, such as the financial control committee or the medical advisory board.

The International Secretariat is the headquarters of the movement based in London. It began in Benenson's office and developed into a complex secretariat with more than 250 paid staff from more than 40 countries. There has been a lot of argument about moving it from London to another country. Benenson, even after he retired, still believed that the Secretariat should not be based in London. However, because of the wide range of activities that London offers, the Secretariat, remained there.

Although it seems that much of the work is carried out by the local groups throughout the world, nonetheless, it is the International Secretariat which makes the crucial decisions and keeps the international sections and local groups up to date when gathering information, and gives directives to them. The Secretariat is divided into different departments and these will be briefly discussed.

The Secretary-General's Office: The Secretary-General and his deputy are responsible for the everyday activities of the organisation. They are involved in making public statements, and give guidance on how to approach governments. The Secretary-General implements decisions of both the International Council and the International Executive Committee, and heads the International Secretariat. His office is involved in co-ordinating different departments within the Secretariat. In doing so, it benefits from the help of two specialised units: (A) The Legal Office which gives advice about international human rights standards and different legal questions, whether they concern Amnesty's statute or the interpretation of the standards that the organisation tries to safeguard. (B) The Documentation Centre which is the main point where all the information is kept. All Amnesty's work is based upon different information gathered and whenever it is needed in the form of archives, video-tapes, or library references.

The Research Department plays a significant role in enhancing the quality of the work produced since it is involved from the first act of collecting information to its publication. Great care is taken in analysing and verifying the information obtained to distinguish between facts and allegations. Thus, all information presented about torture, ill-treatment and capital punishment is accurate, according to Amnesty (Interview 2). It is on basis of the information available that the organisation decides on who can be adopted as a 'prisoner of conscience'. This Department is divided into five sections or divisions (on a geographical base) and each division covers a different part of the world. These include Africa, Asia, the Americas, Europe and the Middle East. Each division is analysed through annual reports produced by Amnesty. This allows each division to work on a particular geographic area to produce more specialised and accurate accounts. The Department also has a wide-ranging network of contacts, as well as making proposals about the distribution of relief and helping prisoners and their families.

The Campaign and Membership Department liaises with different Amnesty sections, groups and members world-wide, co-ordinates their actions or ask for urgent action whenever it is needed. Moreover, it seeks support increasing Amnesty's membership in other parts of the world, apart from western countries where its membership is overwhelmingly concentrated.

The Press and Publications Department is responsible for Amnesty's relations with the press and the distribution of **Amnesty International's** Newsletter. It is in constant contact with different Amnesty sections to assist them in their efforts to publicise the work of the movement. Although the official languages of the movement are English, French and Spanish, this department is responsible for translating publications and leaflets into different languages for use where the former ones are not spoken.

The Administration Department manages the office and the financial procedures. It is responsible for training new personnel, and arranging travel when a mission is to be carried out.

The preceding structural explanation of Amnesty International's hierarchy is necessary to understand the work of this organisation and the extent of its impartiality. The subject of the following section will be Amnesty International's mandate.

Amnesty International: the mandate

This section focuses on Amnesty International's mandate. In other words, on the basis upon which the organisation operates in carrying out its work. One has to understand the mandate in order to better understand Amnesty International's work. Furthermore, this is necessary background to issues which will be raised later in this chapter. Amnesty has limited itself to certain aspects of human rights violations world-wide, and works within these set limits. These aspects are as follows:

To free prisoners of conscience
In the early 1960s, when Peter Benenson wrote his article entitled 'The Forgotten Prisoners', he stated that:

> Open your newspaper any day of the week, and you will find a report from somewhere in the world of someone being imprisoned, tortured `or executed because his opinions or religion are unacceptable to his government (quoted in Sobel, 1978, 1-2).

Even today, more than three decades since Benenson wrote his article, the same abuses and kinds of reports are found daily. Moreover, such practices are likely to continue in the light of the various political, social and economic circumstances of different countries. Amnesty on the other hand is trying to decrease the practice of jailing political opponents by demanding the unconditional release of all the prisoners it has characterised as 'prisoners of conscience'.

It should be pointed out from the beginning that there is not a generally agreed definition of 'prisoners of conscience'. Although Amnesty tries to define them, there remains some ambiguity. According to Amnesty International, 'a prisoner of conscience' is someone who has been imprisoned solely because of holding opinions contrary to those of the state, providing that they did not advocate violence.

However, whether a person has advocated violence or not in expressing their thoughts is not the only determinant factor to judge whether a person should be considered 'a prisoner of conscience'. It is well understood that Amnesty tries to protect this concept by isolating it from any violent or criminal behaviour, so it can work on behalf of any person whenever it hears of anyone being imprisoned. If a person has advocated violence, they will be considered as 'an outlaw' or 'a criminal' by his/her government, and therefore, there will be no room for Amnesty to act since the person is convicted and sentenced because of his violent acts. It is a question of heads you lose, tails I win on the part of these governments. As a result, situations may arise where hundreds of people are jailed or tortured solely for expressing their views, whereas their governments claim that they were jailed because of their criminal activities. Thus, different organisations, among them Amnesty, close their eyes in order to safeguard their image as respectable organisations which do not support 'terrorist acts'. However, the minimum Amnesty claims is that it will make sure that everybody has a fair trial. Nelson Mandela is a good example of a person who was not considered as 'a prisoner of conscience' because he was convicted of sabotage in 1964. At the same time the Universal Declaration of Human Rights, which Amnesty according to its charter seeks to implement, does recognise the use of violence as a last resort. According to the preamble of the Universal Declaration, Desmond reminds us that it 'recognizes that if human rights are not protected by law, then men will be compelled, as a last resort to rebel against repression and tyranny' (1983, 48).

Therefore, 'a prisoner of conscience', according to Amnesty, is characterised by the non-use of violence and imprisoned because of his/her opinions. But is the definition adequate and can one rely on Amnesty's literature? In other words, are 'prisoners of conscience' defined in this way only in Amnesty's publications? The answer of course is no. This term has been used to describe some people being captured, tortured by mistake, or because of their family ties with a genuine 'prisoner of conscience'. Although Amnesty insists on not adopting or considering people imprisoned by mistake as 'prisoners of conscience' (Interview 2), a very convincing example of just that could be found in one of Amnesty's publications itself which states that:

> In El Salvador, two married couples and their young children are staying in a friend's house while she is away, when uniformed members of the security forces burst in, demanding to know where the friend is. They tortured the adults in front of the children, then beat the screaming children - one aged five - before taking all to San Salvador's central barracks. Some days later the children are found in a juvenile reform center. The adults have "disappeared", they became prisoners of conscience (quoted in Desmond, 1983, 47).

In this case, there is no indication of the political or ideological beliefs of the two adults. Nobody knows whether their opinions are opposed to the state or not, or even whether they have any political opinions at all. If a person knows a wanted or 'suspicious' person, it does not necessarily follow that they share that person's opinions. If the owner of the house, in the case above, could be classified as a 'prisoner of conscience', this does not mean in any case that her friends would be. All it says is that these people were imprisoned because they were in the wrong place at the wrong time. Although Amnesty considered them 'prisoners of conscience', their conscience, however, had nothing to do with their imprisonment.

In line with this analysis, the adoption of anybody as 'a prisoner of conscience' imprisoned solely because of their ideas could give rise to different violations of human rights through the widespread advocacy of racist ideas. An Amnesty spokesman has said that Amnesty 'would adopt as a prisoner of conscience a person imprisoned for expressing racist views, provided only they had not advocated violence' (ibid., 50).

Such a position represents a potential threat to other aspects of human rights in today's world. This is especially true in the European context after the re-emergence of extreme right wing groups. For example, what would have been the fate of hundreds of thousands of people in France, especially from North Africa, if a man like Le Pen, leader of the National Front, notorious because of his racist ideas, had won the presidential elections in France? Let us assume that he was imprisoned at a time because of his racist ideas - although it is highly unlikely to happen in a country like France where freedom of expression is guaranteed. Further, he was adopted by Amnesty as 'a prisoner of conscience', since he fitted the standards and was then freed. As President he would have deported almost every immigrant worker under his famous slogan 'La France pour les Francais'. The question to be asked here is, what would have been the position of Amnesty with regard to such violations? Once again, an antagonism between the provisions of the Universal Declaration and Amnesty's work is easily discernible.

Not only is the term 'prisoners of conscience' ambiguous and the criteria by which it is defined are not clear cut or widely acceptable, but some political considerations could be involved in making such a judgement also. Anybody who is in a psychiatric hospital in the West can be considered as just mentally ill, but a similar patient in the former Soviet Union could have been considered as a 'prisoner of conscience', regardless of the norms of the society or its laws. Although Amnesty takes into account the standards developed by the World Psychiatric Association in considering the cases (Interview 2), the practices differ between countries. 'Under the Soviet law if you are said to have committed a crime and if at the same time there is a reason to believe that you were not or are not in your right senses or were not at the same time of committing it, then your psychiatric examination must be ordered' (Dowrick, 1979, 130).

The death penalty

The death penalty is the basic violation of human rights, and all other rights depend on the right to life. It would be absurd to speak about the rights of the people, regardless if they were economic, social or political, if the right to life is threatened. Therefore, Amnesty International is totally opposed to it. Thomas Hammarberg, a former director of the British Section, stated that:

Amnesty International is committed by its statute to oppose by all
appropriate means the imposition and infiltration of the death penalty, on
the ground that it violates the right to life and that it is the most cruel,
inhuman and degrading of all forms of punishment (Amnesty
International, 1979, 1).

However, if Amnesty does not believe in capital punishment and works
for its total abolition, it does not offer an alternative that would be
appropriate. Some argue, among them Amnesty, that the death penalty is a
barbaric act and one of the most cruel punishments, but others see that
imposing it is sometimes the only punishment appropriate to the crime
committed. Moreover, there is no alternative punishment to the death penalty
which satisfies both parties, i.e., Amnesty which calls for its abolition and
societies' demands that the crime committed receives appropriate retribution.
This issue has been raised with Amnesty (Interview 2), and the organisation
thinks that the outcome will very much depend on the situation and the
country itself, though life imprisonment is a viable alternative. However, if
the alternative depends on the country itself, then its abolition or
implementation depends also on the situation of the country and its
particularities. To emphasise total abolition of the death penalty represents
Amnesty's viewpoint, but does not necessarily represent the views of
different countries. Some leaders believe that the death penalty is cruel and
barbaric, but recognise it to be a necessity in some instances. For example,
Amnesty states that:

Colonel Qaddafi called for the death penalty to be abolished and replaced
with life imprisonment. In 1985 he expressed his personal opposition to
the death penalty as a cruel punishment but that it should be used in
certain cases (1988, 3).

There is much controversy about the use of the death penalty. Errors
can happen, and people can be wrongly convicted. Some countries do
implement the death penalty because of their internal situations, others
because of their traditions and beliefs, as will be seen later in the case
studies. However, if life imprisonment is taken as a genuine alternative to the
death penalty, then more questions will be asked about the state of the

prisons and whether they meet certain basic requirements which are not necessarily available in many developing countries. Further, those sentenced to life imprisonment might benefit from the general amnesties whenever presidential elections are won or a human rights day is celebrated.

Nevertheless, one should be objective in determining whether the death penalty is a violation of human rights or not. In other words, do countries which have abolished it have better human rights records than those which have not? Moreover, should it be abolished in the first place? Amnesty think that the abolition of the death penalty is a very significant step in observing human rights. However, it would be better if it remained for some cases. It is absurd that capital punishment is carried out in some countries, such as China, for example, for a wide range of offences which would not warrant this sentence, but that it should serve as a deterrent in order to decrease the overall rate of crimes. It should not be carried out as mass killings such as in Iran or as rally killings in China. A mass killer does not deserve less than capital punishment for the crimes they committed regardless of whether Amnesty thinks that their country does not observe human rights. The right of the collective should come before the right of a person in this case. How important is the life of a criminal compared to the lives of the collective? And to some extent this is the reason behind different opinions advocating the use of the death penalty.

A prompt and fair trial

It should be pointed out from the beginning that Amnesty seeks a fair and prompt trial for all political prisoners. It distinguishes between a 'prisoner of conscience', as discussed earlier, and a political prisoner. The latter is someone who has been imprisoned because of his beliefs and opinions while advocating violence. If a person has advocated violence, Amnesty would not have the credibility to ask for his release (Interview 2), but only for fair a trial. The question is how can this fairness be achieved?

Amnesty believes that a prisoner should have a legal representative and be tried in public. It relies on the expertise of its representative through missions. Missions are frequently sent to different countries to observe trials. The delegates are forbidden from talking to the press, and urged to declare themselves to the authorities and the judges in the courtroom (Amnesty International, 1988, 13). Such practices have proved very successful in ensuring fair trials.

Nevertheless, the differences between the criminal codes and their ambiguity make the task very difficult to state whether a trial was fair or not. A person convicted under article 70 of the Soviet criminal code which deals with Agitation and Propaganda, the punishment of which may be 'imprisonment for a period of from six months to seven years and with exile from two to five years' (Lane, 1985, 273), for instance, could be considered to have had a fair trial from the former Soviet point of view, but not from Amnesty's. Then, the question to be asked is what are the main criteria upon which one might suggest that the trial was fair or not?

There are acceptable general principles of fairness that can usually be applied. Presumption of innocence until proven guilty, equality before the law and the right to a defence lawyer are criteria upon which one can judge whether a trial was fair or not. However, what is considered fair is what can find its justification in the general opinion which believes in that practice, which in turn, finds its acceptance rooted in the social system as a whole. In other words, what is fair is what finds its acceptance and response from the public in a particular area in a given period of time. And, given the diversity of societies and cultures, what could be considered as fair in one country, would not necessarily be considered as such from another point of view or in another country.

Case studies

The choice of countries as case studies has not been an easy task. They are from different political and ideological backgrounds than that in which Amnesty International has developed. Although Amnesty claims to be independent and does not support any political or economic system, the choice of countries should help us to gain a better understanding of the work of this organisation in a different context. First of all the choice of a Communist country is unavoidable, because it has different perceptions and priorities in terms of human rights than those which Amnesty tries to defend. In this context, the former Soviet Union would have been the most natural choice. It was the leading country in experiencing 'communism', and a great deal of literature, especially Amnesty's publications, are available on its record. However, as pointed out in the previous sections, Amnesty International tries to implement the provisions of the Universal Declaration, and its work is based on pointing out the gulf between what countries commit themselves to do, and what they do in reality. Garling states that: 'By approaching governments from the angle of their own prior commitments, Amnesty International has a moral leverage through which to press for the release of individuals or the redress of particular injustices' (1979, 8). However, since the former Soviet Union ratified the two International Covenants, (see chapter five) China would offer, to some extent, the same characteristics but did not ratify either of the instruments. It is thus not legally bound to observe their provisions. Moreover, it has its own perception of human rights, and it is the most populous country in the world, which make its inclusion in this study desirable in itself. The second country chosen is Nicaragua. The choice was made for political reasons, and most notably for the instability of the political system. Nicaragua has experienced a great deal of human rights violations under the dynasty of the Somoza family, and it would be interesting to see how the revolutionary government under former president Daniel Ortega tried to cope with the pressure. Finally, the last case study will focus on the countries in the Middle East. These countries provide a unique environment in which Amnesty works. The influence of Islam, especially on the death penalty, is of paramount importance and the reaching a compromise between Amnesty and Islam on the matter will be discussed.

China

First of all, it should be pointed out that it is difficult, if not impossible, to establish a clear picture of the human rights situation in China, at least till the late 1970s. It was only after the death of Chairman Mao and the relaxation of Chinese politics through 'the Beijing Spring', that Amnesty International produced its first full report.

China was generally agreed to have had one of the worst records of human rights violations, especially during the decade of the 'Cultural Revolution', about which little information was available at the time. According to Lizhi, the Chinese Sakharov, '[T]he true record of human rights in China has been hidden: the Chinese authorities have blocked any communication about it. Some have been misled into believing that China has been free of human rights violations' (1992, 2).

The difficulties in assessing human rights in China are practical. It is, by far, the most populous country in the world, and the flow of information has almost been non-existent - though there have been some improvements in the 1980s as will be seen later. The geographical diversity of the country and the strict control of movement and granting visas to foreigners add to these difficulties. Moreover, China has its own perception of human rights and does not believe in international standard. To apply Amnesty's standards to China was therefore to invite discord. Cohen argues that 'its [the Chinese] official conception of human rights markedly diverges from that of the West. Specifically it does not accept "western human rights standards"... China's own concept of human rights sharply differs from those in the Universal Declaration ... its authorities have had to give precedence to food, shelter, health care and education over the other rights' (1987, 464).

Nevertheless, the situation in China began to change after the death of Mao. The dark years of the Cultural Revolution have been highlighted and different figures relating to the people who suffered have been offered. Thousands of people were granted retrials. Amnesty acknowledged that 'since 1977 the Chinese official press has published a number of cases where violations of human rights committed in the People's Republic of China during the past ten years have been redressed' (1987, p. ix). Moreover, there was a moment of relatively free expression during the 'Beijing Spring', which unfortunately did not last for long.

What should be mentioned in this period is that the Chinese adopted two different constitutions (1978 and 1982) and more significantly, changes occurred in the judicial apparatus. The adoption of a new criminal code in 1979, which came into effect on 1 January 1980 was seen as a significant step forward by the Chinese leadership in the building of a 'socialist democracy'. This criminal code was intended to increase the protection of citizens from persecution and arbitrary detention, in order to put an end to the years of 'lawlessness' which had characterised the Cultural Revolution. However, the question is not whether the Chinese leadership had developed measures to respect their citizens' rights, but how far did they go to respect these measures themselves? In other words, is there a gap between the official commitment of the Chinese government, i.e., the constitution and the criminal law, and what is happening in reality? Did the old practices continue despite the adoption of these new measures?

According to official policy and the official statements by the Chinese government, the question of human rights does not arise in the country. A Foreign Ministry spokesman questioned by foreign journalists in Beijing reportedly said that 'the question of political prisoners and human rights violations did not arise in China as its constitution granted citizens the right to speak, to meet, to demonstrate and to publish' (A. I. Report, 1986, 215). However, one should not only limit oneself to official statements or laws, but to what is happening in reality. Different international reports, especially those by Amnesty International, suggest that in China *plus ca change, plus c'est la meme chose*, at least as far as the judicial system is concerned, which remains a major weakness in observing the rights of the Chinese people. 'According to incomplete statistics,' Lizhi states, 'there at least 976 labour reform camps in China,' and although 'it is hard to know exactly how many people are in them, the inmates of certain camps in Xinjiang Province number between 50,000 and 80,000' (1992, 2). Further, the bloody events that Tienanmen Square witnessed in the first week of June 1989, in which 'at least 10,000 people were killed and thousands injured' (A. I. Report 1990, 65), prove the Foreign Ministry spokesman wrong and show that China has a long way to go to secure such rights. Equality of all the citizens before the law, for instance, although guaranteed by the 1982 Constitution does not exist in the practices of the judicial system. Instead 'political considerations', according to Power, 'have always been taken into account in the treatment of offenders, and this trend has been marked since the Cultural Revolution' (1983, 77).

This was inspired by Mao's teaching when the Chairman declared that the concept of 'the people' varied in different periods of time, and everyone could be subject to the dictatorship of the proletariat depending on the circumstances of that period of time (Amnesty International, 1978, 9). Those who are subject to the dictatorship are deprived of their political and civil rights and therefore considered as having a 'bad political background' or 'bad class origin'. Such labels are carefully scrutinised when conducting investigations. If a person had committed an offence, then the judgement would very much depend on their background. Thus, in its report on political imprisonment in the People's Republic of China (1978), Amnesty stated that:

> ... all cases are treated in the light of political considerations. For instance, petty offenders who have committed minor theft or engaged in speculation may be merely criticized if they have good political or good work records, and good class backgrounds ... On the other hand, the same offence may be punished severely if the offender's social and political background is 'bad', in which case his or her 'crimes' will be considered to be of a political nature (ibid., 13).

This practice, of course, opposes the norms of a fair and prompt trial that Amnesty stresses. The role of the judiciary is clearly defined, but it is heavily under the influence of the Chinese Communist Party. Although the Chinese Criminal Code stresses that nobody should be detained without any charges for longer than 72 hours of detention, the evidence suggests that this rule is not respected (ibid., 46). Perhaps the most publicised case, as far as the French speaking world is concerned, is that of Li Shuang, the Chinese fiancee of Emmanuel Bellefroid, a French diplomat in Beijing. She was arrested on 9 September, 1981 without any charges being prepared against her, and her parents were not allowed to visit her. Two months later she was sentenced to two years of re-education (*Le Monde*, 7 and 12 October, 1981).

A person in detention is asked to write daily reports about his past activities that might help the court to convict him. It is a compulsory act and if someone fails to do so then they are charged with non co-operation with the authorities. It is like a theatrical event where everybody knows exactly what to say and the judgement was sometimes decided before the trial took place (Amnesty International, 1978, 55). The court's judgement depends very much on the defendant's confessions because the official policy stresses that confession deserves leniency, resistance deserves severity which results in people confessing to their 'crimes' to secure leniency. Amnesty reported that 'at the beginning of the trial, Xu Wenli unsuccessfully asked for the presiding judge to be withdrawn on the grounds that the judge had presumed him guilty, having acknowledged his guilt on several occasions before the trial 'to secure lenient treatment' (A. I. Report, 1986, 215). Such an emphasis on defendant's confession led to the use of torture and coercion to extract it. Although such a practice is totally prohibited by law, and 'an official drive began in 1985 to publicise torture and punish responsible officials' (A. I. Report, 1988, 155), it is still a common practice in China's prisons and camps.

The adoption of a new criminal code which was intended to improve the human rights situation in China has not curtailed these abuses. Moreover, it has made things worse in some areas. There are still a lot of people illegally detained and the number has increased over the years. According to Amnesty International during the first half of 1986, 'the number of cases (of illegal detention) nearly doubled over the same period last year, to 949, in which more than 140 were reported to have been tortured' (A. I. Report, 1987, 224), let alone those detained after the Tienanmen Square events solely for expressing their views, and their legitimate demands for peaceful self-expression. However, perhaps the most significant measure is that the new criminal code failed to abolish the death penalty. There is no suggestion that such a practice should be abolished in China, as Amnesty requires, nonetheless, a comparison between the two periods, before and after 1980, suggest that the situation has worsened. Not only has the number of cases punishable by the death penalty increased, but also the speed of sentencing after the judgement was passed. Moreover, different courts, in addition to Supreme People's Court, have become able to pass death sentences without referring them to the Supreme People's Court (Amnesty International, 1984, 53).

The extensive use of the death penalty can be explained in terms of the particularities of China itself. The social and economic situation in which it lives has undoubtedly influenced its position towards capital punishment. While 'most subjected to capital punishment were often accused of internationally recognised crimes', Seymour reminds us, 'but often the offences of economic crimes which could result only in a short prison term in the West' (in Donnelly and Howard, 1987, 84).

Unlike Amnesty International's position, the Chinese officials do stress the importance of the death penalty 'to safeguard social order'. It is used as a warning in order to decrease the number of criminal cases. In November 1893, for instance, the New China News Agency reported that 'criminal cases recorded an overall drop of 46.7 per cent nation-wide from August to September, with a 38.7 per cent decrease in major cases' (Amnesty International, 1984, 80). Nevertheless, despite these measures, China still has a long way to go in observing human rights, not just to international standards, but even to accommodate its practices with its own laws and constitution. The recent events that shook the country may persuade the government to think about new measures and to cope with the demands of the population. The shortcomings of the Chinese government in securing economic and social rights could have an influence on its position. It may perhaps become more flexible in relation to civil and political rights.

Nicaragua

As indicated earlier, Nicaragua was chosen mainly for political reasons (for a general discussion see Walker, 1986). The instability that the country has been experiencing makes the task of evaluating its human rights performance very difficult. Gander argues that 'it is difficult to provide a relatively durable evaluation of human rights in a country undergoing revolutionary transformation. Economic, political and social relations change very quickly, in comparison to more 'stable' systems that have evolved gradually over a century or two' (in Donnelly and Howard, 1987, 253). Nevertheless, an attempt will be made to compare the two periods that Nicaragua has witnessed, i.e., before 1979, during the years of the reign of the Somoza family, and after July 1979, when former President Debayle fled the country to the United States and the revolutionary government assumed power.

'Although it was a matter of public knowledge that the Somoza dynasty had consistently violated the human rights of the Nicaraguan people since its inception,' Medina argues, 'for many years the situation in Nicaragua was not the object of much public scrutiny at international level. In 1978 and 1979 things began to change' (1988, 208). Amnesty International, for instance, sent its first mission to Nicaragua in May 1976. This question was raised with Amnesty and the delay was ascribed to the fact that the Research Department in the International Secretariat did not expand enough, at the time, to cover different countries (Interview 2).

However, one further explanation to this delay may be the fact that the Sandinista National Liberation Front, which took the task of organising the resistance to the Somoza's dynasty, had Marxist-Leninist tendencies. The fear of 'communism' widespread in Latin American led to public opinion turning a blind eye, and the Somoza government was labelled corrupt, rather than one which systematically violated the human rights of the Nicaraguan people. In the mid 1970s, however, the situation dramatically changed. Human rights violations by the National Guard reached their peak and these practices had to be denounced. The indiscriminate bombing of civilians, and the disappearances of peasants in the northern part of the country were very common. In 1979 Amnesty International reported that after the bombing of the civilians from the air 'some 5,000 people had died, 10,000 were injured, 25,000 had lost their homes and 57,000 are believed to have fled into exile in neighbouring Honduras and Costa Rica' (A. Report, 1979, 69).

Such violations happened under the rules of a state of emergency or martial law, which had been in force in Nicaragua since 1974. Many of these violations, according to the Nicaraguan government, occurred in the northern and western states where the guerrilla forces were concentrated. Wholesale killings and disappearances of peasants and farmers occurred because they were supposed to have had links with, or supported the guerrillas. However, this does not in any way mean that the abuses were concentrated in this area only; they covered the country as a whole. Such was the scale of human rights abuses that Republican Congressman Ronald Dellums inserted, in the congressional record on 24 March 1976, a report on political imprisonment in Nicaragua in which he suggested that 'the arrests have occurred throughout the Republic, but especially in the Northern and Western states. It is important to clarify that a very large number of people have been detained in spite of having no connection with the guerrillas in these zones' (in Sobel, 1987, 194). As a result, an in-depth discussion of other aspects of human rights violations such as torture or ill-treatment of prisoners does not arise in this context. This does not necessarily mean that such violations did not occur, but what would torturing a prisoner mean compared to the barbaric act of killing the people indiscriminately? A government which deliberately kills its own people has little respect, if any, for other rights.

After the flight of Anastasio Somoza Debayle and the accession to power of the revolutionary government, a fundamental law was issued on 20 July 1979, which replaced the 1974 Constitution. 'Article 6 of the fundamental law gives full recognition to the human rights established in the Universal Declaration of Human Rights, the United Nations Covenants on Economic, Social and Cultural Rights and on Civil and Political Rights' (A. I. Report 1980, 154). In addition to these developments, the death penalty was abolished to show the goodwill of the new government in observing human rights. However, martial law, which suspended almost all the constitutional guarantees, was restored and thousands of people, most of them former members of the National Guard or members of the Somoza's government, were held in police custody. There was ill-treatment and even killings of the prisoners despite the official policy of the government. 'Immediate steps would be taken to prevent misconduct by the Sandinista forces', declared the new Minister of Interior who insisted 'that no prisoner would be ill-treated and that neither the death penalty nor torture would exist after the revolution' (ibid., 155).

The trials of the Guardsmen continued, especially under *Tribunales Especiales de Justicia* (Special Courts) which lasted from December 1979 to February 1981 (A. I. Report, 1981, 170-1). The sentences they received depended on where they were stationed. Those who served in the rural Northeast part of the country received the maximum prison sentence. It should be pointed out that the country was unstable during the time. The Contras' military opposition, backed by the United States, had undoubtedly made things worse in Nicaragua. Such threats explain the declaration of a state of emergency in the country. Different attacks by the Contras were the origin of the continuity of the martial law in Nicaragua. Human rights abuses under Ortega were, to some extent, linked to the economic and political situation of the country. Part of the information received about human rights abuses suggested that they were, in fact, carried out by the forces opposed to the revolutionary government. Gander rightly argues that 'economic, military and ideological facts must be considered in an analysis of human rights in Nicaragua ... The war created exceptional circumstances in Nicaragua' (in Donnelly and Howard, 1987, 260-1).

The exceptional circumstances that the country was experiencing made it very difficult to evaluate the human rights situation; and even more difficult to apply Amnesty's standards. Apart from the abolition of the death penalty, it is quite difficult to apply the rest of the criteria and base a judgement on them. Any relatively new government having to deal with those responsible for past violations, improving the standard of living, and above all, facing the military threats of the Contras, might reasonably neglect human rights in an attempt to carry the country through a very difficult period until stable institutions are established. These were translated after the 1984 elections which gave Nicaragua a president, a vice-president and a National Assembly (Walker, 1986, 119). Although the situation has relatively improved compared to the Somoza's days - the National Assembly (for instance) passed a decree pardoning 1,894 prisoners who had been convicted by the Special Courts between 1979 and 1981 (A. I. Report, 1990, 177) -, still a lot remains to be done. It should be pointed out at the end of this section that elections were held in Nicaragua in February 1990, which marked the defeat of Daniel Ortega by Violeta Chamorro who represented a coalition of different political parties, and assumed power in April 1992.

The Middle East

This case has been included in the study because of the religious issues involved. Middle Eastern countries are almost exclusively Muslim, which in some senses provide a real challenge to Amnesty's work. The emphasis here will be upon Saudi Arabia since it is one country where Muslim laws inspired from the 'Quran' are applied. In this country, for instance, Amnesty

International makes it clear that 'justice is administered according to a fundamentalist interpretation of the *Shari'a*, Islamic law, based on the 'Quran' and the *Sunna*, the way of life and the pronouncement of the Prophet' (A. I. Report, 1980, 351). However, the information available about human rights in Middle Eastern countries is quite scarce. Amnesty's reports, which are supposed to give brief descriptions of different countries fail to do so in some instances. Saudi Arabia, for instance, was not included in both the 1979 and 1981 Reports: not because there were no human rights violation, but because of lack of information.

For the purpose of this chapter, no investigation of the different aspects of human rights in these countries will be attempted. The survival of governments depends largely on a heavy oppressive apparatus and state police. Freedom of expression is almost non existent, and censorship of the press and political imprisonment on political grounds are very common. Nonetheless, what constitutes an exception is the death penalty which is widely applied in the Middle East, particularly in Saudi Arabia. While Islamic law, upon which some national laws is based, insists on the use of the death penalty as a punishment for certain offences, Amnesty International has expressed its concern and worked towards its abolition. On 11 December 1981, it wrote to the Saudi Minister of Interior urging him 'to give consideration to the question of the death penalty in Saudi Arabia and the possibility of restricting and eventually abolishing it' (A. I. Report, 1982, 344).

However, despite Amnesty's efforts, the death penalty in Saudi Arabia cannot be abolished as long as its laws are based upon the 'Quran'. To judge the record of human rights by the country's use of the death penalty would be unfair, at least in cases where it was imposed on religious grounds. In other words, a comparison can never be fair when it is based upon arbitrary standards. Amnesty believes in its eventual abolition in Muslim countries. This optimism is encouraged, according to Amnesty, by some schools of Muslim jurisprudence which are in favour of its abolition (Interview 2). However, such a claim does not rest on any foundations. The 'Quran' is clear about the question. It insists on it as a punishment for certain crimes and leaves no room for jurisprudence. What might be considered cruel in the United Kingdom, for instance, may not be considered as such in another country. The amputation of the hand for repeated theft is widely accepted in a country where Islamic law is fully implemented. Such a practice, in their view, does not represent a violation of human rights (Interview 3). Therefore, the role of culture and the circumstances under which the 'abuse' occur, have a significant role in determining whether a country respects human rights or not.

Amnesty International and comparative politics

Having discussed the basis Amnesty offers and the obstacles that it faces in carrying out its work, it becomes apparent that it is quite difficult to use Amnesty's standards as basis upon which a cross-national comparison is attempted. On a comparative level, its work does not offer a ranking of countries, and deliberately refrains from such a comparative judgement. The organisation acknowledges that it is does not provide any ranking (A. I. Report, 1978, 1), but its work offers a broad range of evidence and relatively clear reports - depending on the country under scrutiny - upon which an independent observer may make a judgement.

Amnesty is not a do gooder for all possible causes; it has a restricted mandate. It works for the release of prisoners of conscience and against torture and executions, but it is not involved in work against unemployment, starvation and other social diseases. 'Our platform,' Amnesty remind us, 'is the Universal Declaration of Human Rights adopted thirty years ago by the nations of the world. Within that frame Amnesty International concentrates its resources on particular civil and political rights ... This is not because we ignore the importance of all rights, but because we recognise that we can only achieve concrete results within set limits' (ibid.). Nevertheless, this is still unacceptable to different governments which do not believe in the set of rights that Amnesty works upon. Although Amnesty insists on 'achieving concrete results within set limits', its arguments are not entirely satisfactory. Why does it concentrate upon political and civil rights, for instance, bearing in mind that countries which have ratified the Covenant on Social, Economic and Cultural Rights outnumber those which have ratified the Covenant on Civil and Political Rights, let alone countries which did not ratify any of them? How can it apply different criteria to a country which rejects them, and expect to conduct useful comparison and achieve fruitful results?

Amnesty as an organisation 'born' in the West, although claims to be independent from any government or ideology has, in one way or another, been influenced by the philosophy and the norms in which it has developed.

As Desmond rightly puts it 'we have defined as fundamental human rights those rights which can be accorded to people in our society without posing any threat to our socio-political system. It is we who have decided how societies should be judged and since our society is taken as the norm, it is not surprising that we measure up to it better than other societies. The West may be worse than other countries in some respects, but we have decided that those respects are not the important ones. The most important aspect, we have decided, is whether a country recognised human rights as we have defined them. We have decided, for example, that individual freedom is so important that some people must be left free to exploit other people' (1984, 24).

From this East-West antagonism it becomes quite difficult, if not impossible, to compare different kinds of political systems on the basis that Amnesty offers. To conduct a comparison in terms of political prisoners, for instance, between a totalitarian or a military regime and a liberal democratic country would be misleading, and will not lead to useful results. Secondly, what makes a comparison difficult is that Amnesty's work does not take into account the political culture of the country under investigation, its level of development and modernisation and its level of political participation. Gander, for instance, argues that a 'country's progress in human rights is directly related to its level of participation. Nations in which the majority of the population is excluded from any degree of power are more apt to transgress rights than those where people take an active part in decision making and can fight for their rights' (in Donnelly and Howard, 1987, 264). In its annual reports, Amnesty offers pictures of almost every country in the world, conducted on the basis previously discussed.

Human rights abuses are social phenomena, which influence and are influenced by the political and social environment in which they occur, and analysed in that context. Let us try to make a comparison between the United Kingdom, for instance, and an Islamic country such as Saudi Arabia or Iran in the light of Amnesty's work for the past ten years. Although Amnesty opposes the death penalty and works for its abolition, it cannot be widely applicable. In the United Kingdom, for instance, it was abolished in the mid 1970s, whereas in Iran and Saudi Arabia, the death penalty is still carried out and the practice is likely to continue.

Amnesty takes different countries at the same level of development and deals with them equally. Here the emphasis is not economic development, but it is on the political dimension. The backwardness or the development of any political system does, in one way or another, influence the human rights situation. Countries such as the United Kingdom or the United States which have experienced democratic practices for a very long period of time cannot be compared to a country which has achieved its independence three or four decades ago. There are pressures on every government, but the scale and the way in which governments respond to these pressures varies considerably from one country to another. In a democratic country, the system is able to adopt to almost every situation and the succession of different governments is guaranteed smoothly through democratic means. It would be absurd to imagine a coup d'etat in the United Kingdom, for instance, whereas a government in a backward country where the institutions are flexible is less likely to cope with the pressures. This may result in its collapse or it may respond differently to these pressures, which in turn, may affect its human rights record. This point was realised by Amnesty when it stated that:

> We do realise that there is a link between general politics and the rights we try to defend; changes of government often result in arrests or releases. But this fact does not make us change our approach. We simply take facts into account without hiding some of them or emphasising others, according to regime or ideology (A. I. Report, 1978, 2).

However, it would be misleading to simply take facts into account without considering what led to them. Different political systems, especially the changes of the political structure mainly in the 'Third World', do have a great effect on the human rights situation in other countries. It goes without saying facts are important in conducting a comparison, but they can be misleading if they are not understood within the social and political environment in which they have come into being. Thus, investigators must bear in mind the particularities of each country, how developed it is, and to what extent it is able to cope with the pressure from the people to better understand the ways in which governments respond.

Furthermore, it should be pointed out that the variety of political systems around the world makes the comparison very difficult. It is generally agreed that emergency rule and martial law have been frequently imposed by military regimes in Africa, Asia and Latin America. As a matter of fact, the steps taken by the military in assuming power are; suspend the constitution, dissolve the government and parliament, disband political parties and persecute those who oppose the new regime. In such countries which lack stability or legitimacy - in a sense that a government did not come to power through democratic means - protection of human rights will almost always take a secondary place in their political agenda. In addition, they always claim that the situation obliges them to 'sacrifice' human rights for more important issues such as 'national unity' and/or 'economic development'. Benenson eventually acknowledged this point when he recognised 'that there are situations when the security of the state is threatened, in which the governments feel obliged to arrest their opponents' (ibid.).

The 'general interest' and other slogans have been used by some governments to justify their abuse of human rights. It goes without saying that there might be some genuine situations under which suspending some political rights and civil liberties, for a short period of time, might be justified by such wars or natural disasters, however, many 'Third World' countries, such as Algeria in 1992, have stretched this idea to the limit and declared a state of emergency just because the government lost an election.

The above discussion was a brief survey of the difficulties that face a comparativist in an attempt to undertake a cross-national comparison based upon the principles set by Amnesty. The particularities of every country on the one hand, and the difficulties that Amnesty face in carrying out its work properly on the other, make the task difficult. One cannot imagine a comparison being carried out without facts, statistics and supporting arguments which make the comparison meaningful and the results convincing. However, it is not always the case with the work of Amnesty given the sensitivity of the human rights issue in today's politics. No government, to varying degrees, wants its 'dirty linen' to be washed in public. Thus, different steps are taken to curtail the flow of information. The lack of information on political imprisonment in China, for instance, is due among other factors, 'to the restrictions of movement and the lack of free access to information' (Amnesty International, 1978, xii). Such obstacles and how to overcome them are of great importance to Amnesty's findings. After all, investigators will base their judgements upon the accuracy of the information it gives, and conversely 'the effectiveness of Amnesty International depends on the accuracy and the availability of its information' (A. I. Report, 1978, 7). However, many statistics are neither available nor accurate in the work of Amnesty and are given depending on the country and how flexible the flow of information is. Furthermore, Amnesty reports only about the cases known to it. But the proportion, no matter how big or small it is, is not representative of the situation in the country as a whole. When dealing with China Amnesty stressed that 'the death penalty continued to be used extensively' and during 1989 recorded '282 death sentences and 273 executions'. However, it acknowledged that 'the true totals were thought to be much higher' (A. I. Report, 1990, 68).

The lack of information concerning different categories of people imprisoned, combined with the relative availability of information about those who have been granted freedom, still does not give a clear picture even within the borders of the same country. A government which imprisons, tortures and sentences people to death would not publicise its acts since they are not the kind of actions to be proud of. Thus, the cases known to the outside world are still a proportion, and no one knows in terms of percentages how much it represents of the real figures. However, figures concerning people who were granted freedom are publicised to show the goodwill of the government and its wish to gain respect and praise from the international community.

Having said that, it does not automatically follow that the work of Amnesty is misleading. The point that was intended to be stressed is that there are enormous difficulties if a comparative study on a cross-national level on the basis Amnesty proposes is undertaken. The areas of study should be carefully chosen. In this case, they are already set by Amnesty. Moreover, the death penalty is considered a major violation of human rights, and it should be considered as such in all the countries which the comparativist has chosen as a field to his research. Dogan and Pelassy highlight this point when they argue that 'once the comparativist has decided which part of the political system or sector of the society he wishes to study, he has another decision to make. He has to choose the countries to be included in his analysis' (1984, 105).

The significance of a comparison and the validity of the results achieved will depend basically on the countries chosen. To conduct a comparison on such a basis, for instance, between a Muslim, underdeveloped country in which a new government has emerged such as Iran, with the United Kingdom or Sweden would perhaps be of little significance. Different circumstances may, in many instances, help to explain differences in governments' attitudes towards what some see as violations of human rights.

5 The Human Rights Committee

The question of human rights, as we have seen, is one of the most significant issues in contemporary world politics. There is no single agreement on its definition, let alone measurement. Many attempts have been made, both by organisations such as Amnesty International, as pointed out in the previous chapter, and by individuals, as will be discussed in the next chapter, to define and measure human rights on a cross-national basis. Such attempts fall short in terms of their applicability to different countries; not only because they derive from one specific philosophy or culture, which makes them unacceptable in some parts of the world, but because they are arbitrary measures. Such situations make the task of comparing and agreeing on specific standards very difficult, if not impossible.

However, the Human Rights Committee (hereafter referred to as the Committee) has adopted a completely different approach to human rights (McGoldrick, 1991; Decaux, 1980; Robertson and Merrills, 1992, 37-72). The Committee was set up under the provision of Article 28 of the International Covenant on Civil and Political Rights (hereafter referred to as the Covenant). Theoretically speaking, it is not biased: there has been an agreement on a single measure as a basis on which to judge human rights performance. States freely ratified the Covenant which gave power to the Committee and, conversely, made the states party to this Covenant responsible to the Committee through a system of communication. This chapter examines the work of the Committee. It begins with a general account of the establishment of this Committee and its significance. A knowledge of these matters is a necessary prerequisite to a proper understanding and evaluation of its work. A full examination of the two practices under which the Committee operates is provided. The two procedures are: the study of states' reports provided for by Article 40 of the Covenant and individual communications according to the Optional Protocol. In order to provide an appraisal, the Committee's work will be assessed through two case studies. The chapter concludes a general overview of the Committee's work from a comparative perspective.

What is the Human Rights Committee?

This section maps out the origins and the work of the Committee. It attempts to answer the following questions: how did the Committee come into being? How are people elected to it? Is there a geographical distribution in elections of the Committee? For how long are the Committee's members elected? How many times a year does it meet? For how long? Is there enough time for the Committee to carry out its work properly? How many cases does it have to deal with a year? And how impartial are the Committee's members? The answers to these questions should provide the reader with a clear idea about the Committee and enable a better understanding of its work.

The Committee

Article 28 (1) of the Covenant provides for the establishment of the 'Human Rights Committee' to consist of eighteen members and to carry out the functions according to the Covenant and its Optional Protocol. The membership of the Committee, according to Article 28 (2) is made up of 'nationals of the states parties to the present Covenant who shall be persons of high moral character and recognised competence in the field of human rights, consideration being given to the usefulness of the participation of some persons having legal experience'. The members are elected and serve in their personal capacity (Article 28 (3)).

The Covenant came into force on 23 March 1976 when the thirty fifth state ratified it. The Committee was established in 1977 with the functions in respect to the provisions of the Covenant and its Optional Protocol. Its term of office began on 1 January 1977. It is composed of eighteen members, nationals of the states party to the Covenant, elected for a period of term of years, (Article 5 of the Covenant) with half the membership renewed every two years. Article 29 (3) allows the renomination of Committee members. Each state may include more than one candidate, but membership of the

Committee should not exceed one member per state. 'In the election to the Committee' Article 31 (2) stresses that 'consideration shall be given to the equitable geographical distribution of membership and the representation of different forms of civilisation and the principal legal systems'.

Although the Committee was set up under the provisions of a Covenant which does not generally adhere to the former Eastern block orthodoxy, former communist countries were in the majority at the time (1976) compared with Western Europe, Africa, Asia or Latin America. Out of the original ten communist countries, four members only were elected to the Committee compared with five members elected from Western Europe out of the original seven (Jhabvala, 1984, 83). This discrepancy led some writers, especially Jhabvala, to suggest that the membership of the Committee should be reduced for some countries and increased for others for a strict geographical distribution (ibid.). However, the provision of the article above provided for the geographical distribution of the Committee's membership and not for proportional representation. There has been representation of different forms of civilisation and of the principal legal systems within the Committee. These members, as stated above, are of high moral character and recognised competence in the human rights area. They serve in their personal capacity, but the 'Covenant does stipulate that a member must be personally independent of his government' (McGoldrick, 1991, 44). In order to achieve this impartiality, each member has to give a solemn declaration in which he undertakes to discharge his duties impartially and consciously. Such qualities and requirements make the views of the Committee's members homogeneous. Independence of governments' or institutions' influences are fundamental to the effectiveness of the Committee's work. Nonetheless, it should be noted in passing that some disagreements among Committee members on the way they assess matters, have been registered. These disagreements are based on the background of the member making the comments, which, in many cases, represent the views of his own government. A conspicuous example of that was during the discussion of the second periodic report of the former Soviet Union in 1984. While Mr. Tomuschut of the former West Germany concluded that the 'dialogue between the Soviet delegation and the members of the Committee was less than positive', Mr. Graefrath, who represented the former East Germany in the Third Committee of the General Assembly, 'congratulated the Soviet delegation ... [and] regretted that the dialogue had been hampered by politically motivated statements' (Jhabvala, 1985, 480). Moreover, there might be some provocative comments by Committee's members. Mr Bouzidi of Tunisia, when discussing the report of Iran, asked:

> ... what was the Iranian government doing to promote the right of Palestinian and Lebanese peoples to self-determination? Why had the Iranian government not accepted the cease-fire by Iraq, so that Iraq could go and fight the Israelis? Why had Iranian troops not come to the aid of the Palestinian and Lebanese peoples now that the Iraqi army had withdrawn from Iran? (UN Doc. CCPR/C/1/ Add. 58. par. 35)

These kinds of statements put the impartiality of the Committee in jeopardy. There is a standard upon which the experts make their comments, i.e., the Covenant compared with the codes and practices of the country under scrutiny. The disagreements between the experts, as in the case of the former Soviet Union, were mainly based on the experts' backgrounds and the views of their respective governments. The quotation above represents a direct attack on the Iranian government. In other words, a statement such as '... so that Iraq could go and fight the Israelis' does not seem relevant to the work of the Committee. This expert needs to be reminded that the Committee is not an arena for war propaganda. It is meant to promote and help countries to enhance their human rights records, not to urge Iran to accept Iraq's offer of a cease-fire so that the latter could enter into a new war. One member of the Committee assured the author that the Committee had known such practices, and that such practices have changed. Reports are judged more unequivocally by all members regardless of the country's report being discussed. To borrow her words 'the experts are experts more than ever before' (Interview 1).

Sessions

The first meeting of the Committee, in line with the provision of Article 37 (1) of the Covenant, was held at the United Nations Headquarters in New York. Article 39 (2) provides that the Committee draws up the Rules of Procedures according to which other meetings would be held. Thus, Rule 12 provides that the Committee holds two regular sessions a year. However, given the increased workload of the Committee, since 1978 it has been holding three session a year. Even with an additional session, the Committee is still unable to cope with the work it has to do. Three sessions a year comprised of three weeks each has thus been the practice of the Committee, while the number of countries becoming parties to the Covenant keeps increasing every year. As a result, the Committee has found itself with increasingly more work to do in the same period of time. The problem is that it is quite difficult, if not impossible, for it to carry out its work properly and effectively within this short period of time. This is especially true when dealing with countries which delay sending their reports. Additional information is sometimes requested from countries whenever it is appropriate, adding to the already overburdened workload.

There is no doubt that the Committee could be more effective if it had more time to deal with reports, or if it had more resources to recruit personnel to undertake preparation for the sessions. A member of the Committee agrees that there is a lack of time and an adequate balance between time and amount of work is needed (Interview 1). Nonetheless, the Committee has followed a strategy that saves time for the experts to deal with the most important aspects. Thus, a working group is to meet one week before every session to look at the different reports, especially those which appear after the initial ones. These latter are usually shorter, so the discussion within the Committee can concentrate upon 'problem areas', to see if the country in question has made efforts to take into account the Committee's views. This working group looks at personal communications and decides on their admissibility. In doing so, it is helped by a *Special Rapporteur* who deals with the same question between sessions.

This 'focus discussion', having been scrutinised by the working group, although it saves the Committee valuable time, it is still unable to cope with the increased pressure placed upon it every year. Given the fact that the experts are members in their personal capacities, having other professional arrangements, little time is available to study different reports. It would seem that more time should be made available, or that these experts should become full-time staff paid for their membership of the Committee. Robertson, for instance sees that there 'is a strong case for making membership on the Committee a salaried occupation to which members could devote all their time' (in Henkin, 1981, 339), so that it can more easily and effectively carry out its work. However, these are not ideal solutions; for the amount of time to be increased is not necessarily convenient for the experts themselves. As mentioned earlier, they have other professional engagements and may not be able to adjust to the new requirements. Making them full-time staff would require a new budget which the United Nations is unable to secure due to its limited financial resources.

A great deal of research is carried out whenever a country's report is examined. The researchers focus not only on states' reports and their laws, but different sources are used such as non-governmental organisations, newspapers, the State Department Country Reports etc. ... which are certainly time consuming. It might be appropriate, in these circumstances, for a small unit to be permanently created under the auspices of the Committee. Its main task would be the preparation of the Committee's work and the following of developments in different countries.

Finally, Rule 5 of the Rules of Procedure reads as follow:

> Sessions of the Committee shall normally be held at the Headquarters of the United Nations or at the United Nations Office at Geneva. Another place for a session may be designated by the Committee in consultation with the Secretary-General.

Although the provision of this rule specifies that another place may be designated, to the best of the author's knowledge, except for the fourteenth session held in Bonn, Germany, the practice has always been to meet either in New York or Geneva. Although it was originally conceived that the spring session is held at the Headquarters in New York and the summer and autumn sessions in Geneva, due to economic constraints the Committee is forced to hold almost all of its sessions in Geneva. Dr. John Pace, Chief, Research Studies and Prevention of Discrimination at the Centre for Human Rights, the United Nations Office in Geneva, assured the author that many countries, especially those which do not have diplomatic representation in Geneva, wish the sessions to be held in New York. However, from the United Nations' points of view, it is less costly to hold sessions in Geneva where the Centre for Human Rights exists and where all the information and archives are held (Interview 4). It may be suggested that holding sessions where United Nations offices already exist, or at the headquarters of any regional organisation, would be helpful in publicising the work of the Committee. Holding a session in a 'Third World' country such as Kenya or Ethiopia would be a good opportunity to raise the people's awareness, not only in these particular countries, but in the region as a whole, regarding their rights and how their governments should treat them. With the media coverage of the

Committee's activities, more people would be aware that their governments can be held accountable to this body in the event of any abuse of human rights. The Committee's members, aware of this fact, have stressed the importance of holding sessions in countries others than those in which they are usually held. Because of financial limitations, however, they feel bound to hold them in New York and especially in Geneva. They would welcome any invitation from governments to hold sessions in their countries (Interview 1).

Decisions of the Committee

Decisions in the Committee are taken by majority vote, but the practice is to seek consensus first. Rule 51 specifies that the proposal can be put to a vote at the request of any member. Rule 50 states that: 'each member of the Committee shall have one vote.' Bearing in mind that the Committee comprises eighteen experts, the question arises regarding what would happen if the votes were divided into two groups of nine each. This situation did in fact occur during one of the Committee's sessions (ibid.). When taking decisions, the Chairman's vote should be taken into account whenever the votes are equally divided.

The work of the Committee

The Committee performs two roles: an investigatory one and a conciliatory one. Its role as an investigatory body can be seen from the provisions of Article 40 of the Covenant where the reports of states' parties are discussed and under Article 3 of the Optional Protocol to the International Covenant on Civil and Political Rights (hereafter the Protocol). The conciliatory role can be understood in the case of interstate complaints as provided for in Articles 41 to 44 of the Covenant. In what follows, a more detailed analysis of each of the roles of the Committee will be attempted to provide a better understanding of its work as a whole.

The study of states' reports

The main task of the Committee involves the study of reports states party to the Covenant are required to submit. The obligation of reporting is provided for by Article 40 of the Covenant. These reports, it should be noted, can be divided into three types: First, initial reports, according to Article 40 (1) (a), which are submitted within one year of the entry of force of the Covenant for the States Party concerned. Second, the supplementary reports, 40 (1) (b), whenever the Committee requests them. These reports are usually a follow up whenever the Committee is not satisfied with the previous one. Finally the periodic reports are submitted every five years after consideration of the initial report.

These reports include the measures adopted by the States Parties to bring their internal laws in conformity with the provisions of the Covenant. They also indicate the factors and difficulties, if any, affecting the implementation of the Covenant. Because of the inadequacy and the general character of many of the initial reports, the Committee has developed some general guidelines, during its second session in August 1977 (UN Doc. A/32/44 Apx. IV). These guidelines were aimed at helping states to fulfil their obligations and facilitate the Committee's work when examining them.

Nevertheless, although different countries have willingly ratified this Covenant whereby the investigatory body was set up, there has been resistance from these States Parties themselves to the work of the Committee. Some states believe that human rights practices are within their internal jurisdiction and therefore should not be subject to international scrutiny. Others have interpreted the work of the Committee as an attempt on their national sovereignty. The view of the Afro-Asian states, for instance, has been that the 'time has not yet come when the states which had recently gained their independence could give up their sovereignty with complete confidence' (Jhabvala, 1984, 86). These reservations soon began to emerge when States party were reluctant to send their representatives to the Committee, or delayed sending their reports. As early as the third session, 'the Committee was informed that 18 states had so far submitted their initial reports to the Committee, that 20 other States Parties which should have submitted their initial reports in 1977 had not yet done so, and 6 States Parties were due to submit their initial reports in 1978' (UN Doc. A/33/40. par. 33). Zaire represented the worst case of a delayed submission. Its report, due in 1978, was submitted nine years later (UN Doc. CCPR/C/4/add. 10). In spite of these difficulties, the Committee, on the whole, has been able to carry out its work satisfactorily.

There has been a further debate about how the Committee ought to operate. Does it limit itself to the reports submitted by the States Parties only, or does it have to go far beyond that to include reports by the media, or non-government organisations? Some representatives expressed the views that the Committee should restrict its activities to the literal provision of Article 40. The representative of Chile, for instance, said that:

> Consideration of the report of Chile should be confined to the terms of Article 40 of the Covenant and it was inadmissible that allegations should have been made on the basis of information obtained from sources other than those provided in the Covenant (UN Doc A/34/40. par. 107).

Another question needed to be resolved concerning the role of the Committee in relation to the study of states' reports. Does the Committee have to make general comments? Is it empowered to conclude whether a country has satisfied its obligations or not? The role of the Committee has become one of studying reports and making general recommendations of assisting States Parties in fulfilling their obligations and encouraging them to promote human rights.

Once a state's report is received, prepared according to the general guidelines, (according to Rule 70 of the Human Rights Committee's Rules of procedures if, in the opinion of the Committee, a state report does not contain sufficient information, the Committee may require that state to furnish more) it is discussed in the presence of a representative of the state concerned. This is to engage in a friendly dialogue between the experts and the delegation, which will explain different points and/or answer some of the questions that the Committee's members may ask. It also takes notes of the different questions on which the Committee may require some clarification. Professor Higgins, a former member of this Committee, describes its work as follows:

> The total context is one of encouragement rather than condemnation, if that is at all possible. Each delegation will be warmly welcomed, and an attempt will be made to put them at their ease ... It is explained that the Committee's role is not to attack or condemn, or to engage in any sort of political campaign against the state concerned. Rather it is to engage in a constructive and friendly dialogue, to see if the Committee can assist the government concerned in making progress in the realization of human rights in its territory ... The Committee much prefers to know that there are problems and shortcomings, and try to assist in rectifying these, than

to be told that the Covenant is fully implemented and that absolutely no problems exist in respect of human rights (1988, 256).

According to this opinion, the role of the Committee is to encourage rather than to condemn the practices of human rights. Different claims that the Covenant is fully implemented in some countries have been common practice. The former Soviet Union represented the best example of one. Their representative, Mr. Bykov, claimed that with the development of socialism 'the nationality question had been resolved once and for all', while Mr. Gustenko, claimed that 'there were no political prisoners in the USSR' (Jhabvala, 1985, 479). Such claims were not usually true, since the practices of the states concerned fell below what they had committed themselves to do. A self recognition of the shortcomings in the progress of implementing the Covenant is a significant factor to the Committee in helping countries where the changes are needed. The experts, as Higgins puts it:

> do not grade the countries, either issuing blanket condemnation or giving a clear bill of health. Nor do [they] put them on a league table in which they are compared to other countries (1988, 257).

The process has been conducted on the basis of friendly dialogue. Countries are made to feel that no matter what their human rights record is, the Committee is not going to condemn them or make any comparison with others which have better records. On the contrary, it deals with each country on its own, and tries to pinpoint the shortcomings and the different means by which the Committee can assist them. This represents a comprehensive way whereby co-operation with the Committee is maintained.

Despite this friendly approach, there has been some resistance to the work of the Committee. Some states, as noted above, have resisted sending reports or providing additional information. There are still some difficulties in the reporting system or the steps taken by the states towards the enjoyment of human rights. This covers specific areas when there is an antagonism between the provisions of the Covenant and national laws. Nonetheless, the Committee has been successful in many instances. This will be discussed in the next section when dealing with the particular case studies.

Individual communications

Apart from dealing with states' reports as discussed above, the investigatory role of the Committee consists of dealing with individual communications under the Protocol. Article 1 provides that:

> A State Party to the Covenant that becomes a party to the present Protocol recognizes the competence of the Committee to receive and consider communications from individuals subject to its jurisdiction who claim to be victims of a violation by the State Party of any of the rights set forth in the Covenant. No communication shall be received by the Committee if it concerns a State Party to the Covenant which is not party to the present Protocol.

This procedure has further revolutionised the approach to the issue of human rights. The fact that an individual can make complaints against their own state is a very significant step forward towards the full implementation of human rights. However, there are some conditions that are to be taken into account when sending these communications. They must be sent by the person concerned, or by another on their behalf - stating the kind of relationship - and that the matter has exhausted all domestic remedies, so that the Committee can consider whether these individual communications are admissible or not. If a communication is admissible, it is forwarded to the State Party concerned for clarification. Article 4 (2) provides that 'within six months, the receiving states shall submit to the Committee written explanations, or statements clarifying the matter and the remedy, if any, that may have been taken by that state'.

This procedure depends on the publicity given by the State Party to this Protocol. In other words, how many people, or what is the percentage of the population who know that their government has ratified this Protocol? How many of them know that they can complain to the Committee when their rights under the Covenant are, in their view, abused? Governments have willingly ratified both the Covenant and the Protocol knowing the new responsibilities they would undertake. However, it does not necessarily follows that a government respects human rights if it ratifies the Covenant and its Protocol. What is the meaning of a country like Zaire, for instance, ratifying this Protocol? There is little, if any, opportunity for the simple Zairian citizen who is underfed and is often illiterate, complaining against his/her government. How can one expect illiterate people in the 'Third World' to be aware of their rights under the Protocol? In the best of cases where people are indeed aware of this possibility, a fundamental question cannot be avoided: what would happen to the letters, if any, they send to the Committee? In other words, how many communications does the Committee receive from the original number of communications sent? It is very difficult to answer these questions since the original number of communications sent is never known. People living under oppressive regimes would certainly abstain from such exercise fearing their government's response. The process of controlling private mail in a lot of countries, for instance, is a daily event, let alone 'official' mail. Hundreds of these communications never reach the Committee, and thus the number of people who do send these communications is never known.

Finally, the last task of the Committee is to deal with interstate disputes. According to Article 41 of the Covenant, the Committee receives communications from a State Party against another State Party which has failed to take the necessary steps towards observing the provisions of the Covenant. However, to the best of the author's knowledge the Committee has never dealt with such disputes (Higgins, 1988, 254).

Derogation

Article 4 of the Covenant allows States Parties to derogate from the provisions of the Covenant by suspending some guaranteed aspects of human rights in times of public emergency that threaten the life of the nation. Although the article provides for rights that should not be derogated from, and the suspension should strictly be to the exigencies required by the new situations, states' practices have often been open to criticism. It is generally agreed that the worst abuses occur during times of public emergency that make states invulnerable to scrutiny. What violations occur under a state of siege, according to these states, find its explanation in the newly emerged situation. However, the questions which need to be addressed here are: what constitutes a threat to the nation? Is there a real threat and a genuine case where a state of emergency should be declared? For how long should such a situation last?

Since there is derogation in public emergency, states have often used it to justify their actions. Although the Covenant provides that the Committee should be notified of the new situation and the rights that are to be suspended, 'States Parties to the Covenant have tended to provide only delayed and inadequate notices of derogation, or sometimes, none at all' (Hartman, 1985, 99). In some cases, states of emergency have been declared when there is no real threat to the nation, unless this threat refers to the privileged group in power. In other words, states of emergency have been declared because there is a danger that may bring down a government, or governments themselves have created these states of emergency to ensure that their powers are unchallenged. These is especially true in Africa and Latin America, where states of emergency have been declared after the numerous coups d'etat that these countries witnessed. Long lasting states of emergency are another problem, where the reasons behind the declaration of the state of emergency are no longer applicable.

These are several further difficulties in connection with derogation that may arise when dealing with the work of the Committee. These are due to the different interpretations of the term 'threat to the nation'. What constitutes a threat in an underdeveloped country is not automatically one in a developed one. In the former, it is generally linked to the selfishness of the people in power and their desire to ensure their long standing in power. As with the study of states' reports, overcoming these difficulties depends very much on the co-operation of governments, i.e., to assist the Committee by providing the up to date information concerning the state of emergency, and seeking advice and help whenever the governments are in doubt. By joining efforts both governments and the Committee, especially governments, have shown their willingness to promote and respect human rights.

Case studies

This section deals with some particular cases in the light of the Committee's work. The choice of case studies was difficult to make, since there are a lot of countries that could possibly be considered. In this choice Western developed countries were avoided. They have the organisational and judicial organs whereby they implement the Covenant. However, the former Soviet Union, a leading example of communist practice up to 1991, offers a better insight to the Committee work in a different environment. As pointed out in the second chapter, political rights and civil liberties were not particularly stressed in the former communist countries. I shall also discuss the changes, in relation to the Committee's work, which took place in the country after the introduction of *Perestroika*. The other example that will be highlighted is that of Chile: a country notorious for its human rights violations especially after the 1973 military coup. It has also experienced extended periods of states of siege.

The former Soviet Union

The former Soviet Union ratified the Covenant on 16 October 1973 and therefore was among the first thirty five countries for which the Covenant entered into effect almost three years later. What seems to be surprising about the former Soviet Union, as already pointed out earlier, is that the provisions of the Covenant are not in line with Soviet orthodoxy. It stressed the priority of economic and social rights and saw any monitoring of its human rights record as an interference in its domestic affairs. However, what should be pointed out at this stage is that ratifying an international agreement does not automatically mean that the state which has done so observes it. The following discussion will look at the Soviet case to find out to what extent, if any, the Committee was successful in bringing about changes in the Soviet jurisdiction concerning human rights.

Extensive changes in Soviet policies were clearly taking place in the former Soviet Union after Gorbachev came to power. In other words, improvements, if any, in the sphere of human rights could not be solely attributed to the Committee only, but to the different policies introduced by the new General-Secretary. A proper assessment of the Soviet experience would be ideal, but can not be achieved. This is due to the fact that changes were taking place so rapidly in the former Soviet Union and what can be satisfactory today would be out of date in a short period of time. During the discussion of the Soviet third periodic report, Mr. Yakovlev, the Soviet representative, confirmed that 'changes were taking place so rapidly in the Soviet Union that the report was already somewhat out of date, and he would therefore provide some additional information in his introduction' (UN Doc. CCPR/ C/ SR 928/. par. 5).

A close look at the different reports submitted to the Committee reveals that there was a shift in the Soviet government's attitude towards the Committee in the course of a decade: from a hostile self-congratulatory position to a more accommodatory, self-critical one. This defensive position can be seen during the discussion of the Soviet initial report in 1978. The Soviet representative, Mr. Sudarikov, said that his country's 'report clearly showed that all the provisions of the International Covenant on Civil and Political Rights were fully respected in the Soviet law' CCPR/C/1/Add. 22, par. 2). He stressed further that 'due to a high level of development of Soviet legislation, the ratification by the Soviet Union of the International Covenants on human rights in 1973, and their entry into force in 1976 did not entail any essential changes of, or supplements to, Soviet legislation' (UN Document A/33/40. par. 411). However, this position changed and a more open attitude was adopted when Yakovlev, the Soviet representative, concluded that a 'matter of major concern to his government was the lack of effective machinery for the full realisation of civil and political rights' (UN Doc. CCPR/C/SR. 928 par. 8). This marks the step forward towards the improvement of the human rights situation. Given the role of the Committee, claims that the Covenant is fully implemented are not in the interests of the country. Mr. Sadi, a Committee member, re-iterates that 'the Committee was not a tribunal with the power to condemn but rather a body responsible for constructive criticism that would help countries to fulfil their obligations under the Covenant' (UN Doc. CCPR/C/1/Add. 25 and 40. par. 44).

The former Soviet Union, as well as other East European countries, did not at first co-operate with the Committee. Initially they claimed that the Covenant was fully implemented, and that there were different interpretations of human rights depending on the socio-political system. Jhabvala states that:

> During the Committee's discussion of the Soviet Union's report, Committee member Bernhard Graefrath, an East German national, noted that it would be improper for the Committee to define human rights according to the standards of one model social system since different countries have 'different conceptions' of 'public order and morality' as well as approaches to freedom of expression (1985, 478).

Thus, the initial Soviet report was full of claims that the Covenant was fully implemented in the Soviet Union, and that the Soviet peoples, according to the representative of their government, 'were proud of their achievements in human rights and had nothing to hide from world public opinion in that field' (UN Doc. CCPR/C/1/ Add. 22. par. 3). Soviet laws and Constitution, it was agreed, guaranteed the rights set forth in the Covenant. However, there is a big difference between different provisions of the laws and the Constitution and the practices there. Although the Soviet Constitution guaranteed freedom of movement, for instance, how easy was it for a Soviet citizen to travel abroad? From a Soviet point of view, this right was fully guaranteed, and anything that questioned this fact was just a myth. Mr. Sudarikov, the Soviet representative, insisted that 'the situation with respect to freedom of movement was clearly set forth in the Soviet media and by Soviet official bodies. The assertions that millions of persons wanted to leave the Soviet Union was a myth: that was not the case and never had been. The decreasing number of persons who did, however, could request exit visas from the Ministry of Interior' (ibid., par. 33).

The defensive attitude of the Soviet government could be seen as well in the case of self-determination and the secession of the Republics. Members of the Committee questioned the possibility of any Republic wishing to secede from the Soviet Union, and how easy it might be for them to do so. In his response, the Soviet representative confirmed that 'in the first place, it should be realised that it was absolutely inconceivable that a republic would want to secede, since there was an unshakeable bond uniting all the peoples and nations of the state, and they attribute their well-being to the fact that they formed part of the Soviet Union. Nonetheless, the right to secede did exist and could be exercised (ibid., par. 8).

The answer above, and others by Soviet representatives, are very politicised covered with the Soviet attitude of defending their achievements. The answer could have been more fruitful if it had been limited to the question put forward by the Committee members, giving examples, if any, of any attempts to secede from the Union. The 'unshakeable bond uniting the peoples and nations of the state', were often no more than a heavy coercive state machinery ready to interfere whenever a movement aiming at secession emerged. This was especially true, at least in the events that the Baltic Republics have witnessed since 1989.

Having said that does not automatically mean that the Soviet's record was condemned. As with any country, there were some shortcomings in its human rights record. Nonetheless, the former Soviet Union showed its willingness to co-operate with the Committee, not only by ratifying the Covenant which made it accountable to this body, but by submitting its different reports and sending representatives of very high calibre to discuss the matter with the Committee's members. It should also be noted that there were some improvements in the Soviet performance after the mid 1980s. At this stage no talk about any improvement is complete without reference to the policies introduced by Gorbachev. *Perestroika* was a new policy which represented the thinking of the new leadership on the internal as well as the external situation of the former Soviet Union. Many changes took place there, among those in the sphere of human rights.

The willingness of the Soviet government to carry its co-operation with the Committee and its commitment to improve its human rights record could be seen from the shift in its attitudes; stating the difficulties that the country faced, as well as sending its third periodic report, due in November 1988, ahead of schedule (UN Doc. CCPR/C/SR. 928. par. 2). With the different changes that took place, undoubtedly, the former Soviet Union was making significant steps forward towards the full implementation of human rights as more attention was paid to international human rights standards. The Soviet representative told the Committee that 'a teaching course on international human rights standards was to be organised in Moscow in November/December, 1989 by the Centre for Human Rights, with the participation of three members of the Committee, Mrs Higgins, Ms Chanet and Mr Procar, whose presence could be most welcome. The programme included a visit to the Ministry of Justice' (UN Doc. CCPR/C/SR. 928. par. 13).

According to the Soviet representative, the Soviet government had realised that there had been some shortcomings in the area of human rights and different draft laws had been adopted or were waiting to be approved to put an end to that situation. Further, while answering questions put forward to him by the Committee's members, the Soviet representative acknowledged that the legislation in force, regarding freedom of religion, 'was not yet perfect. However, there were no limitations in practice, which evolved more rapidly than legislation, and it might be said that religion has its place in society' (ibid., par. 18). Perhaps the most important measure to be taken was in the judicial field. Mr. Yakovlev told the Committee that:

> Important measures had also been taken in the field of judicial reform. It was realized that without a suitable legal system and independent courts governed solely by the law and protected against interference there could be no effective machinery to guarantee the enjoyment by citizens of their rights and freedoms (UN Doc. CCPR/C/SR. 928. par. 9).

There have also been some changes in different aspects of human rights, mainly freedom of movement, of conscience, expression and ill-treatment in psychiatric hospitals, which were the subject of the 931st meeting. (For a detailed analysis see UN Doc. CCPR/C/SR. 931.) Different shortcomings were acknowledged and remedies were in prospect. Mr. Pocar, a Committee member, 'after having examined the summary records of the meetings devoted to the consideration of the second periodic report of the Soviet Union (CCPR/C/28 Add. 3), ... wished to emphasise that distinct progress had been made, precisely in areas that had caused the Committee concern, namely, freedom of conscience, the treatment of persons interned in psychiatric institutions, freedom of movement and freedom of political activity' (UN Doc. CCPR/C/SR. 931. par. 54).

To sum up, there were many changes taking place in the former Soviet Union which had some effect on the human rights situation. Although Gorbachev's policies were very significant, the role of the Committee should not be neglected. The discussion of the different reports submitted by the former Soviet Union, and the shortcomings highlighted by the Committee's members, undoubtedly helped the Soviet government improve its standards. Satisfaction was noticed on the part of the Committee's members with the third Soviet report. Mrs Higgins, for instance, observed that the report 'and the discussion to which it had just given rise were exemplary. She congratulated Mr Yakovlev and his colleagues on their competence and thanked them for having accepted the suggestions of the Committee on a number of points' (UN Doc. CCPR/C/SR. 931. par. 73). The Soviet delegation, on the other hand, concluded that 'the discussion had been extremely enriching' and that it 'had acquired considerable knowledge that would be useful in the future' (ibid., par. 86).

Chile

The Covenant came into force on 23 March, 1976 in Chile, after the latter ratified it on 10 February, 1972. Nonetheless, substantial changes took place in the period between the ratification of the Covenant and its entry into force. A knowledge of these changes is necessary for a better understanding of the attitudes of both the Chilean government and the Committee's members.

In the Autumn of 1973, the democratically elected government of Chile was overthrown by a military coup d'etat, suspending all the constitutional guarantees despite the Chilean government denials. Its representative to the

Committee maintained that on 'the same day that the armed forces had assumed power, legislative decree No. 1 had declared that the government Junta guaranteed the full effectiveness of the powers of the judiciary and respect for the constitution and laws' (UN Doc. CCPR/C/1/Add. 25 and 40. par. 18). Following the coup, a state of siege was imposed, all political parties were dissolved and major human rights abuses began to take place.

The initial Chilean report, due in 1977, was submitted and discussed in 1979. In the discussion, the Committee's members did not limit themselves to the information and the claims contained in the report, but went beyond that to use the information contained in a report by the ad hoc working group. This led to tensions between the Committee's members and the Chilean government's representatives. The report claimed that the situation in the country was in accordance with the provisions of the Covenant, and that human rights in general were fully respected. The Chilean representative 'pointed out that civil and political rights, and human rights in general were respected only when there was an independent judicial power. That was especially important in the case of Chile, a country with a very old democratic tradition in which the independence of the magistracy had always been unquestioned' (ibid., par. 34). He also stressed that his government had 'informed the Secretary-General which rights had been restricted, thus complying with its obligation under the Covenant' (ibid., par. 23).

In what follows, I shall not engage in a detailed scrutiny of the Chilean report, but examine the improvement, if any, that may have taken place since the discussion of the initial one. The latter gives rise to many controversies. The Committee's members, although maintaining a friendly dialogue, heavily criticised the report showing that it was insufficient (Decaux, 1980, 529), that it did not give a clear picture of the human rights situation and especially that it contradicted the findings of the ad hoc working group. Mr Hanga, a Committee member, remarked that 'there were conflicts between the facts established by the working group and the statement in the report submitted by Chile (UN Doc. CCPR/C/1/Add. 25 and 40. par. 10). His colleague, Mr. Koulishev, also observed that it 'was not difficult to compare the report submitted by the government of Chile with the report of the ad hoc working group. Anyone examining the former could not forget the working group's findings on the increase in detention for political reasons or for reasons of national security and the growing number of cases of intimidation, torture and missing persons' (ibid., par. 30).

Given these facts, the Committee requested a new report. A close look at the reports that have followed the initial one shows that there was a shift in the Chilean government's attitude towards the Committee as well as an improvement in the human rights situation in the country. At the discussion of its third periodic report, the Chairman of the Committee reminded the members who had been present during the second periodic report of Chile of 'the spirit of co-operation and understanding shown by the delegation of Chile in its dialogue with the Committee (UN Doc. CCPR/C/SR. 942. par. 2).

What can be pointed out at the beginning is that Chile had adopted a new Constitution in 1980, which, according to its representative, 'marked the beginning of a transition towards full democracy' (ibid., par. 4), and further steps towards the improvement of its human rights record were clearly noticeable. Perhaps the most significant of all was the lifting of the state of emergency in August 1988 and the plebiscite held in October 1988. Since then many rights, especially freedom of assembly and of opinion, have been restored. The position of the Chilean government has become more flexible, willing to co-operate with the Committee on various issues. Such a position, undoubtedly, helped Chile improve its human rights record. Mr. El-Shafei, a Committee member, summarising the improvement in Chile, observed:

> The third periodic report of Chile, although short, was informative particularly regarding developments which had taken place since the submission of the previous report. The most notable of those developments had been the plebiscite on the presidency, held in October 1988; the promulgation of a number of acts designed to restore a democratic, pluralist regime; publication in the *Diario Oficial* of the text of the Covenant; the lifting of the states of emergency in force since 1973; the publication of the Convention for the Prevention and Punishment of Torture; the closing of detention centers run by the State Security Police; and, finally, the conclusion of an agreement with the International Committee of the Red Cross (ICRC) permitting that body access to detainees (ibid., par. 18).

Having said that, it does not automatically mean that human rights in Chile are fully respected. There are still some shortcomings in different aspects which have been brought to the attention of the Chilean representative. What matters most in this regard is that there have been improvements in this field since the initial report and the Chilean government has shown some co-operation with the Committee. Given the adoption of the Constitution and laws and the restoration of different rights, human rights in Chile can be improved further.

The Committee's work and the comparative study of human rights

Although the Committee does not engage in any comparison or ranking of countries, its work can lead to such conclusions. However, before going into depth in discussing its work from a comparative perspective, it is helpful to highlight further difficulties the Committee faces in carrying out its work properly. First, during the examination of the Committee's work, it was found that some misunderstanding had taken place during the discussion of some reports due to difficulties in the translation. Again, problems of a conceptual nature arise whenever a study of human rights is attempted. During the discussion of Madagascar's report, for instance, the representative of that government said:

> The question which had arisen with respect to imprisonment for debt appeared to be the result of misunderstanding. He explained that the French expression '*contrainte par corps*' used in Article 68 of the Decree No 59.121 (section 7 of the report) did not in fact refer to persons 'imprisoned for debt', as the English translation suggested. As used in Madagascar, it meant simply that persons sentenced to pay a fine could, in a lieu of payment, serve a prison term (UN Doc. CCPR/C/1/Add. 14. 87th meeting, par. 24).

Therefore, it would make more sense if an expert from the state concerned was present during the translation of the report to avoid any misunderstanding that might otherwise occur. The second, pointed out earlier, is that the Committee lacks enough time to sustain the workload put upon it. This is made worse by the fact that some questions are pointed out by more than one member of the Committee. For example, during the discussion of the Iranian report, Mr. Khosroshachi, the government's representative, pointed out that the 'question of the Bahai's had been raised by no less than five members, which seemed a waste of time when one would have sufficed' (UN Doc. CCPR/C/1/Add. 58. par. 53), at the time, when Committee members should have abstained from raising any question already mentioned by one of their colleagues.

The Committee's work is very sensitive and may face a lot of difficulties especially in the 'Third World'. 'The selfish reluctance of the ruling classes or groups', Bandura argues, 'to give up their long lasting privileges' (1989, 6) is very significant in generating opposition to its work. The Committee, as opposed to the different analyses dealt with in this book, has set itself a standard of achievement in the Covenant. Countries have freely ratified it, knowing the responsibilities they should assume. The scope of the human rights is larger, i.e., does not limit itself to some aspects of human rights but to the civil and political rights set. This has led to some difficulties in that the Committee avoids the economic and cultural rights. The formulation of the Covenant was undertaken within a dominant Western orientation, which makes it quite distant from the realities in the Third World. The realisation of the Covenant does require a minimum level of development and of state welfare. This is especially true in the cases of Madagascar and Mali, to name just two examples. The representative of the former publicly pointed out that 'the promotion of civil and political rights in his country had been hampered by the lack of judicial facilities, the sharp rise in crime and the worsening of the economic situation as the result of the world economic crisis' (UN Doc. A/33/40. par. 260). Furthermore, during the discussion of the report of Mali, 'the view was expressed that the report could not be judged in absolute terms or on the same basis as a report from a developed country ... [and that] the economic circumstances of a Sahelian country like Mali could not be overlooked when considering its report; and that it was particularly important to understand the background and the conditions prevailing in the country concerned' (Jhabvala, 198, 103).

There is no doubt about the importance of economic and cultural rights if the Covenant is to be fully implemented. The more people educated in any given country, the higher is their awareness about their rights, and the more likely they are to put pressure on their government to comply with the international standards. Sir Vincent Evans, a former Committee member, for example, questioned 'whether serious attention was being paid in Madagascar to prison conditions and the rehabilitation of prisoners' (UN Doc. CCPR/C/1/Add. 14. par. 31). There is no doubt that such an observation was made along with the Covenant's provisions. A more appropriate inquiry would have been about the living situation of the people in Madagascar let alone its prisoners' conditions. How can someone expect improvement in prison conditions in a poor, deprived country like Madagascar? 'Members of the Committee had often stressed the importance of economic and social factors for civil and political rights [Mr. Hanga argues]; unless there had been economic and social basis, the civil and political rights set out in the Covenant are practically meaningless' (UN Doc. CCPR/C/1/Add. 14. par. 25).

In the light of what has been said, the importance of the Committee's work is evident. It is a body which provides different types information in great detail about what is happening in different countries that have ratified the Covenant. It, contrary to the case studies undertaken in this work, takes into account the difficulties, if any, affecting the implementation of the Covenant. Thus, it is difficult to argue that the work of the Committee is motivated by political considerations. Differences between countries in terms of their understanding of the Covenant, and the different stages of development do exist. However, the Committee does not apply arbitrary measures which make its work hostile in some parts of the world. The stress has always been, as far as the Committee's work is concerned, not upon comparing countries in terms of their observance of human rights, but on helping them to improve their standards. Central to this approach is the knowledge held by the states themselves that they are not going to be condemned but will be offered help whenever they request so. This will not only improve the human rights record in general, but at the same time offers the opportunities for comparison, based on the extent to which countries fulfil their obligations under the Covenant. A comparative study of human rights, based on the Committee's work, is therefore possible. A country's human rights record can be determined by the extent to which it implements the Covenant, co-operates with the Committee and takes the necessary steps towards incorporating the Committee's recommendations in its national laws. Its work also makes an assessment over time possible. By looking at the periodic reports of the countries chosen for investigation, conclusions can be reached on the scope of the improvements these particular countries have made and the problems they have encountered. Such a study can be an over time assessment of one particular country to monitor the improvements, if any, with respect to the provisions of the Covenant. It can also be a comparison between States Party to the Covenant to see whether they have made any progress in the rights provided in this Covenant. Such comparisons would help to detect whether progress has been made or not and which country has been more compliant with the Covenant it pledged itself to respect.

6 Quantitative approaches to the comparative study of human rights: the work of Charles Humana

In the discussion that follows, I shall look at the work undertaken by the late Charles Humana, a British journalist. His was not taken very seriously initially by the human rights community; however, it became a matter of public controversy in 1991 after the UN Development Program, which published the Human Development Report based on his work. Humana carried out three exercises, based on questionnaires, to compare human rights on a cross-national basis in 1983, 1986, and 1992 all of which will be discussed in this chapter. In particular, I look at the validity of these works as quantitative measures for human rights. In this connection, I shall try to answer some critical questions that may influence the outcome of his results. Most importantly I wish to test the objectivity of the questions and the accuracy of the answers. In other words, what are the philosophical foundations or the background to the questionnaire? Is his work applicable to different cultures? Is the study biased, in this case, influenced by the Western culture to which the author belongs? Finally, what are the main difficulties, if any, in applying Humana's inquiries on a cross-national basis?

In order to answer these questions, and for a better understanding of Humana's attempts to measure human rights, this chapter begins with the philosophical foundations of his study. In the second part, the methodology he employs is analysed. The third section focuses on the two different types of assessment of countries employed in his work. Two striking examples are highlighted in this connection; Israel and South Africa. The strengths and weaknesses of applying this methodology to a comparative analysis of countries in terms of their human rights performance.

It is firstly necessary to stress that, contrary to what Humana states that 'the United Nations organisation, though it adopted the human rights treaties, does not issue periodic reports on the extent to which the member states honour them' (1986, 1), the UN Human Rights Committee does indeed report to the UN General Assembly on its monitoring of compliance with the International Covenant on Civil and Political Rights and with the Optional Protocol, and has published reports throughout the 1980s. This was discussed in more depth in chapter five. Furthermore, before going into analysing Humana's work, I shall quote his definitions of the concept of human rights:

> In simplest terms they are laws and practices that have evolved over the centuries to protect ordinary people, minorities, groups and races from oppressive rulers and governments (Humana, 1983, 7).

Philosophical foundations of the study

To understand the philosophical foundations of any study is to be able to predict, to some extent, the outcome of that particular study. When dealing with a sensitive issue like human rights, and trying to develop a set of criteria upon which the ranking of different countries may be based, the variables selected are of paramount importance. The selection of variables is very much influenced by the culture of any researcher. Humana selects the ones he thinks are appropriate, and as such influence the outcome of the study. This first section accordingly analyses the foundations of Humana's study, which will enable the reader to better understand his conclusions and his rankings of different countries.

It should be borne in mind, as already pointed out in this chapter, that Humana undertook three studies to measure human rights on a cross-national basis; these will be examined in order to determine the extent of changes between them or if any occurred at all.

The first inquiry

Humana's first inquiry, published in 1983, was based on a sample size of 107 countries evaluated in two different ways. When there was co-operation with the compiler and data were available, countries were assessed through a questionnaire. When information was scarce or suspect, however, countries were assessed in different, more summary ways. I am particularly interested in the first category, which contains 75 countries (ibid., 24-5). This group offers the reader opportunities to follow the methodology employed to obtain the results, and to pinpoint the shortcomings, if any. I shall look at the questions and examine their applicability on a cross-national basis.

The questions: A close look at the range of the questions used by Humana reveals that the validity of some is doubtful. In other words, they do not derive from the usual sources of human rights agreements. He claims that his guide is not 'bound by what is acceptable to all and is therefore free to extend its inquiry with explicit questions about divorce and abortion, about compulsory military service and maximum sentences for standard offences' (ibid., 8). This does not automatically mean that what derives from the usual sources. i.e., international documents on human rights, is always accepted, but at least it rests upon a fair and widely acceptable foundation. However, in this inquiry some of the questions are arbitrarily selected and are culture bound, representing the values of western liberal thought. Problematic questions such as: drink and the purchase of alcohol, or the number of police and military and weapons normally carried by civil police, do not relate to the subject. Moreover, they may favour the ranking of some countries and disfavour others. The questions related to drinking and purchasing alcohol may very well fit in a tourist guide, rather than a serious attempt to measure human rights. Some countries in the world, i.e., Islamic ones, prohibit this practice and are therefore culturally different from the rest of the world in this respect. The same applies to the remaining questions. There is a need to look, for instance, at the causes of the higher number of police and military and what roles these two institutions perform in their respective countries.

Humana seems to believe that the higher the proportion of police and military personnel to the number of citizens in a country, the lower the country ranks in terms of human rights. A country such as Syria, for example, is seen to be behind many countries on Humana's scale. This phenomenon can be explained, at least from a Syrian point of view, by the fact that Syria neighbours Israel and there is a constant threat from the latter to its territory. The comparatively high number of the Syrian military and police may find a reasonable explanation in terms of national security. The high number of police and military is not then a violation of human rights, nor can the country's record be judged upon such a variable. These two institutions may be, and indeed are in some countries, agencies in the hands of governments whereby torture and coercion are carried out, but this has nothing to do with their number. Another question is about the weapons normally carried by the police. In Algeria, for instance, they carry sidearms, while in Papua New Guinea they carry batons only. Given this information, the former ranks lower than the latter on Humana's score. Once again the question that needs to be asked is not what kind of weapons are normally carried by the police, but how likely or how often they use them? If in a country police carry pistols or sidearms, this does not automatically mean that they use them against citizens. Perhaps gun control may also be a reason why police need weapons. In the US they are armed, however citizens are allowed to own firearms also.

In addition to some of the questions not pertaining closely to human rights, Humana's survey also suffers from a degree of repetition. The issue of military service, for instance, is the subject of two different questions in the study. Although there is room for argument that 'freedom from military service' may be used as a variable-objection to military service and seen as a human right (see chapter three), there is certainly an objection to the inclusion of another question relating to 'maximum punishment for refusing military service'. It is common knowledge that in some counties citizens are free from military service: Canada, Japan, Senegal and Papua New Guinea to name just a few, and if they are free, there will be no punishment whatsoever for refusing it. The opposite could be said about countries where military service is compulsory and, if someone refuses it, he will be punished accordingly depending on the country. Faced with this situation, it seems that there is a tendency in the part of the compiler to favour countries which have no compulsory military service.

Finally, the questions employed by Humana and which have some legal basis derive mainly from the International Covenant on Civil and Political Rights. This Covenant, although ratified by different countries in the 'Third World' and in the former Eastern Europe, represents the traditional perception of human rights, associated with Western liberal thinking.

Humana, nonetheless, undertook a second, and eventually a third, inquiry to measure human rights. He may have done so to overcome the difficulties and contradictions found in his first inquiry; a close analysis of his second study will help to establish the extent to which he has been able to do so.

The second inquiry

Raymond Gastil argues that:

> Charles Humana's World Human Rights Guide, a comprehensive attempt to review the state of human rights, is now in its second edition. Humana's selection of forty questions of detailed country by country examination is buttressed by citation of the international human rights documents that support each (1987, 87).

Humana sought to avoid arbitrary questions, and in this inquiry all the questions used in the questionnaire were based upon different articles in international agreements. However, this does not mean that the questionnaire is immune from criticism or that it can be relied upon as an objective measure of comparative human rights.

A critical look at the questionnaire, in the second inquiry, reveals that 57.5 per cent of the questions are drawn from the Universal Declaration of Human Rights, 35 per cent from the International Covenant on Civil and Political Rights, and only 7.5 per cent from the International Covenant on Economic, Social and Cultural Rights. Such a distinction greatly influences the outcome of the inquiry. Although Humana drew his questions from legal documents that countries had agreed upon, the result of the questionnaire would have been different if the distribution of the questions had been in favour of Economic, Social and Cultural Rights. Civil and Political Rights had little significance in practice in the Eastern bloc because of the priorities they had at this time adopted, and in most countries in the 'Third World' because of historical and practical reasons: historical reasons, such as poverty and illiteracy and the commitment of governments to overcome these problems, and practical reasons, such as the form of their governments (usually military dictatorships). Thus, a questionnaire based on civil and political rights will, without any doubt, favour western countries.

Although the questionnaire is based on international instruments, nonetheless, it fails to overcome the fact that these rights represent the values of the liberal democracies. Some of the rights in the questionnaire are only indirectly supported by international instruments. Humana derives the right to be free from capital punishment, for instance, from article 6 of the International Covenant on Civil and Political Rights which stipulates that '... sentence of death may be imposed only for the most serious crimes in accordance with the law in force at the time of the commission of the crime and ... shall not be imposed for crimes committed by persons below eighteen years of age and shall not be carried out on pregnant women'. However, if the Covenant does not prohibit the imposition of the death penalty, and merely stresses the exceptions for it, why should Humana class countries which have failed to abolish it below those which have done so. The term 'most serious crimes in accordance with the law at the time' is a very vague and complex one. What is considered as a most serious crime under Iranian or Saudi Arabian laws, for instance, does not mean anything in another society with a different culture. Adultery, for instance, is a very serious crime under Islamic law and is punishable by the death penalty, whereas the sentence, if any, is less severe in most other countries. What should also be borne in mind is the crimes committed during states of emergencies. Experience has shown in many countries in the 'Third World' that some of the worst human rights abuses have occurred during states of emergency. The point that needs to be stressed here is that the Covenant does not prohibit the use of the death penalty in principle, and some of the violations are within the law at the time they are carried out.

The third inquiry

The third edition of Humana's work has introduced several new elements. For a start, it concentrates on 104 countries with populations over one million assessed through a questionnaire, and none in summary forms. Most importantly perhaps, is that he limited his questions to internationally binding treaties to which all states have committed themselves. In other words, his study 'simply sets their performance against their obligations'. This, according to Humana, 'should dispose of complaints that cross-national comparison of human rights 'appear to favor more prosperous countries' (1992, 7).

However, at this stage two reservations should be noted. The first is that not every country included in the study is a member of the United Nations: Hong Kong and Switzerland for example. Secondly, not every country, of the 104 included in the study, has ratified the two International Covenants upon which his entire exercise is premised. Humana has assumed that every country included in this study is committed to respecting the provision of these international treaties, which in turn, makes his study immune from any criticism. The contrary is true. Brazil, Kuwait, Pakistan and the United States are countries, among others, which have not ratified any of the international documents on which Humana's study is based.

Like the second inquiry, the third suffers from inequalities in the distribution of questions between the relevant international documents in favour of the Covenant on Civil and Political Rights. However, the point that needs to be stressed is: not every country has ratified both Covenants. Some countries have ratified only one of the two Covenants, and subjecting them to the provisions of the unratified one means that the argument of performance versus obligation is no longer valid. Guatemala, Honduras and Uganda are examples of countries which have only ratified one covenant on economic and social rights.

To sum up, the examples discussed above show the internal contradictions of Humana's attempt to measure human rights on a cross-national basis. In the first inquiry, some of the questions were irrelevant to the subject, and in the second and third, although partially based on or supported by international agreements, they tended to be western culture-bound. Upon these questionnaires, Humana tried to develop a strategy whereby human rights are measured internationally; this will be discussed in the section below.

The strategy of assessment

Humana has developed a comprehensive method whereby he assesses countries' human rights performances. The strategies he follows are very similar in the three inquiries. However, as we shall see later, in the last two he introduced a system of weighting.

The method

The method used is quite simple. Humana proposes a scale of four points from zero (0) to three (3). The score that each country receives depends on the answers to each of the forty questions. In the questionnaire, each question receives a score depending on the severity of the government's action towards that particular issue. For the purpose of this study, I shall refer to these categories as: top, upper middle, lower middle, and bottom respectively. A country's human rights ranking is determined by the scores obtained from the forty questions. This can be seen from the illustration shown below:

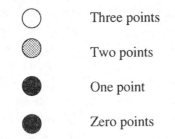

○	Three points
◎	Two points
●	One point
●	Zero points

The scores and countries' rankings depend on the nature of the questions asked. As pointed out earlier, the questions are influenced by western values, so it will be no surprise to see Western countries enjoying leading positions compared to the rest of the world. The scores given to any question depend very much on the availability of data and the co-operation of governments around the world. So, the source of information is a very important factor in assessing the validity of Humana's approach. He states that:

> the accuracy and objectivity of the answers to the questionnaire have been considered of paramount importance. In most instances information has come from the most authoritative sources and is the latest available at the time of compilation (ibid.).

However, when dealing with the human rights issue, a very sensitive question in contemporary politics, even 'the most authoritative sources' do not necessarily have accurate and objective data and information. Governments, especially in the 'Third World' and indeed in the former communist countries, tend to conceal facts relating to different aspects of social and political life, let alone questions relating to human rights. Some feel that they are not accountable since the matter relates to internal competence. Further, the accuracy of data from a developing country like Ethiopia or Niger cannot be as accurate as those of a developed country like the United States or Germany.

Such factors should have been considered by Humana when making his compilation. I shall give the example of Algeria (ibid., 33). As far as military service is concerned there are two questions related to this area. Although one objection to the second question was raised, I shall deal with both of them here to highlight that some of the answers are misleading and therefore may influence the ranking of countries.

Concerning the question related to 'freedom from military service', in Algeria citizens are not free from obligations of this kind. Every man, aged eighteen or over and who is not disabled is required to do military service. The answer in Humana's inquiry was that everybody has to do six months' military service and thus Algeria was ranked lower middle. It would be of particular interest to know the source of this information. Algeria stipulated compulsory military service of two years at the time of the compilation. This was decreased to eighteen months in January 1990. Thus, according to Humana's system of scoring, Algeria should have been ranked at the bottom and not the lower middle. The same measure could apply to the question dealing with maximum punishment for refusing such service. Humana states that the maximum punishment is one year's imprisonment. However, if the period required for compulsory military service was two years, how could the punishment for refusing it be just one year in prison? The punishment for refusing it is much more severe when it is tied to curtailment of civil liberties, such as movement outside the country or the acquisition of a passport and application for jobs. In these cases confirmation of a citizen's status vis-à-vis military service is a necessary prerequisite. Thus, Algeria, instead of being in the upper middle category, should have been in the bottom one.

Another contradictory area of the comparison is the question of the death penalty. In some instances, where the answers were similar, the scores given to the countries concerned were different in 1983. For example, the answers to the question on the death penalty for France and Italy were respectively: recently abolished, and, abolished in 1944. The answers show that both countries do not carry out this kind of punishment any more.

Nonetheless, the 1983 ranking of the two countries differs. France was ranked at the top, whereas Italy was ranked upper middle. The scores, however, were corrected in 1986 (compare the scores of the two countries in ibid., 187-199). The two countries should have been in the same category, i.e., at the top, following Humana's line of argument.

His strategy of ranking or giving scores to each country depends on the relative position of the state. But, the decisive question to be asked here is how can someone assess the position of a country concerning the death penalty? I believe that this question should not have been assessed on a four point scale as Humana did. What is the attitude of governments which have been ranked at the upper middle or lower middle? As far as the death penalty is concerned, there are two extremes and nothing in between; the state carries out the death penalty and is ranked at the bottom, or it does not carry out the death penalty and is ranked at the top. The crux of the matter is not whether the death penalty is an established violation of the right to life or not, but the way by which Humana has tried to assess it. If the state carries out the death penalty, the damage is done. There is nothing relative that gives any room for argument as is the case with other rights. Algeria for instance, has been ranked lower middle, but, it should have gone down to bottom.

Finally, the results or the scores of the different questions are turned into percentages. Each country that was assessed through this questionnaire was given a percentage which indicated its position compared to other countries and to a world average. I shall be discussing the world average at a later stage. What matters here is how Humana achieved his percentages in the three inquiries. In the second and third studies there is a clear indication of how the figures are turned into percentages using a system of weighting. However, there is no indication to this effect in the first one. Humana fails to show how countries are ranked this way: how a particular country is ranked above or below another country. It would have been very helpful had Humana explained how these percentages were calculated, and how he established the basis on which the performance of countries was to be compared.

I have tried one possible and logical way to achieve his percentages. In his first study, there are fifty questions. The first forty are the ones which receive scores, the remaining ten are divided into two categories: the first five 'are given simply as an indication of the severity or otherwise of the penal code' (Humana, 1983, 27), whereas the last five are compulsory documents for citizens.

The percentages are reached by adding the scores of each question multiplied by one hundred (100) and the result is divided by one hundred and twenty (120), which is the maximum possible score for the 40 questions. I have tried this method on two countries; Algeria and Sweden. The results were slightly different: in the case of Algeria, for instance, the finding was 62.5 per cent, and therefore its percentage should have been 63. In the case of Sweden, however, the finding matched the number Humana proposed. Probably this is the method since the difference between the actual percentages and the findings is just slight. But, it is possible that the rest of the questionnaire might have some influence on the final percentage. When his percentages for the year 1986 are applied to different countries, the situation in the histogram below is reached.

Histogram (6) 1: Percentages of human rights in selected countries

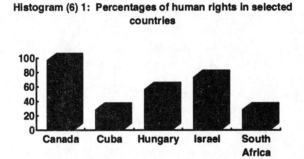

This is the position and the ranking of selected countries as far as human rights are concerned according to Humana. A comparison between counties based on this histogram can be easily made and a conclusion of which country better complies with Humana's scale is clearly visible. Nonetheless, these results are doubtful, not only because the questions are not acceptable to all, but because they are sometimes misleading. In this context Algeria provides the best example. Its score should have been lower since Humana attributed some answers with scores higher than his system warranted.

The system of weighting

Humana introduced a system of weighting in both his second and third exercises. Although he did not introduce weighting in his first, he considered doing so. He states that a 'system of weighting each of the questions was considered. In human rights terms some are undoubtedly more important than others'. However, he decided against it to 'avoid the impression of an arbitrary selection on the part of the compiler' (ibid., 11). Through the introduction of this system, some rights apparently become more equal than others. Among the range of the forty questions employed in the inquiry, he chose seven weighted ones. This weighting system means giving each of these seven questions three times the weight of each of the remaining thirty three. Here, a crucial question cannot be avoided: Where is the willingness to 'avoid the impression of arbitrary selection on the part of the compile'? The questions that Humana weights are freedom from:

-Serfdom, slavery, forced or child labor.
-Extrajudicial killings or "disappearances".
-Torture or coercion by the state.
-Compulsory work permits or conscription of labor.
-Capital punishment by the state.
-Court sentences of corporal punishment.
-Indefinite detention without trial.

Certainly the rights mentioned above are very important. In terms of human rights some rights are more important than others, and, indeed, some may depend on the others. It would be absurd to talk about human rights when the basic right, i.e., the right to life, is violated. The reason behind this system of weighting is the endurance and the pain to which the individual is subject. Humana argues that:

An individual screaming while subjected to torture or locked for years in an unlit cell because of his or her opinions is enduring a degree of physical or mental suffering greater than the denial of a vote or of having his or her newspaper censored (1983, 3-4).

Humana's argument that there is, in principle, a difference in the importance of human rights may be accepted. Extrajudicial killings and torture are more important than, for instance, freedom of association. By the same token, it may be argued that the seven weighted rights are not all important to the same extent. The point that needs to be stressed here is that if Humana's hierarchy of human rights is taken seriously into account, then it is possible to find rights either within the seven weighted or the remaining thirty-three rights that are more important than others in the same category. Within the seven weighted rights, for instance, freedom from capital punishment by the state, it might be argued, is the basic human right without which human rights would have little, if any, meaning. By the same token, extrajudicial killings and torture, for instance, are arguably more important than indefinite detention without trial. In these two instances, there is a difference in the extent of physical suffering inflicted on the individual. A person detained without trial is physically suffering less than one who is tortured. The same argument could be made about the remaining non-weighted rights. As a result, when a comparative study of human rights is undertaken, every right should be considered as equal as the others. In this context Donnelly and Howard argue that 'Although no rights can be enjoyed unless one is alive, the right to life has no moral priority; it may be a prerequisite to enjoying other rights, but does not make it a "higher" right'. (1986, 215). Furthermore, Yoram Dinstein, a prominent international lawyer from Tel Aviv University, in a talk at the Department of Law, Glasgow University, about 'Human Rights in Israel', stressed:

> Each state should be credited for honouring and respecting any aspect of human rights, and should be blamed for failing to do so. [He continued:]. In Israel the state does not carry out the death penalty, but at the same time some practices of demolishing Palestinians' houses are witnessed. There is no way to suggest that the state is observing human rights since the right to life is respected, which is above all.

Thus, according to this system of weighting, the percentage that each country receives is calculated as follow:

$$\frac{[(33 \times 3) + (7 \times 3) \times 3)] \times 100}{162}$$

Thirty three refers to the number of the non-weighted questions multiplied by three, which is the maximum score for each question. From this formula the highest possible number accounting can obtain is ninety nine. Seven, is the number of the questions that are weighted by being multiplied by three, and the result is multiplied again by three - as these rights are more important than the others according to Humana. The maximum score for this section would be sixty three. Converting these scores into percentages is achieved by adding the two sets of results, multiplied by one hundred and the overall is divided by one hundred and sixty two, which is the maximum score for the forty questions after weighting.

The conclusion reached from the above is that not only the choice of questions is debatable, but there is also a discrepancy within the questions themselves. Or, how can it be explained that the maximum a weighted right receives equals the maximum score of three non-weighted questions put together? Thus, according to the methodology suggested by Humana, if a country performs well in the weighted rights, it will have a big advantage over others which did not observe human rights in general. These particular weighted rights, moreover, are widely enjoyed in all Western countries. They constitute a necessity, whereas they are a luxury in most, if not all 'Third World' countries.

Let us try to imagine a situation where two countries A and B are subjected to the questionnaire, and see their ranking position using this system of weighting. Country A scores the maximum points for the first twenty questions, and none for the second twenty. On the other hand, Country B scores none for the first twenty, and the maximum for the second twenty. Needless to say, according to the questionnaire, the weighted rights are within the first twenty. Normally, they should be at the same level within the ranking table, since both received maximum points for twenty questions and none for the other twenty. However, it is clearly visible that country A is well ahead of country B, thanks to this system of weighting, as follows:

Country A:
$$\frac{(13 \times 3) + (7 \times 3) \times 3) \times 100}{162}$$
$$\frac{39 + 63 = 102 \times 1000}{162} = 62.96$$

Country B: $(20 \times 3) + (7 \times 0) \times 3) \times 100$

162

$\dfrac{60 + 0 = 60 \times 1000}{162}$ $= 37.03$

To see the discrepancy between the two countries, these percentages shown above will be highlighted in this histogram.

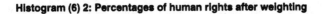

Histogram (6) 2: Percentages of human rights after weighting

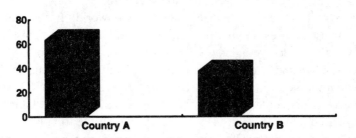

This histogram shows the inequalities between the two countries. This inequality that I shall refer to as 'spurious lead' would not have existed had Humana not introduced his system of weighting. Although he intended to highlight that some rights were of genuine importance, applying them world wide would be exalting some countries against the others. Therefore, even a system of weighting of this kind, however plausible, introduces an element of arbitrariness into the entire exercise.

The world average

In his assessment of human rights situations, Humana has developed a minimum standard of achievement referred to as the world average: In the first inquiry the world average was 64 per cent, in the second it dropped to 55 per cent, and in the third it was 62 per cent. In other words, countries scoring above this percentage may be regarded as better than those below it. In his comprehensive table of countries assessed, the ranking position of each country is determined relative to this world average.

The first inquiry's world average of 64 per cent was surprisingly high as Humana himself conceded. He gave two main explanations for this phenomenon, stating that:

The first is the earlier reference to regional, religious or social distinctions which establish certain areas of tolerance in different groups of countries. The second, ... is that the efficiency of a state usually falls short of controlling all aspects of life (1983, 11).

Nonetheless, another possible explanation to this and it is not less important than the two mentioned above - the size of the sample. Humana established a world average for human rights taken from the seventy five countries assessed through his questionnaire. So, it does not reflect a comprehensive overview of human rights in the world. If the study had included more countries, the world average would have fallen. This helps to explain why the world average has fallen in the second inquiry to 55 per cent, since the study included eighty nine countries; fourteen new ones had been added. The third inquiry, 1992, saw the world average go up to 62 per cent. This increase is undoubtedly due to the changes that have been taking place in the former communist countries since Gorbachev came to power in March 1985, and any cross-national measurement of human rights on a continuous basis, taking into account these changes, is bound to suggest an overall improvement in the human rights situation in the world. However, the high percentages received by the former communist countries in Humana's study undermine the findings of the study as a genuine attempt to reflect the world's human rights situation. Humana seems to be overimpressed with what has happened in these countries, and to have assumed that post-communist regimes will further improve their human rights records. No one denies how dramatic these changes were, but they led Humana into overlooking putting the situation in perspective. If this was not the case, how can it be explained that the former Czechoslovakia, for instance, scored 97 per cent, a higher percentage than more established liberal democracies such as Austria with 95 per cent, France with 94 per cent and Switzerland with 96 per cent? Other examples include Romania with a score of 82 per cent, and both Bulgaria and Poland which scored 83 per cent each.

However, there is no explanation as to why the world average was 64, 55 and 62 per cent in 1983, 1986 and 1992 respectively. In other words, why did he establish these percentages and not others? The explanations given above help illustrate the 1983 average attained its level and dropped in 1986, but they do not tell us how the world average of 64 per cent, for example, was obtained in the first instance.

The only possible formula is to add the score of each country, and decide the result by the number of countries assessed. I tested this hypothesis on the two inquiries. In the first one, the findings were slightly over the number Humana gave. According to this strategy, the world average should have been 65 per cent rather than 64 per cent. This is because the test resulted in 64.6 per cent, and this figure is nearer to 65 than to 64. However, in the second inquiry, the gap between the findings and the figure given by Humana creates doubt as to whether the formula is the appropriate one. I added the score received by each country, and divided the result by 89 - which is the number of countries assessed under the questionnaire. The world average reported by Humana was 55 per cent, but my finding was 61.8 per cent. Thus, the world average should be 62 per cent, if the formula is correct. It would have been appropriate if Humana had explained how his results were achieved.

Even if there was consensus on the method used to establish the three world averages of 64, 55 and 62 per cent, agreement on the use of this system as a whole is very difficult to achieve. Human rights, in this view, are a kind of test a government has to take: if it achieves the minimum requirement it passes, and if it does not it fails. Professor Yoram Dinstein observed that:

> Human rights are not a balance between credit and debit. If a government does not violate one right it should be credited for it and if it does it should be debited for it. At the end if the credited side is higher than the debited one, we cannot say that the country is observing human rights.

The same argument could be applied to this use of a world average. Countries which have reached the average might be thought to be more observant of human rights than those which received lower averages. On the contrary, every government violates human rights in one way or another, and the enhancement and enjoyment of human rights is a continuous process. It does not mean that countries like the United States, France, Sweden and Norway which scored high, far beyond the world average, are not questionable in terms of their performance. This application of a world average makes them less vulnerable to scrutiny at a time when they should work harder towards improving the standards already achieved. Therefore, the world average should have been omitted from the two inquiries, because it is not fully representative, and because it invites non-constructive comparison between countries' scores and a spurious global norm.

Types of assessment

This section examines the different types of countries considered in the two inquiries. Humana has selected two criteria for assessment: countries assessed under the questionnaire and others assessed in a more summary form, both of which will be analysed below.

Assessment under the questionnaire (the cases of Israel and South Africa)

Seventy-five, eighty-nine and one-hundred and four countries respectively were assessed through the questionnaires in the three inquiries. The kind of questions that constituted the questionnaires and the method developed to rank countries have been discussed in some detail. The focus here is on two countries which pose a lot of difficulties: South Africa and Israel. It is generally agreed that, relatively, some of the worst human rights violations occurred in these countries. For historical reasons these two countries are peculiar, and whatever strategy is followed to assess human rights in them will have its shortcomings. Humana has applied two different strategies; one for each country. For the former, the compiler asked:

> How does one, for example, apply a single questionnaire to South Africa with its bewildering contradictions of human rights for its white citizens and the denial of most of the non-white two-thirds of the population who do not qualify, because of their colour for citizenship? As the Guide accepts the premise that in the field of human rights mankind is one, the only honest treatment of South Africa is to apply the questionnaire to the least favoured of the population. And this approach has been followed (1983, 11).

Whereas, as far as Israel is concerned in Humana's study, another approach has been followed. The justification was that:

These [The Occupied Territories] are administered by a separate military government, and law enforcement and breaches of human rights are much more repressive than in the liberal state of Israel. For the purpose of this Guide Israel has been assessed without the Occupied Territories (ibid., 12).

Histogram (6) 3: Human rights in South Africa and Israel

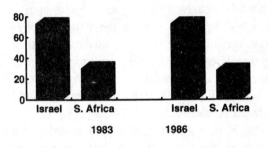

This histogram, a result of Humana's inquiries, shows the differences between two countries with notorious records of human rights violations. After the elimination of the Occupied Territories for Israel, it is clear that the latter is ranked much higher than South Africa. Had it not been for this discriminatory strategy, these countries would have had the same scores, i.e., well below the world average. If 'in the field of human rights mankind is one' - as Humana has suggested - why is it then that Israel was assessed without the Occupied Territories? Why were the Occupied Territories assessed by themselves in the second inquiry? Who is responsible for the violations that the Occupied Territories witness daily? The answer is obvious: the Israeli government. These are practices by a state against individuals; if they are positive acts it should be credited, and if they are not, the state concerned should be blamed. Humana defined human rights in his introduction, as 'laws and practices ... to protect ordinary people, groups and races, from oppressive rulers and governments', and since they were not considered, where do the Palestinian people in the Occupied Territories fit, if they do not belong in these categories? Moreover, where are the laws to protect them against abuses and by which standards should we judge the oppressor?

Therefore, what is the purpose of a guide which assesses Israel without the Occupied Territories?

Conversely, why does the questionnaire in South Africa apply to Blacks only, 'the least favoured of the population'? The standard of 30 per cent in South Africa does not reflect the real situation in the country as far as the white citizens are concerned. If the same questionnaire was to be applied, using the same techniques that Humana suggested, to white citizens only in South Africa, the outcome of the inquiry would be completely different from the one Humana achieved. The same could apply to Israel; the high percentage is not representative for the unprivileged Arabs. If mankind is one, then one questionnaire only should be applied to different groups or segments in the society. Although the questionnaire in both cases was applied to the majority of the population, applying the questionnaire to all the population within the jurisdiction of the state would have been able to produce a clearer picture.

The important question that should be asked in this instance is why were the Occupied Territories independently assessed in the second inquiry? The Occupied Territories, at the time of the compilation, did not qualify as a state since there was no legitimate sovereign government enjoying acceptance within the international community. Power in these territories was concentrated in a military authority, which was responsible for what was happening. It would be absurd, then, to examine the Occupied Territories as independent from Israel, with the latter's performance not influenced by the abuses in the Occupied Territories. Otherwise the result would hide facts or mislead readers to believe that Israel performs well and observes a wide range of human rights. The situation in this area was very difficult; the Arabs did not recognise the state of Israel, while the latter claimed sovereignty over some areas through military authorities. Therefore, it is quite difficult to find an accommodation that would satisfy both parties. Nonetheless, in the area of human rights where human beings are supposed to be equal, the same treatment should be applied to both of them. Thus, Israel's performance should have been lower than what Humana proposed.

The summary forms

Countries where information was scarce were assessed in both studies in a more summary form. In other words, the questionnaire was not applied to them, but the compiler tried to give a general picture about the situation in each of the countries considered. After that, he divided the countries into three different categories: 'Bad', 'Poor' and 'Fair'. These categories are comparatively acceptable, but did not mean anything in terms of percentages in the first inquiry. In the second inquiry, and in order to make the picture clearer, Humana tried to define his categories further by giving them percentages. Thus, 'Bad' is the category where the percentage is 40 per cent or lower, 'Poor' is between 41 and 75 per cent, and 'Fair' is over 75 per cent (Humana, 1986, 4).

These are the categories and the percentages representing each. Humana felt that the categories were vague in terms of significance, and tried in his second inquiry to make them more understandable. Nonetheless, the matter is not clear, especially in the lower and the middle categories. There is a gap of 40 per cent, and another of 34 per cent in both categories respectively, which poses a lot of difficulties. In other words, how is it that the two countries are ranked in the same category with one scoring 73 per cent and the other just 41 per cent? Since both of them have scored between forty one and seventy five per cent, they are both in the 'Poor' category according to Humana.

It would have been more appropriate had these countries been ranked in different categories or clusters of six or seven: to narrow the gap between different categories and make the comparison more meaningful. However, if this cannot be done, and the compiler felt that countries should be ranked in just three categories, it would perhaps make more sense if these categories did not have these high percentages. The reason behind this strategy is the lack of information concerning the attitudes of governments towards their citizens. In the area of human rights, governments try to hide or falsify facts related to abuses in human rights. That is not the kind of publicity that governments will normally seek. So, the assumption is that, when there is no co-operation with human rights organisations, the country's record must be quite bad. Therefore, it came as a surprise to see some countries, assessed through summary forms, in the middle category, 'Poor', indicating that they scored a percentage between 70 and 75 per cent.

Humana's work in comparative perspective

Humana had tried to develop a comprehensive strategy whereby the human rights performance of every country is measured. It has been suggested elsewhere in this chapter that the criteria he developed are not necessarily acceptable as a basis of comparison on a cross-national basis. He himself acknowledges the fact when he says that:

> One of the purposes of this Guide is to make possible comparison between countries. Such comparisons, by the distinctive nature of each society, can be only approximations, and objections to such an exercise can be predicted and understood (1983, 9).

To start with, Humana defined human rights as 'paws and practices'. However, in his application of the questionnaire he scarcely takes into account practices. It is acknowledged that the laws are necessary to establish standards and to obtain reparation, nonetheless, the practices have tended, for different reasons, not to take into account the provisions of the laws. What is the meaning of freedom of movement in a country where the acquisition of a passport is very difficult? In Algeria, for instance, 'Algerians are free to travel within Algeria and outside, although travelling abroad is made difficult by strict currency controls' (Freedom House, 1990a, 30). This may be the case; but if citizens do not have any access to foreign currency, what does freedom to travel mean to them?

In his definition of human rights, there is a reference to time when he says: 'They[human rights] are laws and practices that have evolved over the centuries.' This in turn poses some difficulties in comparison. The development of the laws differs from one country to another. The evolution over the centuries did not follow the same course in different countries. In this context the age of a nation has some significance. How can it be possible to apply the same standards to countries which have existed for centuries such as the United Kingdom, France or the United States to the majority of 'Third World' countries which have existed for only a few decades. Rhoda Howard, among others, has 'made compelling arguments that in effect measuring all countries by the same definitional standards is grossly unfair to developing nations' (quoted in R. Goldsmith, 1986, 612).

Clearly it is difficult to achieve high standards of human rights in countries with a long tradition of arbitrary and authoritarian rule and oppression. Human rights, as they are enjoyed in today's West, are the product of a continuous process that has been progressing over the centuries; and, relatively, the same process is taking place in the underdeveloped world. It is difficult to apply standards developed in the West, and thought to be the best, to describe situations in different countries in the world. Dogan and Pelassy argue:

> Is it possible to analyse, with concepts formulated in Europe, in a completely different context what is now happening in Burma or Zaire? What is a 'nation' or 'a social class' in Sub-Sahara Africa? Are not the words we are using surreptitiously leading us to misinterpretation? (1984, 22)

To achieve valid results when comparing human rights, ethnocentrism has to be avoided. In other words, the establishment of a set of variables and a minimum standard of achievement, referred to as the world average in the inquiries, and attempts to apply them on a cross-national basis will not solve anything. It will, on the contrary create a lot of controversies. When attempting to measure human rights, a clear definition of the concept has to be provided as well as the different variables upon which judgement is to be based. A small set of variables can give a relatively clear picture of the situation in any country. Nonetheless, these variables should not be in contradiction to the political system of any country. A secret ballot, for instance, affords the opportunity to reject a single party. However, in his second work, although Humana states that former Czechoslovakia is a one-party communist state, he uses a question about multiparty elections by secret and universal ballot as a variable upon which he judges the performance of this country (1986, 72).

It is quite difficult to reach an accommodation as far as this area is concerned. What constitutes a human right in one country may not be quite so fundamental in the other. What has to be taken into account are the social and economic conditions as well as the cultural factors whenever human rights are discussed. They do not develop in a vacuum. They influence, and are influenced by the environment in which they exist. Different attitudes can be understood by looking at the political culture of the society itself.

To understand the economic factors better, Algeria provides an example *par excellence*. The country witnessed the worst human rights violations since independence when government troops indiscriminately massacred its citizens in October 1988. Since that time, it moved from a one-party system to multi-party 'democracy'. Algerians currently enjoy different forms of freedom that did not exist before: freedom of expression, independent newspapers, associations etc.... In both instances (before and after October 1988) it was due to economic factors. Protests against unemployment, corruption and the failure of the economic system led to these demonstrations ending in bloodshed. The inability of the government to provide materially what it did previously, and to manage the increasing demands of the people, led to these reforms as a strategy to gain legitimacy. The question that needs to be asked here is; would these violations of human rights, and the flexibility on the part of the government have existed, if it was not for the failure of the economic system?

Therefore, many factors are involved when human rights are discussed. However, it should be made clear that Humana's inquiries are not without value. They are above all comprehensive inquiries; he tries to develop a strategy by which one can measure human rights, in principle, on a global basis. As already mentioned, however, they are heavily influenced by Western thinking, which finds little, if any, significance in different parts of the world.

One of the purposes of these guides is to make possible comparison between countries in terms of human rights. Nevertheless, concepts and statistics do not provide sufficient data to allow for a meaningful comparison. To make the best possible use of Humana's inquiries, a selection of the countries to be studied should be made first. The adoption of the method is a very significant step in the process of comparisons. The cross-national approach that Humana followed in his inquiries led to disagreements on the range of the questions asked on the methods of assessment. The inclusion of different countries, with their differences in cultures and backgrounds, further added to the difficulties which might be encountered when measuring human rights. It would have been more helpful had Humana restricted the application of his strategies to countries from the Western world. If the concepts concerned are not judged and valued within the same context, the result of any inquiry would not be very convincing. Human rights are a social phenomenon that influence, and are influenced, by the environment in which they occur, as well as the culture of the actors involved whether in violating or assessing them. Therefore, it would not come as a surprise to find a completely different picture had the inquiries been carried out by a scholar from the former Eastern Europe or the 'Third World'. The argument and variables he would use would, undoubtedly, differ from those seen in Humana's inquiries.

7 Comparative measures of democracy

The past two decades witnessed dramatic moves towards democratisation in many regions of the world. The mid 1970s saw the collapse of military dictatorships in Southern Europe and similar events took place in the majority of Latin American countries in the first half of the 1980s. The end of the decade saw the collapse of communism in East and Central Europe. These changes have led to substantial research by political scientists and historians alike to study and document these events. As a result, the study of democratisation has become one of the fastest growing areas in political science. More importantly, with these new waves of democratisation, this interest does not only lie in what brings countries to democratise, but measuring this level of democracy also. However, the questions that need to be addressed are: can the level of democracy be measured at all? If so, by what degree of precision? What variables or criteria can be used in an exercise of this kind? Are the variables used, often by Western scholars, universal or culture specific? Can the same variables be used to assess developed and developing countries alike? Do we need a different set of criteria for different countries? These theoretical and empirical questions will be addressed in the following discussion to highlight the problems associated with any exercise of this kind.

Measuring democracy has a relatively long tradition in political science. Perhaps the most influential work to date is Robert Dahl's *Polyarchy* (1971), which attempted to measure democracy by using its two dimensions: competition and participation. Later work includes that of Kenneth Bollen (1979, 1980); Charles Humana's approach, as pointed out in the previous chapter; Freedom House's, as will be seen in the next chapter, and that of Vanhanen (1984). In this Chapter, and in an attempt to answer the above questions, I shall concentrate on both Dahl's and Bollen's studies to measure democracy on a cross-national basis. I begin with Dahl's study. I shall look at the definition he gives and the conditions upon which he judges whether a system is democratic or not. Then, I shall turn to the study undertaken by Bollen. The third part of the chapter contains a comparative analysis of the two inquiries. In other words, it highlights the characteristics shared by the two scholars in measuring the degrees of democratisation. The chapter concludes with some critical reflections on the shortcomings of the two inquiries discussed and a general assessment.

Dahl's measurement of democracy

It should be noted at the outset that Robert Dahl believes that no political system in the contemporary world is fully democratic. Since, in his view, 'no large system in the real world is democratised', he prefers to call them polyarchies. 'Polyarchies, then, may be thought of as relatively (but incompletely) democratised regimes, or, to put it in another way, polyarchies are regimes that have been substantially popularised and liberalised' (Dahl, 1971, 8). In subsequent work, he defined polyarchy as 'a political order distinguished by the presence of seven institutions' which are - elected officials, free and fair elections, inclusive suffrage, the right to run for office, freedom of expression, alternative information and associational autonomy (Dahl, 1989, 221). In what follows, I shall use these terms interchangeably.

Definition of democracy

What should be borne in mind is that there have been many definitions of the term democracy since its evolution over the centuries. What concern us, in this respect, is the definition used by Dahl. As suggested above, he believes that no system in today's world is democratic. Nonetheless, he suggests that 'democratic theory is concerned with the processes by which ordinary citizens exert a relatively high degree of control over leaders' (Dahl, 1956, 3).

This suggests that, where citizens have a relatively high degree of control over their leaders, that country is democratic. In other words, governments are not in office to exert authority over their citizens, but to be responsive to the demands formulated by them. Dahl observes that: 'The key characteristic of democracy is the continuing responsiveness of the government to the preferences of its citizens considered as political equals' (Dahl, 1971, 1).

Such a distinctive characteristic of democracy leaves the door wide open to debate and offers grounds for questioning the statement itself. The questions that need to be clarified in this respect are: what kind of responsiveness of governments exist in relation to the preferences of their citizens? And how far do governments go in responding to these preferences? He assumes that for a government to be responsive to the preferences of its citizens, they should be offered opportunities (1) to formulate their preferences, (2) to signify their preferences to their fellow citizens and the government by individual and collective action and (3) to have their preferences weighted equally in the conduct of the government, that is, weighted with no discrimination because of the content or source of the preference (ibid., 3).

When scrutinising these requirements (which will be the basis for his measurement of democracy, as will be seen at a later stage in the chapter), the right to vote, freedom to form and join organisations and freedom of expression would be at the centre of democracy. 'In so far as democracy is concerned with the issue of rule and control or decision-making', Graham argues, 'it is perforce concerned with freedom and liberty; and at least to the extent that no one is excluded from a share in decision making some rudimentary notion of equality is implicit' (1986, 13).

Although there is not much ground upon which to disagree with Dahl, it is difficult, if not impossible, to achieve in practice. When these conditions are applied to the real world, no country in the world meets these requirements properly. Dahl's model appears utopian. What should be borne in mind is that although these characteristics are vital to a democratic system, they are insufficient as countries differ in the extent to which they meet them. This is especially true of some systems which are democratic but do not have all these kinds of rights. The United States is an example par excellence. There is no doubt that the USA is considered among the most democratic countries in the world, and, one would suspect, that the different requirements that Dahl proposed for democracy were met within the American system. However, in the process described above, freedom to form or join organisations is not well established; a fact when it comes to organisations of communist persuasion. The same objection to such organisations was, until recently, found in the former West Germany. However, before looking at Dahl's attempt to measure democracy, I shall first consider the conditions that favour it.

Conditions of polyarchy

The measurement of democracy depends on its existence in the first place. It would be absurd to think of measuring this phenomenon unless it existed. In this respect, it is of paramount importance to observe whether the conditions favouring polyarchy, and whether the variables used have any connection with these conditions. Democratic political systems do not exist as such, but there are some conditions which favour their emergence. These conditions, according to Dahl, can be summarised as follows:

Historical sequences: Historical events that countries experience may play a crucial role in determining whether a country moves towards polyarchy or not. According to Dahl, countries where competition precedes inclusiveness are more favourable to polyarchy than those where the process is the other way around. Obviously competition has to precede inclusiveness if the system is to develop smoothly into a polyarchy. Little by little, more and more citizens are included in the system. However, if one takes this for granted, many questions arise that need to be clarified.

Applying this condition would mean omitting many countries from the political map. Historical sequences could be applicable to different countries which have existed for centuries, which have experienced different periods of transformation and social change. In this respect, what would someone say about different countries in the 'Third World', especially in Asia and Africa, which are the creation of foreign domination? How would one account for Tunisia or Zimbabwe, for instance, countries which have achieved independence recently whether competition preceded inclusiveness or the other way around? Is it fair on developing countries to be judged by the same criterion as developed ones? I am not suggesting that countries in today's Africa should be compared to nineteenth century Europe as suggested by the theorists such as Rhoda Howard (Goldsmith, 1986, 612). This is methodologically difficult, if not impossible. What needs to be stressed here is that the development in the majority of 'Third World' countries did not follow the same path, was disturbed by different foreign dominations and has evolved over a shorter period of time.

The socio-economic order: In societies where access to violence and economic sanctions is monopolised, the chances for polyarchy, in Dahl's view, are lower. Both economic sanctions and violence are two important tools whereby one group, segment or class influences the decisions of others. In a society where these powers are concentrated in the hands of the government, the chances that it will tolerate the emergence of opposition are very weak indeed. The government has free access to these tools to curtail the opposition when it is unable to cope with the increasing demands.

They are two ways by which governments respond to the continuing demands of their citizens. The first includes positive response when the institutions are adaptable to the new situations, i.e., the feedback of the government in terms of laws and decrees which would meet the increasing demands of the citizens. The second is the use of violence and economic sanctions. In this instance, it does not automatically follow that this condition should be taken for granted. What should be borne in mind, however, is that equal access amongst government and opposition to violence and economic sanctions may be a very good condition favouring democracy, but seeing it from another angle it may also be an outcome of democracy. Would it be safe to assume that if access to violence and socio-economic sanctions was neutralised, a country would become democratic? On the other hand, would not this concentration of sanctions in the hands of the government lead to democracy?

As for the type of economy, Dahl believes that if it is agrarian, the free farmers type is more favourable than the traditional peasant, whereas decentralised direction in a commercial industry would favour polyarchy rather than centralised direction. Dahl's view of democracy, which he shares with Bobbio (1987, 26), is that it goes hand in hand with the type of economy. That is, a competitive politics requires a competitive economy.

However, the concentration of violence in the hands of the government, although a condition unfavourable to polyarchy according to Dahl, might be seen as a path to polyarchy. In almost every country in the world, legitimised access to violence and to economic sanctions is monopolised in the hands of governments. The point to be made here is that, 'legitimised access' in the

Weberian sense, is the determining factor in favouring polyarchy. Moreover, the concentration of these powers in the hands of government, and their steady use against opposition groups may lead to uprisings and disturbances that would compel authoritarian systems to experiment with some forms of liberalisation.

The level of socio-economic development: Dahl observes that when the GNP per capita is high (over or about $700-800), at the time of writing (1971), it favours polyarchy, and when it is low it does not. Such a variable was, to some extent, ignored by the different attempts to measure human rights. Having said that, it does not automatically mean that the higher the level of socio-economic development, the higher the respect for human rights. Nonetheless, this factor should be taken into account when dealing with the issues of human rights and democracy. It is borne in mind that this high level of socio-economic development is very much related to the richness of the country itself, whereas the treatment of the citizens such as granting them freedom of speech, assembly, etc. depends on the goodwill of the government. The higher the level of socio-economic development in a country, the more opportunities are available to the citizen to learn, to travel, and to communicate. Such development enables the citizen to become aware of what others enjoy in different countries. Neubauer rightly argues that:

> It is quite clear, one may say obvious, that extremely poor, traditional societies characterised by illiterate, rural population in which intergroup communication is barely developed and national identification and national institutions barely extant, will have considerable difficulty in establishing and maintaining political equality (1967, 1008-9).

What needs to be stressed here is that the role of socio-economic development in a country is so crucial that it cannot be neglected, and to some extent, should be considered as the driving force for any changes that may occur in political systems. Many social phenomena, to take a Marxist approach, find their explanations in the economy. Further, 'the data show rather conclusively that: the higher the socio-economic level of a country, the more likely it is to have a competitive political regime' (Dahl, 1971, 64). However, it does not necessarily follow that when a country is rich, it is democratic. There are many examples that refute this hypothesis such as South Africa, before the abolition of Apartheid and all the Gulf states.

Equalities and inequalities: Extreme inequalities, according to Dahl, in a country do not favour polyarchy. By contrast, the lower the level of inequality, the higher the chances for polyarchy to develop. Inequalities in this context are seen mainly from an economic point of view. The allocation of wealth, income and social status to a particular group within a given society would privilege them and enable them to gain more influence. The accumulation of these economic resources in the hands of a small number of citizens may be turned into political resources which can influence, at a later stage, the kind of political system. In such a situation, polyarchy is unthinkable. A system would develop which would safeguard the privileges already realised by this handful of citizens. It is only an industrial society, according to Dahl, which can decrease these inequalities. He argues that:

> If industrial societies do not eliminate inequalities they significantly reduce them. As average income rises with advancing technology and growing productivity, more and more advantages hitherto abrogated to small elite come within reach of an expanding proportion of the population. In loose language, then, one might say that as a country approaches high levels of industrialisation, extreme inequalities in important political resources decline (ibid., 86).

Here, two questions ought to be answered. The first would be: if inequalities do not favour democracy, do equalities inevitably lead to it? Then, if extreme inequalities decline in a country when it approaches high levels of industrialisation, does this imply that an agricultural country, or one without high levels of industrialisation cannot decrease these inequalities and therefore cannot become democratic? To answer these questions two countries spring to mind: the former Soviet Union, a country with high levels of industrialisation and low inequalities, but still considered to be far from democratic; on the other hand India, a poor agricultural country with a relatively high level of democracy.

Subcultural Pluralism is one of the most significant dangers that any political system may face. A country with deep divisions is vulnerable to violence and instability. Dahl rightly argues that:

> There are conflicts, that a competitive political system does not manage easily and perhaps cannot handle at all. Any dispute in which a large section of the population of a country feels that its way of life or its highest values are severely menaced by another segment of the population creates a crisis in a competitive system (ibid., 105).

Generally speaking, in countries with such peculiarities, loyalty is to the group or the segment rather than to the country, and this therefore makes the country's political system very inept at coping with different changes and demands. However, having said that, it does not necessarily mean that a country with different segments cannot be democratic. Many are considered as such while having these divisions, Belgium and Canada to name just the two.

Although it is not difficult to agree with Dahl that this condition does not favour polyarchy, what should be borne in mind is that: when the persons who constitute the segments in a society have reached a degree of compromise and tolerance and learned that the interests of the country should come first, then this condition may not assume great importance. There are many grounds for optimism in saying that a kind of democracy may succeed in such countries. Consociational democracy is a system for countries with subcultural divisions, where some conditions have to be met to ensure the success of the political system. Any imbalance or shortcomings in these conditions would put the system in jeopardy. Lebanon and Switzerland provide the best examples of two countries with deep subcultural divisions, with completely opposite outcomes as regards the stability of their systems.

Domination by a foreign power: A country dominated by a foreign power is influenced, depending on the extent of that domination, by the policies and structures in the dominant country. That is to say, the people are not really free to choose the type of political system by which they want to be governed. This, in turn, will very much affect the chances of polyarchy. Such a variable is used by Raymond Gastil in the Comparative Surveys of Freedom that Freedom House produces (see chapter eight).

There is no doubt that the domination of a foreign power in any country affects its political system. However, taking this variable into account, although convincing in principle, would overlook a group of countries. In other words, foreign domination cannot be clearly identified when it comes to countries in the developed world. This in turn leads to more issues which need clarification, such as what is meant by foreign domination and in what forms this foreign domination may be said to exist. It involves more figures than was traditionally thought, i.e., military occupation of territories other than those of the dominant states. Dahl believes that, among other factors, if foreign domination is strong and persistent, it disfavours polyarchy, and if it is weak or temporary it favours it. In this case, one cannot avoid asking questions about the kind of foreign domination in countries such as the USA or the UK.

Beliefs of political activists: The beliefs of political activists together with the level of socio-economic development are perhaps the most significant conditions favouring democracy. The level of socio-economic development is very important not only for the stability of a country, but for its development also. The higher this level in a country, the more chances a citizen has for a better life, and the more resources the government has to respond to the demands of its citizens. The higher this level, the more responsive a government is to social and economic rights. As Dahl suggests:

> Looking more closely we see that the claim to primary social rights can be justified on one or both of the two grounds. They may be necessary simply in order to make it possible for citizens to exercise their primary political rights, or like the primary political rights they may be directly necessary in order to satisfy the criteria of democratic process (1980, 14).

To some extent the stability of the system is ensured since the need for material goods is met by the country. However, a higher level of socio-economic development does not automatically lead to democracy and the stability of the system. Although the level of economic development is a very significant factor, it is not sufficient. It would make more sense if it were coupled with the beliefs of political activists.

The legitimacy of institutions is another factor under the heading of beliefs of political activists. Dahl feels the legitimacy of institutions favours polyarchy and is effective in solving major problems. However, the legitimacy of institutions does not necessarily favour the establishment of polyarchy as much as its continuation.

The measurement of democracy

Dahl was quite reluctant to engage in any kind of quantitative analysis of democracy since the data that would support his conditions for polyarchy are difficult, if not impossible, to come by. Data concerning the level of socio-economic development or equalities and inequalities are comparatively easily obtainable and more convincing than the other variables which are difficult to quantify. However, in his appendix an attempt at measurement was made by Dahl and two associates, Norling and Williams (Dahl, 1971, 231). There are two dimensions upon which the classification of countries was undertaken: classification of countries according to their eligibility to participate and the degree of opportunity available for public contestation. In Dahl's view, democratisation refers to the developments on both these dimensions. In the remainder of this section, I shall look at his measurement of polyarchy more closely and assess the validity of the measures used as well as the reliability of the data, which are the sole basis for the whole operation.

The variables

It should be borne in mind that a definition of the concept under study influences the choices of variables used in the measurement. At the centre of Dahl's definition of democracy are elections: participation and the opportunity for opposition. This depends on the range of variables chosen which should be met to determine the degree of democratisation in any country. Then the question arises do the variables used by Dahl and associates to measure polyarchy correspond to the theoretical definition of the concept given earlier? This question cannot be answered unless an attempt is made to consider the variables used. They are:

Freedom of group opposition,
Interest articulation by associational groups,
Freedom of the press,
Representative character of current regime,
Current electoral system,

Interest articulation by political parties,
Party system: quantitative,
Constitutional status of present regime,
Interest aggregation by legislature,
Horizontal power distribution,
Current status of legislature.

In an attempt to measure polyarchy in terms of variables for which data were available, Dahl and his associates sought to take them from Banks and Textor's *A Cross-Polity Survey*, which aimed at quantifying 115 countries on 57 characteristics as of about 1960-62 (ibid., 235). The choice of these variables was carefully undertaken to correspond to the theoretical definition Dahl gave to democracy. When applied, they lead to a ranking of countries in terms of degrees of democratisation.

As pointed out earlier, the data were for the years 1960-62, but updated as to 1968, before the classification of countries was attempted. This led to one of the variables above (Representative character of the current regime) being dropped as redundant. Since the categories considered under this variable were: polyarchic, limited polyarchic, pseudo polyarchic and non polyarchic (Banks and Textor, 1963, 85), it provides an answer to the number of polyarchies.

A close look at the variables chosen reveals that they are quite difficult to assess, and the number of categories into which each variable was broken varied from one to another. 'The variable considering the degree of freedom of the press contains four categories, the constitutional status of the current regime variable contains three categories whereas the party system-quantitative variable contains six categories' (Dahl, 1971, 238-9; Banks and Textor, 1963, 67-97). One can conclude that the scores vary from 1 to 6 depending upon the categories that break down each variable. Thus countries with the highest scores are placed in the top category. (For a better understanding of the breakdown of the variables into different categories, see Dahl, 1971, 238-40.) However, this poses a problem as far as one variable is concerned. The party system-quantitative variable contains 'multiparty' as the first category, and 'two party' as the second. The two kinds of political system can both be considered democratic since they allow opposition to the government and offer opportunities to participate. It would have been more appropriate had these distinctions not been introduced. Nonetheless, and according to this hypothesis, countries within these two categories should receive the highest scores.

To determine whether this hypothesis is true or false is quite difficult, if not impossible. This is especially true bearing in mind that the updated data upon which Dahl and associates based their ranking are not available. In addition, more issues need to be clarified, among which are: how can someone assess, for instance, freedom of the press? Does this mean freedom from government ownership and should the press be privately owned? They found that in 40 countries freedom of the press was complete (Dahl, 1971, 238). The question that needs to be answered in this respect is: to what extent can we say that freedom of the press is complete? And with what degree of precision? Do the forty countries guarantee freedom of the press to the same extent? There is a kind of censorship on every press, however, the degree of such censorship or control varies from one country to another.

Furthermore, the breakdown of the variables 'interest articulation by associational groups', 'interest articulation by political parties' and 'interest articulation by legislature' resulted in the following categories: 'significant', 'moderate', 'limited' and 'negligible'. Dahl and associates do not provide the reader with a set of criteria upon which to make judgement. In other words, there is no clear cut threshold, between the different categories. When does 'moderate' finish and 'limited' begin? This would perhaps suggest that some of the variables are based on judgemental rather than hard data. It is left to the judgement of the reader, based on the information gathered and his background or previous knowledge of any country, to decide what the country's score should be.

Before going into the different aspects of the scale represented by countries, two points of caution should be noted. The first is that Dahl treats every variable equally compared with others. In other words, he does not introduce a system of weighting that would favour one variable as against others. There is no necessary correlation between them. Contestation may increase without a parallel increase in participation. Conversely, participation may exist without an automatic increase in political choice. Since the classification is based on the opportunities to participate and to oppose from the greatest to the least, the highest score is given to the variables that provide the greatest opportunity and so forth. These in turn would represent the scores received by every country. The second point of caution is that I do not display all the countries, but only a few of them which are of a particular interest to this study. The countries are placed on a scale from 1 to 31, but since no countries were found on scales 2 and 21, it was decided that the perfect scale would be of 29 (Dahl, 1971, 241).

Table (7) 1: Selected countries ranked by opportunities to participate in national elections and to oppose the government, circa 1969

Opportunities for political opposition	Elections not held	Percentage of population eligible to vote			unascertained uncertain *
Scale Types		- 20 %	20-90 %	+ 90 %	
Greatest opportunity					
1			Switzerland	Belgium	
				Denmark.	
				Sweden	
3b			Chile		
			USA		
6			France		Turkey
			Lebanon		
11			Bolivia		
			(France)		
14		South Africa			Mexico
23	Indonesia				Algeria
					Tunisia
27	Syria				Senegal
					Soviet Union
29					Albania
					Bulgaria
30	Cuba				
Least opportunity 31	Nigeria				
* Includes countries where a constitutional government or elections have been suspended or nullified at least once since 1960, the constitution has been suspended, a state of siege declared, or massive violence has occurred.					
Source: Based on Dahl ,1971, 232-4.					

The table above suggests that Dahl, as pointed out earlier, reserves the term political democracy for popular sovereignty as understood by its two elements of participation and public contestation. The study has emphasised the electoral processes by which citizens can exert some kind of control over their leaders. The assessment of whether such a component alone is valid and leads to meaningful conclusions will be dealt with at a later stage in the chapter. What matters in this respect is that the ranking of some countries seems to be of debatable validity. The most obvious one is that of France. In this table, France appears twice; in point 6 along with Turkey and Lebanon, and in point 11 with Bolivia, well below some 'Third World' countries such as Colombia, Venezuela and Costa Rica. This may perhaps suggest that there is a kind of ambiguity in the system of ranking as a whole, or a bias in the treatment of the data available. Gastil argues that 'France was placed in the same category as Bolivia in both 1962 and 1968. Since intuitively he saw an error, Dahl took France out of this category and placed it much higher. In this case the "data" used as well as the final aggregation seem to have been at fault' (1978, 248). It might further support the claim that the judgement and the personal knowledge about any country will influence either positively or negatively the scores and the rankings of countries. There is a prejudice about the safeguarding of different rights and liberties in every country. It may seem that France was judged severely as far as some variables are concerned. Dahl argues that 'one does not have to be biased in favour of France to conclude that France was badly misplaced' (Dahl, 1971, 243). However, this may suggest that there is no exact scale, or a better scale that can be devised, for judging or weighting different social phenomena. A country with a history of safeguarding these rights and liberties, for which the outcome of the inquiry does not match the general impression, would be judged severely compared to others. Dahl concluded that:

> Its [France] dual location will perhaps serve as a visible warning against taking the ranking in table A-1 [table above] as if it had been engraved in stone by the hand of God. Doubtless, there are other errors. Nonetheless, the ranking, I believe, is useful (ibid., 244).

The usefulness of any ranking depends on whether or not countries are appropriately ranked. In Dahl's study, some countries do not seem to be. Countries which share the same characteristics are placed at different points.

The table above shows that Ghana, Syria and Nigeria, for instance, are countries were no elections were held. One would expect to see these countries at the same point in the scale. However, they were at 26, 27, and 31 respectively. Regardless of the different variables discussed above, if the table is taken into account, then the question about the discrepancy in the ranking of these countries arises. If no elections were held, how would one know about the opportunities available to adult citizens to participate in national elections and to oppose the government? Furthermore, there is no indication of the eligibility of the adult population to vote, in the first column. The fact that no elections were held in any country does not mean that adult citizens are not eligible to vote.

To follow the same line of argument concerning the eligibility of adult citizens to vote, there is a point concerning the classification in the table above worth mentioning. The third column includes countries where the percentage of adult population eligible to vote is between 20 and 90 per cent. 'This indicator [per cent of adult population eligible to vote],' Neubauer argues, 'is basic to the concept of "democrativeness". The variation between nations on this measure indicates the percentage of population which excluded from the suffrage for whatever reasons (sex, race, residence, literacy, etc.)' (1967, 1005). Although it is a base upon which one can distinguish political systems, it would have been more fruitful had Dahl and associates provided detailed information about these countries and what the actual percentages were (it is worth mentioning that Dahl does give some information concerning what he called 'special cases' about Chile, Switzerland and the United States in his list of polyarchies).

It can be argued that countries with the highest percentage of adult citizens eligible to vote had more opportunities to participate. However, this depends on several factors such as variations in the minimum age of voting and whether voting is compulsory or not, which in turn, influence the percentage. Nonetheless, the point that needs to be clarified here is: was South Africa, at the time of the ranking, for instance, more democratic than Tunisia or Nicaragua?

The answer to this question is obvious. The ranking of countries was hierarchical; from the top down to the bottom. The nearer the country is to the top, the greater the opportunities to participate in national elections and to oppose government, and therefore the greater its degree of democracy. However the ranking of South Africa, a country where just under 20 per cent of adult citizens were eligible to vote, in a position well above countries like Tunisia and Nicaragua, where over 90 per cent of adult citizens were eligible to vote is questionable.

It is borne in mind that countries with very high percentages of adult citizens who are eligible to vote are not necessarily 'democratic', since different factors are involved in the high percentage. In addition, the ranking was based not only on the elections and the percentage of adults eligible to vote, but on different variables that would make such a process meaningful. The question that cannot be avoided is: how democratic is a system where more than 80 per cent of the adult citizens are not eligible to vote? What would freedom of the press, of group opposition mean, and whether the electoral system is competitive or not in such a country? Elections are one form of expression. They are channels whereby a citizen can express his choice and preference: choice of candidates and policies in a multiparty election, and freedom to agree or disagree when such a choice exists. What would freedom of group opposition lead to if the majority of the citizens, who support this opposition, do not have the right to bring it into office? Any system where the majority of the citizens is not eligible to vote is undemocratic regardless of the other variables that may exist. Therefore, South Africa, in this ranking, should have been at the bottom of the scale, i.e., with the least opportunity to participate and to oppose.

Moreover, one would question the placing of countries in the right-hand column of the table. According to Dahl, they are 'countries where a constitutional government or elections have been superseded or nullified at least once since 1960, the constitution has been suspended, a state of siege declared, or massive civil violence occurred' (Dahl, 1971, 234).

The high number of such countries is not surprising, but predictable. It should have been higher. The majority of 'Third World' countries have experienced states of siege and massive violence. Nonetheless, how can one account for countries like Algeria or Nigeria, for instance, which should not have been included within the category of countries in the right column? Algeria had a coup d'etat in 1965 following which the 1964 Constitution was suspended, and the National Assembly was dissolved. Nigeria also experienced coups d'etat (January and July 1966) as well as a massive violence during the Biafra War 1966-69. These events do not make them any different from those in the right-hand column and raises the issue of whether the data were updated. Dahl and associates do not seem to take into account these facts. The placing of these countries in the 'wrong' column makes the system of ranking doubtful.

Coups d'etat are illegal and yet the most common way by which leaders in the 'Third World' seize power. It is against this background that such countries should be ranked. Ironically enough, countries in which the succession to power did not follow a smooth and normal path have been ranked well above others which are stable, bearing in mind that the most significant, if not the only, dimension in Dahl's definition of democracy is popular sovereignty as understood in the electoral process.

In an attempt to clarify further the ranking, Dahl proposed a detailed table of different variables and categories used in the ranking of countries as well as the number and percentages of countries representing each category, and went on to provide a list of polyarchies and near polyarchies. His cut-off line was point 8 on the scale represented in table 1. The list of countries which Dahl calls fully inclusive polyarchies contains 29 countries, with three countries (Chile, Switzerland and the United States) considered to be special cases for electoral restrictions as mentioned earlier. (For a full list of these countries see Dahl, 1971, 248.)

In order to conclude whether his list is meaningful and was achieved according to the data given, it was thought that a look at the variable used might yield useful conclusions. Since the primary objective is to measure democracy and distinguish between polyarchies and non polyarchies, it was decided to use only the number of countries in the categories that matter to this study. In other words, since each variable is broken down into a number of categories, I select the number of countries in the highest category which are considered to be democratic. However, there is one variable - 'Party system: Quantitative' - which raises some problems. To overcome these problems, I decided that the scores received by the two categories: 'Multiparty' and 'Two Party' will be considered as one - by adding the two scores and dividing the result by two. This has resulted in the following table:

Table (7) 2: Variables used as indicators of opportunities for opposition

No.	Vari.	Variable descriptions and categories
	13	Degree of freedom of the press
40		1- Complete (no censorship of government control either on press on foreign correspondents)
	26	Constitutional status of current regime
53		1- Constitutional (government conducted with reference to recognized constitutional norms).
	29	Current electoral system
47		1- Competitive (no party ban, or ban on extremists or extraconstitutional parties only)
	30	Degree of freedom or group opposition
41		1- Autonomous groups free to enter politics and able to oppose government (save for extremist groups where banned)
	33	Interest articulation by associational groups
19		1- Significant
	37	Interest articulation by political parties
17		1- Significant
	40	Interest articulation by the legislature
12		1- Significant
	41 *	Party system: Quantitative
25		1- Multiparty (coalition or minority party government normally mandatory if parliament system).
12		2- Two party or effectively two-party (reasonable expectation of party rotation)
	48	Horizontal power distribution
32		1- Significant (effective allocation of power to functionally autonomous legislative, executive, and judicial organs)
	50	Current status of legislature
28		1- Fully effective (performs normal legislative function as reasonably 'coequal' branch of national government).
Source: Based on Dahl, 1971, 238-40. I am only interested in the first category of each variable. However, for variable 41 (Party system: Quantitative), the score represents the average of the two categories: 'Multiparty' and 'Two-party'.		

The above table suggests that the number of 'polyarchies' varies from one category to another depending on the severity of the government in curtailing or respecting these variables. To establish the number of polyarchies, which Dahl puts at 29 including the special cases, I added the number of countries in these categories and divided the result by ten, which is the original number of the variables employed. Then the result of such an exercise is compared with the number of polyarchies provided by Dahl to determine whether his proposed number of polyarchies is acceptable. The result achieved, after this operation, shows that there are 30.7 polyarchies in the world according to the data used by Dahl. This number is higher than the one given by Dahl (ibid.). This number may be compared with another list by Rustow. Although the basis of consideration differ, Rustow's study concluded that there were thirty-one democracies (Rustow, 1967, 290-1; Dahl, 1971, 249).

The inclusion of two more countries within Dahl's list of polyarchies will make the number of such countries correspond to the one achieved after close scrutiny of the variables used. Some have criticised Dahl for not placing Ceylon, for instance, within the column of democratic countries. Gastil suggests that 'the reluctance of Dahl and associates to place Ceylon in the democratic column was not founded on comparative evidence. In fact, in 1968 Ceylon (Sri Lanka) was one of the very few underdeveloped nations to have changed the party in power by democratic processes since independence, a change that did not occur in India until 1977' (1978, 24-6).

Dahl does provide answers about not including some countries included in Rustow's list. However, it seems possible to add to his list two countries from his list of near polyarchies. These two countries could be Colombia and Venezuela, which come at point 9 on his scale, along with others (Ecuador, Guatemala, and Honduras), but with no restrictions (Dahl, 1971, 248).

If one recalls the discussion earlier, Dahl's list of polyarchies was based on a cut-off point in scale type 8. This cut-off point is questionable since it had no reasonable explanation upon which one can judge its validity. It may make more sense to suggest that the cut-off should be scale type 9, and therefore all countries, up to this scale type, in column four should be classified as polyarchies. These countries, in addition to the three special cases of electoral restrictions, total 31 countries: a number which corresponds to the average countries included in the different categories of the variables used to measure this phenomenon.

Bollen's measurement of political democracy

Among the scholars who have dealt with the measurement of political democracy, I shall look at the work undertaken by Bollen. I focus on his proposed index for measuring democracy. Bollen states that 'validity concerns whether one is really measuring a concept' (1986, 587). Thus, before going into his proposed index of political democracy and more importantly determining how valid it is, a definition of the concept itself should be given. He defines political democracy as follows:

> It is these differences in the political power held by the elite, relative to the nonelite, that helps identify how democratic a nation is. I define political democracy as to the extent to which the political power of the elite in minimised and that of the nonelite is maximised (1980, 372).

This definition of political democracy suggests that the electoral process is at the centre. Like Dahl, Bollen stresses the importance of the electoral process in the definition of political democracy, although Dahl attributes more conditions to the elections themselves. He sees political democracy as a balance between two powers; the elite and the nonelite. For democracy to obtain, the power of the former must be minimised and of the latter maximised. This situation can only be achieved through elections and through the manner in which they are conducted. That is, political democracy can materialise if elections are carried out and the conditions necessary for bias-free elections are met. Political democracy in this way involves two main dimensions: popular sovereignty and political liberties (Bollen, 1979, 578-80; Bollen, 1980, 375-6), which constitute the basis for Bollen's index of political democracy.

A close look at the two dimensions proposed by Bollen reveals that aspects of human rights, represented in political liberties, are a major component in the study and measurement of political democracy. The inclusion of this dimension undoubtedly influence the ratings of countries when the measurement of their political democracy is attempted. Political liberties are traditionally associated with the Western developed world, and have little significance in the 'Third World' or the former East European countries. Therefore, it would not be surprising if the outcome of this study confirms the general assumption that Western countries are more democratic than the rest of the world.

Political democracy index

Bollen suggests an index for political democracy that fits his definition given above. He believes that the two dimensions (popular sovereignty and civil liberties) will enable the reader to understand how that balance is kept and therefore measure the degree of democratisation of countries.

Popular sovereignty

The first dimension Bollen considers is popular sovereignty. This is understood within the context of the electoral process. Scrutiny of the electoral process would reveal how much power the nonelite have over the elite. Selection to the key posts, such as the executive and legislative bodies, are at the centre of the process. Bollen suggests three indicators dimension, which are: fairness of elections, executive selection and legislative selection. I shall examine them in what follows.

Fairness of elections

Among the first variables one looks for when distinguishing democratic countries are elections and how fair they are. Elections and their fairness have been the centre of attention for those who deal with the issue of democracy, such as Dahl. This indicator in Bollen's attempt is measured on a four-point scale to determine whether elections are free from corruption and coercion or not. He observes that:

> The scoring of this variable is based on whether or not alternative choices exist, and on whether or not the elections are administered by a non-partisan administration. Also considered are whether or not the elections are rigged and if the results of the elections are binding on all parties (1980, 376).

It is not an easy task to determine whether elections are free from corruption and coercion. First of all, we have to determine what is meant by corruption. In addition to that, we need to ask if the criteria discussed above are met, could we safely conclude that elections are fair? Even in a situation where these conditions are met, elections may not be completely free from corruption. Is it not a form of corruption if one party had a monopoly over the mass media or the most significant ones, such as television? In such a case, it would have more opportunities to transmit its message and programme than other parties. The elections in Russia of June/July 1996 provide the best example of this kind. There is no doubt that such a system is democratic since it offers alternative choices. However, such a choice is merely a facade for the sake of international prestige. It is also quite difficult, if not impossible, to compare degrees of corruption across elections or countries. This depends on the availability of data and the flow of information, as well as the background of the judge who will analyse the data. Kurian, for example, suggests that 'many developing countries manipulate data to suit their self-image. There is a prohibition against collection and publication of data in some developing countries. There are at least two countries where the publications of national statistics is considered a punishable criminal offence: Guinea and Kampuchea' (1984, xii).

The inclusion of alternative choices in elections suggests that all the one-party states are excluded from the measurement of political democracy. Elections, as they are traditionally known, do not exist in these countries. The greatest choice that might exist is between two candidates from the same political party up to the parliamentary level. In this way, and according to the definition forwarded above, these countries would score very low on the four point scale proposed by Bollen.

Executive selection

To determine whether a country is democratic or not, we need to know how its chief executive has come to power. Obviously, in a country where the chief executive has assumed power through elections, the country is considered more democratic compared to one where the chief executive has come to power through a different means. It is not difficult to agree with Bollen on this point. However, some peculiar cases make this variable questionable. The chief executives of most countries in the world are elected, including those considered to be undemocratic. Although there were no alternative choices, many one-party states have seen their chief executives elected to their posts. The highest organ of the party elects the chief executive. Further, there are two examples of countries which had chief executives nominated for life because of the services rendered to their respective countries; Bourguiba in Tunisia and Tito in the former Yugoslavia. In other countries, Egypt for instance, the chief executives have been nominated by their predecessors. This is especially true for Sadat who was nominated vice-president, and assumed the responsibility of chief executive after the death of Nasser. It is also the case for the present president who was nominated by Sadat. The final case is that of monarchs. The king in certain monarchies such as Saudi Arabia, Jordan or Morocco is the chief executive, who was not elected but assumed this responsibility by inheritance.

It has been pointed out that Bollen focuses on whether the chief executive was elected or not. Nonetheless, there are many ways, apart from *coups d'etat*, whereby many chief executives in the world today have assumed their responsibilities. Bollen does not distinguish between these kinds of processes. He does not offer the reader a scale upon which the to differentiate between systems which arise from elections and those that are not. The score as well is not given. One has only to assume that when the chief executive is elected, the country receives the highest mark, whereas the score is nought when the chief executive is not elected. Even if this assumption is true, it would be unfair to place different countries in the nought category. There is a difference between a chief executive who came to power through selection at the highest organ of the party, one who assumed power through a coup d'etat, and one who was directly elected by the population at large.

Legislative selection

This variable is measured on the basis of whether the legislature is elected and effective in determining policies. Again, election in this context needs to be defined. Does it, for instance, mean that the legislative is elected from candidates representing different political parties or just one, as is the case in one-party states in the communist and developing countries? Surely the legislative body of a country like Algeria throughout the 1980s, for instance, was elected since it resulted from the popular will. The electorate had a choice of candidates from the same party to the Parliament. In addition to this, we need to know what is meant by national policies, and how can one determine whether the legislative was effective in determining them?

It seems quite difficult to know exactly what national policies are. This depends very much on the circumstances of the country itself, and the view point from which the matter is seen. What is a national policy for the dilemma facing some of the 'Third World' countries? To have a market economy, open its borders to international investment and enter the international economy. This would mean more opportunities for jobs and the availability of goods. But at the same time, result in the widening of the gap between rich and poor and its dependency international monetary institutions as far as its political decision making is concerned.

Under the dimension of popular sovereignty, Bollen failed to stress the importance of the independence of the judiciary. The variables discussed above are of paramount importance to the proper working of a democratic system, nonetheless, the independence of the judiciary is at the centre of democracy as well. After all, the legitimacy of the political system as a whole is based on the idea of justice in general. These variables cannot work properly unless coupled with more requirements. The other dimension that Bollen proposes, which is discussed as follows.

Political liberties

Bollen suggests that:

> Political liberties exist to the extent that the people of a country have the freedom to express any political opinions in any media and the freedom to form and participate in any political group (1986, 568).

Unlike Dahl, who suggested that his dimensions can exist independently of each other, Bollen's dimensions cannot be treated individually. One can not possibly think of fulfilling the requirements for popular sovereignty without making these political liberties generally available (Bollen and Grandjean, 1983, 138-9). As such these two dimensions are interdependent: popular sovereignty needs political liberties to work properly, and the latter will undoubtedly lead to the former. In the following, I shall look at the indices Bollen suggested, for the political liberties dimension.

Freedom of the press

The press is the most common channel whereby people become aware of what is happening around them. In countries where freedom of the press is guaranteed, people tend to be more conscious of their rights and the shortcomings of their elected representatives. There is constant pressure from the press on the people in office which tends to curtail their powers on the one hand, and increase those of the nonelite on the other. It is not surprising therefore that the press is known as the fourth power, in addition to the three traditional ones: executive, legislature and the judiciary.

Bollen measures this indicator on a nine-point scale (1980, 375) which is attained by looking at the degrees of control exercised over the press. This control may have different aspects such as censorship and interference with the daily work of the media. Like Dahl, he stresses the significance of freedom of the press to the proper working of a democratic system. However, the scale upon which they judge it differs. It would have been more useful and easier had Bollen included his nine-point scale in the appendix to enable the reader to better understand the variety of controls exercised on the press and how he weighted them.

Freedom of group opposition

One of the ways by which the power of the elite is decreased, and that of the nonelite is increased, is through group opposition. A democratic system is judged on, among other factors, the degree to which opposition groups are allowed to emerge. Bollen used a four-point scale for this factor (ibid.).

A society in which everybody agrees on everything does not exist and is not likely to. An opposition to the elite would work better if citizens organised themselves into political parties or pressure groups, to better challenge the elite and curtail their powers. A country's degree of democracy is judged upon the extent to which these opposition groups are allowed to emerge and exert their normal activities. As a result, the higher the levels of tolerance of group opposition, the higher the degree of political democracy. However, the extent to which opposition groups can emerge depends not only on the character of opposition groups themselves but also on how institutionalised a country is. An institutionalised country refers to one whose institutions are able to cope, adapt and be flexible whenever situations change. I shall return to this point later.

Government sanctions

Both Bollen and Dahl include this variable when measuring political democracy. It refers to different actions, whether violent, economic or 'legal', by governments towards the limitation and curtailing of activities of groups or parties. In the case of Bollen's study, this variable seems only to confirm the previous one. If government sanctions are very high in a particular country, it would be absurd to think of freedom of group opposition in the said country. It also seems that the variables included in the political liberties dimension are quite difficult to assess. Most of the data concerning these aspects are reported by the media or the international, regional specialised agencies. A practice by a country with a long tradition of depriving its citizens of these rights would certainly not attract the same attention that would be given to another which was known to be 'moderate' or generally protective of these rights.

To go back to the point made earlier, both government sanctions and freedom of group opposition depend very much on how institutionalised a country is. 'The political institutions of developing societies,' Beitz, argues 'tend to be weaker than those of developed societies in terms of variables such as adaptability to varying types of challenges, organisational complexity, autonomy from other social groupings, and consensus on basic operating procedures. As a result, the political institutions typically found in developing countries are comparatively inefficient and unreliable. They perform their principal functions poorly (including importantly the maintenance of public order), and they do so at great cost' (in Gastil, 1978, 155). There are different pressures on every government. However, the response to these pressures differs from one country to another. There is a limit to the extent of tolerance in every country. A country with inflexible institutions, which are unable to adapt, would be much more vulnerable to the use of sanctions compared to countries with flexible ones.

Bollen's index of political democracy, as seen earlier, is composed of six variables. When these variables are present, i.e., when a country safeguards these rights, the country's percentage of democratisation is high. He tested his index against different attempts to measure democracy, and concluded that it was the most valid. According to him, it was the only index which offered the reader the ground, for which adequate data was available, upon which the comparison of political democracy on a cross-national basis can be conducted. He observes that:

> A number of these measures are limited to certain types of countries. For instance, Adelman and Morris (1971) and Coleman (1960) consider only LDCs (Less Developed Countries). If the researcher wishes to restrict his/her attention to countries of particular type (e.g., LDCs), then one or more of these indices may be suitable. But if the generality of hypothesis of comparison of different countries in different regions or at different level of development is sought, then these indices will not do. In summary, a comparison of POLDEM (Political Democracy Index) with nine other measures shows that it is the only index that reports an estimate of reliability. In addition, POLDEM is available for a greater number of countries than are the others (1980, 380).

Since the intention is to measure political democracy on a cross-national basis, there is no doubt about how important Bollen's index is in carrying out such an exercise. All the attempts with which Bollen compared his work had taken the segmentation approach, i.e., limited themselves to a particular region or types of countries. However, it does not automatically follow that if Bollen's index of political democracy is the only approach which would enable the researcher to conduct a comparison on a cross-national basis, that he has to take it. There are some shortcomings which will be highlighted in the next section. He also proposes a ranking for different countries on their percentages of political democracy for the years 1960 and 1965. The scores received by each country are displayed in the following table:

Table (7) 3: Bollen's ranking of countries according to their degree of political democracy for the years 1960 and 1965

Standard country code as listed by Russet et al (A.P.S.R.)	Country	Political Democracy 1960 and 1965	
002	USA	94.4	94.6
145	Bolivia	36.2	56.8
100	Columbia	71.4	69.7
010	Venezuela	73.4	72.5
211	Belgium	99.9	99.7
220	France	90.8	89.7
560	S. Africa	58.9	64.7
780	Sri Lanka	85.9	94.0
265	GDR	22.1	23.8
365	USSR	18.2	20.4
670	S. Arabia	09.7	12.0
Source: Based on Bollen, 1980, 387-8			

As suggested elsewhere in the chapter, it would have made a big difference had Bollen included a system of scoring and indicated how countries are assessed on each variable. The analysis of the indicators used to measure the two dimensions of political democracy reveals that his scale for 'freedom of group opposition' was four points; nine points for 'freedom of the press' but he gave no indication on the scale upon which other variables are measured. This of course poses a problem when cross checking the results and how his percentages and ranking, in the table above, are achieved. This ranking confirms the general assumption that Western countries are more democratic than the rest of the world. However, what is difficult to accept is the placing of South Africa on this ranking. Bollen's index of political democracy was based on two dimensions: popular sovereignty and political liberties, which were not particularly enjoyed in that country at the time of the ranking. Dahl stressed that less than 20 per cent of the adult citizens were eligible to vote, which made popular sovereignty a meaningless dimension on Bollen's index. In addition, the use of force and violence, seen as part of the government sanctions, were daily events in South Africa which weakens the claim for the enjoyment of any political liberties. Thus, if the two dimensions of political democracy appeared to be absent in South Africa, how would someone explain its relatively high ranking in this table? This might suggest that the standards applied were not for all the citizens, but for the white minority, which would make the country relatively appear more democratic than it should have been. At the same time one would question the dimensions of democracy, and the validity of the variable used when they lead peculiar cases like that of South Africa.

Comparison, critics and assessment

Both Dahl and Bollen's definitions of political democracy are quite similar. They are concerned with the distribution of power between the elite and the nonelite. They both emphasise popular sovereignty as exercised through the electoral process, and Bollen stresses the need for political liberties. If one goes deeper into the analyses of Dahl's measurement of democracy, one finds that political liberties are another implicit dimension within his theory. Among the variables or conditions Dahl puts to the study of the electoral process, and therefore popular sovereignty, are:

> Countries hold fair, competitive elections, they allow their citizens access to alternative sources of information, and they permit people to organise themselves to express policy preferences (quoted in A. Goldsmith, 1986, 520).

As suggested elsewhere in the chapter, it would be absurd to think about popular sovereignty without political liberties. If people had no access to alternative information and no right to organise, fairness of elections would be meaningless. Political rights are another way by which citizens can exert some control over their elected representatives and without such rights popular sovereignty would not be effective. Further, since the two dimensions are at the centre of their analysis, the results obtained suggest that both Bollen and Dahl measure the same concept and reach similar conclusions. The following table presents the ranking of different countries from each of the two studies:

Table (7) 4: Comparison between Dahl's and Bollen's ranking of selected countries

Countries	Dahl's ranking: From the greatest to the least opportunity	Percentages in Bollen study: 1960 and 1965	
Belgium	Scale 1	99.9	99.7
USA	Scale 3	94.4	94.6
France	Scales 6 and 11	90.8	89.7
South Africa	Scale 14	58.9	64.7
Bolivia	Scale 11	36.2	59.8
Saudi Arabia	Scale 31	09.7	12.0
Costa Rica	Scale 8	90.1	91.3
Source: Based on Bollen, 1980, 387-8 and Dahl, 1971, 232-4.			

While Dahl and Bollen see political democracy from the same viewpoint and their results are quite similar a word of caution, regarding the validity of the results, should be noted. The cases of France, Bolivia and Costa Rica suggest that there are some differences between the methods or the variables used. In Dahl's table, France appeared twice, on points 6 and 11, on a scale of 29 points. This raised suspicion as to whether that approach was valid or not. What interests us more in this respect is France's appearance on point 11, alongside Bolivia and behind some 'Third World' countries such as Venezuela and Costa Rica. Dahl believes that this placing was doubtful, and took it to point 6 on the scale. To this point, there is not much ground upon which to disagree with Dahl. However, after the study undertaken by Bollen, one side of the results obtained confirms the ranking position of France. The periods covered by the two studies are relatively similar and therefore lead, if the phenomenon dealt with is the same, to similar results. If we look at the percentage scored by Costa Rica and France, the difference was 1.6 in favour of the former in 1960, and 0.2 in favour of the latter in 1965. To simplify the matter, I decided to draw an overall percentage for the period studied; by adding the two percentages and dividing the results by two. This led to 90.3 and 90.7 per cent being the averages for France and Costa Rica respectively. That result confirms the ranking of France at point 11 behind Costa Rica. On the other hand, the score received by Bolivia in Bollen's study weakens the claim that France and Bolivia should be at the same point in the scale. The table above reveals that the average percentage of Bolivia is 43 per cent, which is less than half the one scored by France. This in turn, leaves no room for suggesting that these countries should be regarded as equally democratic.

The point that needs to be stressed is that, although there is ground for argument that France was in a peculiar place in Dahl's study, there are some doubts about it. A comparison with Bollen's study confirms this peculiarity further. The objection to the ranking of France was because it was ranked at the same point as Bolivia, not because it was ranked below some 'Third World' countries such as Costa Rica. The percentages given by Bollen support this claim. Costa Rica, in another study undertaken by Kurian, is rated above the United States of America on an index of democracy (1984, 104).

Whatever shortcomings occur, the most straightforward points to be considered are the variables and methods used to reach the conclusions. The most significant question that arises is: do the variables used confirm the theoretical definition given to the concept? In this case, the degree of control exerted by citizens over their leaders is at the centre of the definition of the concept of democracy. The most straightforward way of establishing this degree is through elections, we conclude that the variables used confirm the definition of the concept. Against this background we should ask, is this definition acceptable to all? Does not political democracy embrace more dimensions than the above?

The definition of political democracy, and the variables employed in measuring it, incorporate liberal values that are difficult to apply in reality to different countries. Like Dahl, Bollen observes that his index would enable the researcher to 'compare different countries in different regions or at different stages of development'. Would not this be practically difficult and leading to unconvincing conclusions? If the aim is to make a comparison on a cross-national basis, then Bollen's index will enable the researcher to do so. However, if the goal is the consistency and reliability of the results, then this index will be doubtful. How can someone compare, for instance, two countries at different stages of development in terms of political democracy? The term development, in this connection, is not limited only to economic, but to political development also. And as a result, different variables should be taken into account when dealing with the issue of political democracy.

The level of socio-economic development helps the system to develop into a democracy. A country at an advanced stage of development would offer more opportunities to its citizens, as compared to a poor country at a lower stage of development. Among the opportunities the former can offer is education, which could not be possibly available to every citizen in the deprived areas of the undeveloped world. It is also important to stress the crucial role education plays in raising the awareness and consciousness of the people. Democracy requires democratic behaviour. What would democracy mean to an illiterate individual? How can such individuals organise an opposition to face its own government in a peaceful way? What would elections mean for them, or freedom to choose between candidates at an election? Apart from the classical meaning of education, it also means the inclusion of the people in the daily life of the government and to be part of the decision making process. Mr. Loubenchenko, the Soviet representative to the United Nations Human Rights Committee, argues that:

> It was also essential to educate the people who, for many years, had taken no direct part in the political decision making. There was a danger that, without adequate preparation, the direct exercise of democratic rights might harm democracy instead of enhancing it (UN Doc. CCPR/C/SR. 928. par. 57).

In addition to high literacy levels in the advanced countries, the population is urbanised, and the systems of communications are more developed. These realities enable citizens in these countries to know more about what is happening around them, in sharp contrast with the remote areas in an underdeveloped country. If democracy involves alternative sources of information, how would it be accounted for in a country where just one source of information is difficult to come by? What has been considered in the studies above, is the measurement of democracy as perceived by the two scholars, using variables which corresponded to their definitions, and the application of these variables on a cross-national basis. The phenomenon they studied is as it is perceived in their own country, and the outcome of such a ranking favours the countries sharing the same characteristics as theirs. Likewise different studies which dealt with the observance of human rights were culture bound. However, the question that should be asked here is: are there not any other definitions of democracy parallel to those given above? The definition of democracy proposed by both Dahl and Bollen suggests that it does not exist beyond the Western developed world and a handful of 'Third World' countries. The term, however, has been widely used to describe different countries either in the 'Third World' or in the former communist countries in which the variables required are not provided for. Would not it then suggest that democracy may exist in another form? And if so, is it safe to call it democracy?

Marxist regimes, as they are and according to the definitions, are not democratic. There are no civil or political liberties. However, from a Marxist perspective, a Communist country is the ultimate democratic system. Marx observed in his Communist Manifesto (1848) that the 'first step in the revolution by the working class, is to raise the proletariat to the position of ruling class, to win the battle for democracy' (quoted in Macpherson, 1972, 15). This system eventually develops into a democracy because it represents the majority of the people. This suggests that democracy, in this respect, is taken in the broader sense of the term, which differs from the one seen earlier. It is taken to mean equality and social justice, which only an egalitarian regime can provide. Macpherson also believes that a Communist country can be labelled democratic, providing that some conditions are met, even in the narrow sense of the term. He argues that:

> one party state can in principle be democratic even in the narrow sense provided (1) that there is full intra-party democracy, (2) that the party membership is open, and (3) that the price of participation in the party is not a greater degree activity than the average person can reasonably be expected to contribute (ibid., 21).

It is quite difficult, if not impossible, to state whether these provisions are available within a one-party state or not. However, what matters is that, even if systems differ from the ones referred to by Dahl and Bollen, they can still be called democratic. This in turn suggests that democracy exists, or may exist, in different forms not necessarily the one dealt with by the two scholars. The same argument can apply to 'Third World' countries which have followed the same political system as in the Communist world. To the extent that the conditions are provided for, the degree of democratisation is measured. Thus because democracy is defined/interpreted differently, any measurement of it should not be carried out against an abstract set of indices but take this fact into consideration.

Finally, it should be borne in mind that, democracy is regarded in these studies as the perfect system that everybody has to adopt. Another view might be that it is a necessity in some countries or regions in the world, but a luxury in most 'Third World' countries. From this point of view democracy is not the ideal system in many 'Third World' countries given their present circumstances; another, more authoritarian form of government, would perhaps be better equipped to deal with daily events and to prepare for an eventual transition to democracy. Huntington, for instance, argues that 'the process of political change includes two stages. One is the creation of authoritative political institutions; the other, the growth of political participation. The sequence of these components processes matters. Huntington holds that the more important process in developing societies is the creation of political institutions which is undermined by the premature expansion of opportunities for political participation. It is necessary to have strong, widely accepted, and efficient political institutions before people can be permitted to participate in politics; otherwise he claims governments will be unstable and inefficient' (quoted in Beitz, 1978, 155). It should be stressed that practical conditions in many 'Third World' countries could hinder any development of a system towards democracy. Moreover, it appears difficult to overcome the problem of operationalisation of the concepts dealt with on a cross-national basis.

8 Freedom House and the comparative study of human rights

The Comparative Survey of Freedom occupies a prominent and sometimes controversial place in the cross-national study of human rights. Sponsored by Freedom House, an independent New York-based organisation established in 1941 to promote freedom around the world, the Survey followed the 'Balance Sheet of Freedom': an annual assessment of gains and losses in political rights and civil liberties; the first of which was published in 1955, and has been published every year since 1973. The findings of the Survey were incorporated into the publication of the *Annual Development Report on Program Performance* (1994) by the US Agency for International Development and also formed the basis of the indices of political rights and civil liberties that appeared in the third edition of the *World Handbook of Political and Social Indicators* in 1983. The Comparative Survey of Freedom is the only attempt, known to this author, to measure freedom on a cross-national and continuous basis. At least in principle, the Survey must therefore represent an important source of information for a researcher concerned with comparing political systems in terms of their levels of freedom. The Survey is published regularly, takes account of current developments and highlights gains and losses in freedom during each of the periods that it reviews. This in turn enables the researcher to carry out an analysis over time, to compare development and pinpoint losses and gains in freedom in the countries that are being considered.

However, it does not necessarily follow that the Survey's findings should be taken as authoritative, and that discussion must be limited to its ranking of countries and the results it provides. On the contrary, the analysis has to go far beyond that and question the validity of the results themselves. What, for example determines a country's ranking on this league table? Any ranking of this kind obviously depends on the variables used in the study; and the scrutiny of the variables should in turn help to establish whether the Survey is a valid comparative measure. Equally, the sponsoring organisation itself, Freedom House, must be examined, in order to determine its degree of independence as a non-governmental organisation. Ideological and financial independence are the key elements in any discussion of this kind. How did Freedom House come into being? Who are the people associated with it? How is it financed? Where do the data come from? Does it carry out its own research as does, for instance, Amnesty International?

The following discussion examines the work of Freedom House more closely than has been attempted in previous work of this kind, and looks particularly at the validity and reliability of the Survey as a quantitative measure of human rights on a comparative basis. After the discussing of historical setting to Freedom House, I discuss freedom as it is understood by Freedom House, then look at both the dimensions that are employed by the Survey and scrutinise the variables included in each. The methodology and the ranking of countries are then analysed. The variables used and the method whereby countries are ranked are crucial to an understanding of the Survey and its shortcomings, and are necessary to any discussion of the reliability, over time, of any assessment based on the Survey. Following this, I shall apply the Survey in more detail to a small number of countries considered as case studies. The chapter concludes with a general assessment of the Survey and whether the task it seeks to undertake, to measure freedom on a cross-national and continuous basis, is a feasible one.

Freedom House: a historical setting

The Comparative Survey of Freedom is published under the auspices of Freedom House, which makes its study vital to the proper understanding of the Survey and the results obtained. It is only against a background of this kind that one can properly understand the criticisms to which the Survey has been subjected.

In *Freedom in the World 1989-90,* Freedom House defined itself as follows:

> Freedom House is an independent non-profit organisation based in New York that monitors political rights and civil liberties around the world. Established in 1941, Freedom House believes that effective advocacy of civil rights at home and human rights abroad must be grounded in fundamental democratic values and principles (1990a, 1).

As a non-governmental organisation which monitors civil rights and political liberties, Freedom House, from the outset, seems to have been linked with official American policy. Although it defended human rights in general, it was very much directed at defending and encouraging, the words of its former president, Richman, 'liberal elements of our [American] society' (Freedom House, 1989, 3), and attacking communist and fascist regimes. Although its ostensible purpose is to enhance global freedom by pointing to shortcomings and abuses whenever they occur, it is nonetheless, in practice, very much concerned with defending American interests and the American model of freedom. This is especially true when one looks at the members of the board of trustees and their posts within the American government. This fact confirms the contention that this is an organisation very much linked to the American view of freedom. Any list of the members of the board of trustees, at least since 1979 'included a significant number of individuals who are readily identified as having held high government positions past and present' (Scoble and Wisberg in Nanda, et al, 1981, 161).

On this evidence, it might be argued that the activities of Freedom House reflect particular interests and biases. However, there is another vital aspect which is worth investigating to determine the impartiality of any organisation, which is its funding. It goes without saying that if any non-governmental organisation receives or accepts substantial sums of money from any government, this will potentially jeopardise its impartiality and the objectivity of its judgements. Amnesty International, for instance, deliberately excludes any funding of this kind. Official funding may lead to the organisation being manipulated by the funding government, and undermining the efforts of such an organisation. In the case of Freedom House, it can be argued that it is financially independent of any government. Although information on this matter is scarce, the organisation claims that:

Freedom House receives funding from private individuals, corporations, labor unions, and foundations for all its activities. It especially wants to express its gratitude to the Pew Charitable Trusts for its support for the survey project over the many years (Freedom House, 1990a, 1).

However, if it is independent from any government, this does not automatically mean that it is independent and impartial in its judgements. Even if it is sponsored by corporations and individuals, serious questions arise concerning the nature of the sponsors and the amount of money received.

Although there is a file about every country that is considered in the Survey, and area experts are consulted whenever they are needed, Freedom House does not undertake its own research. Scoble and Wisberg state that 'Freedom House itself is not a research organisation. It does not directly gather the raw data employed in its ranking of nations; instead it relies on observations obtained by others, primarily scholars and journalists, mostly Western, among whom Americans predominate' (in Nanda et al, 1989, 155).

Such reliance on what is reported by journalists and scholars makes Freedom House very vulnerable to seeing matters from the point of view that is implicit in its sources of information. Experience has shown in many cases that what is reported in the news does not actually represent facts. The limitation of foreign journalists to specific areas in a given country makes the task very difficult to provide a full and unbiased picture of what is happening. Some of the facts reported are merely based on guess work and personal judgement rather than hard evidence.

Dimensions of freedom

This section will focus on the dimensions of freedom upon which countries are ranked. This may make it easier to understand the basis of Freedom House's work and to see the shortcomings in the compilation of the Survey. As a result, the dimensions of freedom selected clearly relate to the manner in which freedom itself is conceptualised. It may, therefore, be appropriate to consider the definition of freedom, as proposed by Freedom House, to see whether the dimensions studied correspond to the definition. Freedom House defines freedom as follows:

In the Survey freedom is defined in terms of those political rights that allow people to participate freely and effectively in choosing leaders or in voting directly in legislature, and those civil liberties that guarantee freedoms such as speech, privacy, and fair trial ... nor does it include welfare interests, as in the rhetorical extensions 'freedom from fear' or 'freedom from want.' In this definition independence may contribute to political freedom, but an independent state is not thereby free (Gastil, 1979, 4-5).

This definition of freedom suggests that the Survey focuses only on civil liberties and political rights as dimensions of freedom. It takes the view that they are universal and as such that everybody should enjoy them. Welfare rights, or social and economic rights, are not included. Moreover, independence is not a primary indicator upon which the degree of freedom is judged. Although it is not difficult to agree with the Survey that independence does not automatically mean freedom, as defined above, it is nonetheless a very significant factor. Moreover, certain economic rights are of paramount importance to the proper working and the enjoyment of civil rights and political liberties as they are defined in the Survey. In addition to this, as will be seen later, some indicators used to measure degrees of freedom around the world are taken from the two exceptions, i.e., welfare interests and independence.

To shed more light on the definition of freedom, the discussion that follows scrutinises the dimensions as identified by Freedom House. This will help provide a better understanding of the ranking of countries at a later stage.

Political rights

The initial Survey observes that:

When a country's standing in *political rights* is analyzed, attention is first directed to general elections. We want to know how recently there has been an election, and whether there was any competition. We want to know if there is a one-party system. A one-party system allows the least chance of opposition, while more than one party allows the most. In an election we want to know the percentage of voting for a particular party or candidate for head of state. If contested, a vote with over 90% for one side is probably meaningless, while majorities over 70% seem suspicious. We also want to know how often the same results occur, and whether parties or leaders have replaced one another by democratic process. We are also interested in whether there is a regional or local elected government. Unless the country is very small, the more secondary elections there are, and the more power the winners gain by election, the more democratic we assume the society. In all elections we want to know what percentage of the people participate, and how exclusions are created (Freedom House, 1973, 20).

The assumption is that a country is free whenever the above requirements are fulfilled. In other words, the wish of the people is respected regarding the kind of government under which they want to live. However, some requirements for this indicator seem to be vague and difficult to assess. This is readily apparent when looking at general elections and how recently one has taken place. 'Recently' in this context is quite a flexible concept. What can be considered recent in this year's Survey, for instance, may not be considered as such in five or six years. If this is the case, where can France be placed, where general elections are held every five years, as compared to other countries in the western world such as the USA where they are usually held every four years? If this indicator is used to judge the degree of freedom in two countries, the USA and France for instance, for a hypothetical period of twenty years, the results would indicate that the former has held six elections, whereas the latter had only five. However, would it be fair that France scores less on this indicator? Therefore, some clarification of what is meant by 'recently' would be helpful. A more appropriate description would be 'regularly'.

Elections obviously involve competition, and the existence of more than one party offers more competition. Nonetheless, the competition that a two-party system offers differs from that of a multiparty system. While limited numbers of political parties imposed in some countries perhaps helps to explain the percentage of the people who participate in elections, at the same time it offers a basis for understanding how exclusions are created. Although it can be argued that there might be competition even within a one party system, this system clearly offers the fewest opportunities for choice. Does a two-party system like the one in the USA, for instance, offer the same chances to people as a system of the kind that existed in Nigeria? In an attempt to return to civilian rule in Nigeria in 1993, the military government introduced a multi-party system. However, the law limited the number of political parties to just two (for more details see Akinlo, 1990). People had no choice but to affiliate to one of these parties, or not to participate at all if no party represented their views. However, in theory there would have been competition had elections been held. Nonetheless, the questions to be asked here is: would the situation have changed if more political parties had been allowed to emerge on the political scene?

How, for instance, would the score of the USA on this variable compare to the score of Nigeria had elections been held in that country in 1992? This kind of restriction might explain the percentage of people who participated and the reasons for exclusions. It is difficult to agree with the Survey on the inclusion of this variable on different grounds, mainly because such an index does not really reflect the level of freedom enjoyed in any country. The percentage of people who participate in elections and how exclusions are created can be interpreted in different ways. If the percentage of people who vote in country A is higher than in country B, it does not automatically follow that the former is freer than the latter. There is a significant difference between the United States, for example, and European turnouts attributable to registration procedures. In the United States, Powell argues that 'turnout is advantaged about 5% by political attitudes, but disadvantaged 13% by registration laws ... and that 'perhaps two-thirds of eligible citizens [only] are registered' (1976, 17-24). The minimum age of voting differs from one country to another, as does the measuring of the vote; some countries see voting not only as a right but as a duty, and in some, such as Australia, it is compulsory.

However, what should be pointed out at this stage is the fact that, although the Comparative Survey is, in theory, a way to monitor the state of freedom around the world on a continuous basis, 'but the ratings and criteria of judgement have been continually revised' (Gastil, 1978, 4). Thus, the fifth Survey (1975) concluded its description of the political rights dimension by stating it is 'also interested to a lesser degree in the existence of local or regional self-government, of freedom from military participation, or of foreign pressures on the system' (Freedom House, 1975, 3).

It seems clear that two additional aspects were included in the political rights dimension; freedom from military participation, and/or foreign pressure on the system. The Survey does not offer any explanation of what is meant by these variables and how they should be used to judge systems until two years later (1977), when it stressed that:

> Foreign control is defined for this purpose rather narrowly, emphasising the extent to which the government and people of a state are free to publicly criticise a hypothetically dominating state, or how much the government is allowed to diverge from dominating state's position in international consultations and organisations (Freedom House, 1977, 6).

In addition to these variables, the Survey seems to have added another variable; a recent shift in power, when discussing political rights (Gastil, 1987, 15). However, what is meant by a recent shift in power should be clarified. This should be done not only in terms of time, but power itself should be defined. Does it mean the leader or the chief authority or the political party in power?

A shift in power, if any, does not really depend on how free the country is. If power is meant to be the chief authority, then this shift in power depends very much on the country's constitution. In a country like the United States where the Constitution prohibits the president to rule for more than two mandates, as compared with another which does not, this shift in power is bound to take place. However, if power means the political party, then the Survey seems to forget the achievements and popularity that a party in power might enjoy. It may well be argued that there has not been any shift in power in a given country over a period of time without affecting its degree of freedom. The majority of the people may be satisfied with the records of those exerting power on their behalf. In this connection, Sweden provides the best example, where the Social Democratic Party enjoyed a period of virtually continuous rule (up to 1991) without any suggestion that the country was less than a model democracy.

A close analysis of the different Surveys Freedom House published, reveals that new variables have emerged in the discussion of political rights. The quotation above from the initial Survey differs in the variables included from the list in the later Surveys. In the mid 1980s, more new variables have been included to determine the score of every country on political rights. These include 'whether as with the Kurds in Turkey, there is an important group that is denied a reasonable degree of self-determination' and 'whether there is an informal consensus underlying the political system such that even those important segments of society formally out of power still have an important input into the political process' (Gastil, 1985, 7).

Having dealt with the first dimension in the Survey's definition of freedom, I turn now to a critical scrutiny of the second dimension to see if more variables were added to the initial definition of civil liberties.

Civil liberties

In the initial Survey of Freedom civil liberties are defined as follows:

> We are interested first of all in freedom of the press. Is the press critical? Does it support persons who might replace those in power? Alternative systems? Is it independently controlled? Or privately owned? Beyond the press, we want to know how much government control there is over television and radio. Unfortunately, even in countries where the press is relatively independent and untrammelled, the often more popular radio and television systems are frequently under government control. Although this control may be carefully hedged about with legal restrictions, only in a few states with long and continuous democratic traditions of democratic abstinence, such as in Great Britain, are we reassured by legal guarantees of impartiality, particularly for free judiciary. It also seems reasonable to consider freedom from harsh and unusual punishments and torture. Another evidence of civil liberties is offered by a defined and restricted sphere of government attention (Freedom House, 1973, 20).

Before considering these criteria more closely, it may be worth pointing out that civil liberties, according to the quote above include four variables, which are: free press, independence of the judiciary, freedom from cruel and inhuman punishment, and a restricted sphere of government. Whether civil liberties include only the four items mentioned above or not is not the issue. What matters more is the number of items the Survey considers in the ranking of countries when using this dimension, and whether more items have been added since the initial Survey. This will undoubtedly help to establish whether a diachronic analysis of this dimension is possible or not, since the addition of one new item may influence the ranking of different countries if they score well on the added items. However, before looking at the later Surveys, I shall scrutinise the above quotation.

The Survey puts a heavy emphasis on freedom of the press. Different requirements are used in the Survey to determine whether the press is free or not, such as whether it is privately owned, critical of government or supports persons who may replace those in power. However, the standards upon which to decide whether a press is free or not are not clearly set out in the Survey. The Survey seems to suggest that if the press is privately owned and independently controlled, it is therefore free. However, a press owned by the government may also be critical of the system and may favour different alternative policies. The degree of control over the press in general is easy to determine. The Survey does not offer any boundaries as to where this control can be located. On a more global level, censorship and the unbalanced flow of information are significant features of both developed and developing countries, including communist states. The manipulation of the news by a few international news agencies creates a one-way flow of information and feedback is almost non-existent.

However, in the Seventh Survey (1977), and in addition to the items considered above, the civil rights discussion concluded with the following:

> In addition to these four, we consider two types of supporting or subsidiary freedoms. First are those from totalitarianism: economic independence of the media from government, and freedom of individuals to move about, choose among educational systems and occupations, obtain private property, operate in the market freely, or organise and join private organisations of choice. These latter freedoms include freedom of religion as well as freedom to organise and join unions (Freedom House, 1977, 8).

The above quotation suggests that by 1977 the civil liberties dimension included more items than it did in the initial Survey. Furthermore, some of the items discussed in this dimension really depend on the socio-economic level of the country. In other words, social and economic rights are very much at the centre of this dimension and may influence the ranking of countries. The survey clearly stated that 'when governments do not care about the social and economic welfare of large sections of the populations, the human rights of the people suffer' (Freedom House, 1990a, 200), a circumstance the Survey initially dismissed as not relevant. It did acknowledge the importance of social and economic welfare at a later stage, however, and unsuccessfully tried to justify its position by stating that:

Civil rights are also affected by the presence or absence of nongovernmental, environmental inadequacies, such as illiteracy and debilitating poverty. Questions of illiteracy and poverty bring us back, of course, to the positive rights which we argued above should be outside our concern. Yet they must be taken into account in so far as they affect a population's ability to express opinion or vote effectively (Freedom House, 1977, 8).

While the Survey recognised that these 'positive' rights may affect the state of human rights in any country, it leaves unexplained how important they are and how they can be judged. Can they influence the ranking of countries? Are they, for instance, just complementary to the other rights? Are they scored on the same basis as the other rights? How can a country's low score be justified on economic and social grounds?

No ready answer to these questions is available as the Survey has not attempted to provide one. It simply gathered the information concerning the two dimensions of freedom, added different items to the initial list, and tried ranking countries based on scores of the two dimensions discussed above. The methods used and the ranking of countries are discussed as follows.

The method and the ranking

It should be pointed out that the scores for both dimensions range from 1 to 7, with 1 being the most free and 7 the least. Then, depending on the score received by each country, the final ranking is attempted; which can be either 'free', 'not free', or 'partly free'. In terms of categories, the 'free' category is either 1 or 2, the 'not free' is 6 or 7, whereas the 'partly free' category is somewhere in between. However, it should also be noted that the reliability of the Survey is questionable. In 1992 this scoring system was abandoned in favour of a new one. This seems to be the result of the change of the Survey's Director. While previous surveys were identified with Raymond Gastil, those published since 1992 are linked with Joseph Ryan. In Freedom Review (1992, 13) Ryan states that 'other changes [which] reflect methodological refinement [were] developed by this year's Survey's team'. As a result, countries and territories are placed in the same three categories, but differ from the previous methodology in the fact that a country placed in a particular category is a result of averaging 'the numbers they received for political rights and civil liberties. Those whose category numbers average 1-2.5 are considered 'free', 3-5.5 'partly free', and 5.5-7 'not free' (Freedom House, 1992, 14). A discussion of the methodology used follows and an in-depth analysis of the different categories and how the boundaries between them are drawn.

The method

On first sight the method used by Freedom House in ranking countries appears simple. However, this impression can be misleading. The aim of the Survey's method in ranking countries was, initially, to assign each item on the two dimensions (political rights and civil liberties) a 'high', 'medium', 'low' or 'very low' score compared to the checklist. This checklist, it may be noted in passing, remained unpublished until the mid 1980s. Nonetheless, although the four indices may help to assign a country to one category or another, in borderline cases the boundaries between categories are left unexplained. The method itself seems to be doubtful for several reasons.

Firstly, the checklist for the two dimensions, and the exact number of indices included in each, was not made available, at least for the first ten Surveys. This would have enabled the reader to check and recompute the standards upon which the Survey drew its conclusions.

Secondly, it seems that the number of indices on the checklist has increased, or changed since the initial Survey. Although it was not made available, the addition of different items to the lists of the two dimensions automatically means the addition of a number of items to the checklist.

Thirdly, the seventh Comparative Survey of Freedom (1977) states that: 'This year a number of changes of this kind occurred because of the introduction of a new and more adequate checklist for comparative examination' (Freedom House, 1977, 8). Such a statement confirms further the discontinuity of the method and the results achieved. The self-confession concerning the introduction of 'a more adequate check list' confirms this claim. This means that the old checklist, used in the six previous Surveys prior to 1977, was inadequate and therefore the results obtained from it were less representative of the actual situation.

Finally, not only were the number of items on each list changed, but the actual strategy itself seems to have changed. The strategy followed was to assign each item on each dimension a 'high', 'medium', 'low' or 'very low' rating, and the number of items was 11 for political rights and 14 for civil liberties according to the checklist that was published in 1987. However, the 1990 Survey states that: 'The team assigned initial ratings to countries by awarding from zero to two points per check list item, depending on the degree of compliance with the standard. The highest possible score for political rights is eighteen points, based on up to two points for each of the nine questions. The highest possible score for civil liberties is twenty six points based on up to two points for each of the thirteen questions' (Freedom House, 1990a, 21).

Faced with comments of this kind, the consistency of the Comparative Survey as a genuine attempt to measure freedom on a cross-national basis is questionable. The constant changes to the basis of the ranking suggests that the process as a whole is subjective, depending very much on the judgement of the people involved in the Survey. How else can one account for the Survey's statement that it sometimes decides that it has 'been regarding an issue from the wrong point of view' (Freedom House, 1977, 8). South Africa is a very interesting case. Although it was assigned (5) and (6) for political rights and civil liberties respectively for the years 1980 and 1982, nonetheless, it was first ranked 'partly free' in 1980 and 'not free' in 1982 'due to revaluation by the author'. The availability of one more piece of information may change the ratings of a country, however, being 'regarded from the wrong point of view' is unclear and suggests that the Survey exercises a necessarily arbitrary judgement.

The ranking

The countries investigated in the Comparative Survey of Freedom are placed in one of the three categories: 'free', 'partly free', and 'not free'. The placing of countries in such categories depends very much on how well they score on both dimensions of freedom. It is worth noting that these categories cannot be defined exactly, but it is of comparative significance in determining whether state A, for instance, falls within the same category as state B, below it or above it (Freedom House, 1989, 48).

As suggested earlier the ranking is based on two dimensions, therefore some questions ought to be clarified in order to understand why state A, for instance, is ranked below state B, when it has scored the same points for both civil liberties and political rights. Are the dimensions (that is, political rights and civil liberties) treated separately or not? Is more weight put on one dimension than the other? Do dimensions influence one another? And how is the rating achieved?

The first Survey seems to have taken each dimension separately and given it a score ranging from 1 to 7 to determine the degree of freedom of the countries concerned. It stresses that its judgements are not based on quantitative techniques; nonetheless, at a later stage, when its results differ, it uses this technique to obtain the average status of freedom (Gastil, 1978, 22). Moreover, its strategy of ranking countries seems to have changed over the years. This will be looked at closely at a later stage in this section. However, what does matter at this point is that the Survey has ignored one problem in its ranking of countries at least up to the sixth Survey (1976). Up to that year, a relatively simple procedure was used to determine where countries were placed 'free', 'not free', and 'partly free'. However, borderline cases are not easily ranked, i.e., countries which can qualify to be ranked for more than one category, which were pinpointed for the first time in the sixth Survey (1976). The Survey states that 'while a (7) and (5), for instance Chile, is bound not to be free in our ratings, one marked (6) and (5) may or may not be. In making this judgement, we must consider how a state stacks up against other partly free or not free states overall, and consider where it would fall in a finer analysis within the still rather broad ranges of categories (6) and (5)' (Freedom House, 1976, 16). Although it is recognised as difficult to explain the placing of countries in categories, no attempt was made at all to explain how the placing of such countries might be in these categories. The Survey eventually realised the need to clarify this point, and in an attempt to help the reader understand its judgements and explain these borderline cases stated that 'although political rights are given slightly more weight in borderline cases, such cases are generally decided by a judgement of the position of a state within the numerical categories. For example, (6) and (5) may lead either to a rating of "not free" or "partly free", depending on whether the (5) and (6) are a high (5) or low (5), or a high (6) or low (6)' (Gastil, 1978, 22). A very clear example of these borderline cases can be found in the 1980 Survey. Countries such as the former Yugoslavia, Hungary, Ivory Coast and Liberia have scored (6) for political rights and (5) for civil liberties, nonetheless, the first two were ranked within the not free category, whereas the two last were ranked partly free (Gastil, 1980, 17-9).

In an attempt to clarify the borderline cases and explain the methodology of ranking them, the Survey made things more complicated and created some ambiguity surrounding the process as a whole. As suggested earlier, the first six Surveys seem to have dealt with political rights and civil liberties separately, whereas in 1977, it seems to have linked them together by placing more emphasis on the civil rights dimension (Freedom House, 1977, 6), and a year later (1978), as seen in the previous quotation, the weight was put on political rights.

The question now is what might be meant by 'low' and 'high' in this connection. How did the Survey achieve such results? Upon what basis did it make its judgement? The arguments the Survey used in ranking countries are comparative in nature. In other words, they are not made against absolute standards, but just to determine how state A should rank against state B. Nonetheless, if there are no clear-cut thresholds among the categories, how can it speak about a sharp distinction within the units making the final ranking in the categories? If the Survey can make a distinction between 'low (6)' and 'high (6)' for instance, to determine whether a country should be classified 'not free' or 'partly free', this will automatically lead to an exact distinction between the categories and a sharp drawing of boundaries, and therefore any argument concerning borderline cases becomes redundant. The placing of borderline cases, as described above, suggests that the four-fold method, assigning each item in the category a 'high', 'medium', 'low' or 'very low' rating, has been followed. Nonetheless, if the method has changed, how has the placing of countries been affected?

The change of method has indeed led to a change in the ranking of countries in the Comparative Survey of Freedom. In 1989, the Survey abandoned the three categories by which it ranked countries for a new one. The basis remained the same: a list for both civil and political rights ranging from 1 to 7 each is produced. However, instead of a categorisation into three, the Survey placed different countries on a 13 point scale, ranging from 2 to 14 to determine their freedom, with 2 being the least possible score a country could obtain (i.e., 1 point for each of the two dimensions), whereas 14 was the highest (representing 7 for each). On this scale, the nearer a country is to 2, the freer it is. This new method and ranking has resolved many of the ambiguities that surrounded earlier Surveys. However, and as stated earlier, the changes in the Survey's team resulted in another change in the methodology employed to rank countries. While the method is still based on scores up to 2 points for each of the 9 questions on the political rights dimension and the 13 question on the civil liberties dimension; the maximum points attained would be 44 (18 and 26 for the two dimensions respectively), the ranking of countries, however, depends on the total raw points. Those 'with combined raw scores of 0-14 points are "not free", and those with combined raw scores of 15-29 are "partly free". "Fee" countries and territories have combined raw scores of 30-44' (Freedom House, 1992, 14). This new methodology, clearly, is an improvement in the Survey's attempt to overcome many of the shortcomings it has been experiencing, and helps to assign every country to a particular category without any arbitrary judgement.

Case studies

The Survey states that it 'attempts to judge all places by a single standard, and to point out the importance of democracy and freedom' (Freedom House, 1990a, 1). In what follows, an attempt will be made to apply the Survey in a more detailed fashion to a group of countries. This should help the reader to understand the difficulties that may arise whenever countries, at different stages of development and with different traditions, are compared using the same standards. Thus, this section will follow the Survey's accounts of the United States of America and Ethiopia.

The first impression and logical reaction to any attempt to compare these two countries is absurd. To the layperson, let alone the specialist reader, when a comparison is made between the United States and Ethiopia in terms of freedom, democracy or human rights, taking into account whatever variables, it is likely to be of very limited validity. However, it has been included to show that the Survey has assumed the very delicate, if not the impossible, task of measuring freedom on a cross-national basis regardless of the differences that may exist between countries.

The United States of America

Founded over two centuries ago, the United States is often regarded as the most democratic and free country in the world. The freedoms it enjoys are the envy of millions of people elsewhere in the world. Having said that it does not automatically mean that in the US everything is perfect, nor that every other country should seek to achieve the American standard. It has been mainly included in this study because it represents the model upon which the Survey was based. Hence it is a logical choice in any attempt to determine the Survey's shortcomings.

Having been taken as the model upon which freedoms are measured on a cross-national basis, it is not a surprise therefore to see that there has been no change in either dimensions. In other words, a close look at the Surveys since 1973 reveal that the US has scored 1 each on both dimensions for the series of Surveys in question, making it among the freest countries classified. It would be absurd to expect otherwise. Nonetheless, it should be borne in mind that these achievements do not exist in a vacuum. They are the result of social progress over the centuries. In addition to that, economic conditions helped such a process. According to Freedom House, the current system of government began functioning in 1789 (ibid., 259), which suggests that there are established traditions and institutions by which the country is governed, and through which demands and pressures are channelled. Moreover, the way in which conflicts are resolved is already established and leaves no room for violence or instability. These traditions are coupled with the fact that the US is one of the richest countries in the world, which makes social and economic conditions available for the granting of such freedoms. These traditions, or even social and economic conditions, simply do not exist in the majority of 'Third World' countries, which have only achieved nationhood within the last few decades. Many African states, for instance, achieved their independence in the late 1950s or early 1960s.

Many, if not all, the freedoms discussed in the Survey are now taken for granted by Americans, and become part of their daily life. Such a fact makes the aspirations of these people very different. The people in the 'Third World' are longing for civil and political rights, whereas those in the developed world are interested in different issues which curtail their personal freedoms. In assessing freedom in the world in 1990, Freedom House stated that: 'Environmentally, many parts of the US have serious problems. Unacceptably high levels of air, water and ground pollution threaten inhabitants with higher disease rates, and may lead to reductions in personal freedoms in the 1990s such as restrictions on the use of automobiles and water supplies' (ibid.). Issues such as the environment are simply not a concern to the people in a poor country like Chad, Sudan or Ethiopia. What matters more to them is when and where the next meal comes from.

Ethiopia

The first impressions associated with Ethiopia are: famine, disease, illiteracy and civil war. It is one of the poorest countries in the world, where politics is characterised by massive violation of human rights, continuous killing by both government and rebel forces, and the political system itself is very corrupt. Perhaps the most publicised case of today's Ethiopia is famine, which has been threatening the country especially since the mid 1980s.

Given such circumstances, it is hardly a surprise to see that Ethiopia has, up to the early 1990s when it was initially judged 'partly free', always figured in the 'not free' category. According to the Surveys that have been examined, the best standard the country achieved was in 1975; (6-), (5?) for political rights and civil liberties respectively, which arguably could have earned it a ranking among the 'partly free' (Freedom House, 1975, 5-6). However the situation has worsened since, and the reluctance of the Survey to reduce Ethiopia's rating can perhaps be ascribed as well to the fact that it witnessed a coup d'etat against Haile Selassie which brought Lt. Col. Mengistu to power in 1974. This shift from an emperor to a military dictator obviously did not help the development of democratic institutions or traditions.

Living under a military government with the constant threat of famine and a massive and costly civil war in the north, it is quite difficult to imagine the people of Ethiopia enjoying the freedoms discussed above. There are some objective circumstances which act as obstacles towards the achievement of a democratic society in Ethiopia. Above all, Ethiopia lacks the economic and social conditions that would favour such a transition. Moreover, the country lacks democratic traditions. Giorgis, a former commissioner of relief and rehabilitation in Ethiopia and a member of the Central Committee of the Workers' Party of Ethiopia, stresses that: 'In 1974 there was a popular revolution and a military coup. In the absence of any tradition of democracy and political organisations operating freely in the country, the military had to take power, and Mengistu was a member of the armed forces' (Freedom House, 1990b, 12). In addition to the economic and political conditions that prevail in the country, it is worth mentioning corruption and the heavy reliance on the secret police to crack down on any attempt at opposition.

Under such conditions it would be absurd to think about changing the present leadership in a constitutional way, let alone granting civil and political rights. The only way government could come to office is through a military coup, which may perhaps lead the country towards constitutionals. However, experiences have shown, in many African countries, that military regimes rarely evolve in this manner.

The aim behind presenting these cases is to illustrate that it is difficult to compare different countries, with different circumstances and use the same standards of measurement. The reader would have understood by now that freedom as conceived in the Survey may be fully applicable to a handful of Western developed countries. The rights enjoyed by these countries should be enjoyed by every human being but special circumstances of individual countries make it impossible.

The Survey's assessment

In assessing the Comparative Survey of Freedom, two vital questions will be answered to help the reader evaluate the validity and the reliability of the ranking. Brymer and Cramer (1990, 70) identify two major aspects of reliability. The first is external and deals with consistency over time. The second is internal and deals with whether a single scale is measuring a single idea. Hence the discussion that follows assesses the Survey on these lines and asks whether it is possible and useful to measure freedom on a cross-national basis? It also questions whether the model, suggested by Freedom House, is universally applicable? Having answered these questions, the reader will be able to judge whether the ranking and percentages of countries as given by Freedom House are persuasive, and whether an assessment over time of one or more countries is possible. I shall try to highlight what can be considered as shortcomings in the Survey, and the discussion will accordingly emphasise defects to an extent that would not be true of a dispassionate assessment of the Survey.

To begin with, the question of a longitudinal assessment should be attempted for both categories and countries. If someone is interested, for instance, in trends in the proportion of people world-wide who are 'free' or 'not free', then it is time-series statistics of this kind that must be employed. But how reliable are those provided by the Survey? For the categories, for instance, it may be helpful to consider table (8) 1.

In this area the Survey is very weak and unreliable. It was pointed out earlier that it kept adding different indices to both its dimensions of freedom, which would make the results obtained on the basis of the initial list different from the ones on the new lists. This in turn explains why the categories are not successful in representing the gains and losses of freedom around the world. The changes in the indices considered in measuring freedom in the world will go hand in hand with the changes in the percentages themselves. Moreover, the non-publication of the original checklist, and the introduction of a new and more adequate one, will confirm further the claim that an analysis over time of the gains and losses of freedom, based on the Survey, is a meaningless exercise. This makes it difficult to argue that there is continuity between the findings of the Surveys.

Table 8 (1): Percentages of the 'free', 'partly free' and the 'not free' people in the world for selected years

Years	Free	Partly Free	Not Free
January 1973	32.00%	21.00%	47.00%
January 1975	35.00%	23.00%	42.00%
January 1981	35.90%	21.60%	42.50%
January 1985	34.85%	23.30%	41.85%
January 1993	24.83%	44.11%	31.06%
January 1995	19.97%	40.01%	40.02%
Source: Based on Freedom House, 1988, 21 and Freedom House, 1995, 7. For the purpose of this study, I have selected only the percentages of each category.			

It might be argued, for instance, that although it appears that 32 per cent, 35.90 per cent and 19.97 per cent respectively represent the percentages of the free people in the world for the years 1973, 1981 and 1995, nonetheless, this difference should not necessarily be seen as a global gain or loss of freedom. While over a third of the world's population was free in 1981, less than a fifth only was free in 1995. Given the dramatic changes which took place in the former communist countries and their re-classification as 'free', the assumption would be that the percentage of the free people in the world would rise. However, because India, the second most populous country in the world, was placed in the partly free category, the overall percentage fell. As a results, it might be argued, that these percentages represent quite different situations. The indices, and therefore the checklist, upon which the former percentage was obtained differed from the basis upon which the latter one was conducted. Further, it is clear that the actual technique whereby the scores of countries and these percentages are obtained has changed, which makes analysis over time quite an impossible task. The Survey argues that 'hundreds of millions classified as free were just marginally so, and almost as many classified as partly free, could with slight shift of arbitrary category boundaries, have been considered not free' (Gastil, 1978, 4), the changes in the strategy introduced by the new Survey's Director certainly influenced the classification. In addition, the emphasis changed from civil to political rights in 1979, which suggests that there was a cut-off between the results or categories achieved before and after this date. A country which had been ranked 'partly free' could have well been ranked 'not free' compared to one which had received the same score if it was not for this emphasis or weight. Two examples highlight this case: South Africa and the former Soviet Union, although their total for the two dimensions was 11 each. Nonetheless, South Africa was classified 'partly free' since it received 6 and 5 for civil and political rights respectively; whereas, the former Soviet Union received 5 and 6 for the two dimensions respectively and was classified 'not free' (Freedom House, 1990a, 23). This situation leads to questions about the system of weighting. Although the interdependence of the two dimensions is taken into account, a system of weighting should not be introduced as a means to distinguish certain categories. The inconsistency of the Survey in the weighting of its dimensions adds to these difficulties.

Turning now to the question of the applicability of the model developed by Freedom House in all countries of the world, a deeper problem is associated with the ethnocentrism of the Survey: its ready association of freedom with Western institutions and values coupled with its willingness to attack other systems and values. As the 1981 Survey made clear, there was a need to 'identify the most powerful organised, international threat to freedom' as this was 'the communist movement, and particularly that part of it backed by the Soviet Union' (Gastil, 1981, 10). It need not necessarily be biased judgement that western liberal democracies have in practice offered better opportunities for self-expression and wider range of freedoms with which the Survey is concerned. Nonetheless, the Survey has, in these cases, departed from its original purpose of providing an objective measure of human rights performance on a cross-national basis. The Survey's sponsoring organisation, Freedom House, has, in addition, engaged in a number of acts of directly political intervention. Its former director wrote to President Vaclav Havel of the former Czechoslovakia in 1990, for instance, urging him to reappraise the relationship of his country towards Cuba, and 'to bring to an end its representation of Cuban diplomatic interests in the United States' (*The Washington Post*, 9 January, 1990).

The ethnocentrism of the Survey is seen in how countries are ranked. There surely is a distinction between what people want in different countries. The Survey seems convinced that everybody, wherever they may live, would want the freedoms it specifies if they had the chance to choose. Nonetheless, it is not always the case. The priorities that are selected depend very much upon the circumstances of the countries themselves. There is no denial of how valuable civil and political rights are to the enjoyment of freedom; nevertheless, the enjoyment of the basic needs as well are of paramount importance and may affect freedom itself. What would be the situation of a country governed by a chief executive who assumed power through a coup d'etat, who worked for the benefit of his people and whose people agreed with the way he managed the affairs of the state? What would have been the situation of a country where a coup d'etat had just occurred and the majority of the people agreed with it? The Survey seems to have set a standard, which was thought to be the best, and countries are judged on whether or not they approach it, leaving out of consideration the particularities of each country.

The Survey gives the impression that a great deal is known about different countries through the gathering of the information upon which it made its judgements. However, what it not considered is how these phenomena are viewed in a different context. Does it really matter for people in Ethiopia, for instance, if they are denied the right to free speech and assembly? Probably such an issue does not matter as much as many other, more basic, issues such as food. The granting of such freedoms is a long process, and depends not only on the will of governments, but on how prepared people are to accept these ideas and practices. These freedoms may be the ultimate goal, and many people may envy Westerners for these freedoms. As the Survey makes clear, and without apology, its model 'is that of Western constitutional democracy, and we are asking to what extent the countries of the world accord with this model' (Freedom House, 1975, 3). However, such enjoyment is a result of an evolution over the years, if not centuries. Many 'Third World' countries lack the institutions and the appropriate channels through which such a change may take place. Economic conditions may also make it difficult for them to enjoy these freedoms. In other words, there are some practical obstacles that many countries face in the 'Third World' in achieving a high level of freedoms.

Political rights and civil liberties need a material base in order to work properly. It would be absurd to talk about a people enjoying civil and political liberties at a time when the very same people are illiterate. How does it affect the status of a group of people living in remote rural areas, illiterate, and with virtually no access to the mass media, if the chief executive is elected or not? There are still many areas in different countries in the 'Third World' without access to newspapers or television programmes. These people are not free because they cannot be free. Freedom, as understood in the Survey, requires a citizen in the model of J. S. Mill, someone who is active, informed and knows his/her duties and rights. At the same time, it also requires institutions already set to channel different demands, and a government which respects the 'rules of the game'. Unfortunately, these are rarely encountered in the majority of 'Third World' countries. The Survey, in fact, is highly ethnocentric and difficult to apply on a cross-national basis. It represents the American model of freedom, which hinders the chances of countries such as Ghana, China, Ethiopia or Nigeria, with their traditions of totalitarian rule. Each of these has its own circumstances which may lead to such freedoms being denied, or provided in a different form.

The point that needs to be stressed here is that although the Survey may be successful in assigning countries to the different categories seen above, except initially perhaps for the borderline cases, it fails to account for the social and economic circumstances, and traditions of different countries. As pointed out earlier, Ethiopia had special circumstances; it did not have 'any tradition of democracy and political organisation'. Such statement is undoubtedly crucial to the understanding of why the ranking of these countries, as well as others, has been that way.

The Survey has simply selected a set of variables that corresponded to its theoretical definition of freedom, and tried to apply them on a cross-national basis. The ranking for each year may be appropriate, nonetheless, the question that needs to be asked here is: do the variables or the concepts used in this Survey have the same meaning in the different countries under consideration?

Another point of interest is freedom from foreign control. This control may influence the degree of freedom in any country being subjected to it.

Nonetheless, the question that needs to be answered here is, what harm has a country done in being subjected to such a control to see its score reduced? It should be the other way around. No country in the world can live by itself. There should be contact and interdependence between them. Such interdependence varies, of course, between them to the point of domination or control. What is the difference between a chief executive of a country in black Africa, Nigeria for instance, who assumed power through a coup d'etat, and one in Latin or Central America who came to power through corrupt elections financed by the US or was simply put in office by the Americans, as with the case of Panama?

Constant interference in the internal affairs of 'Third World' countries endangers the transition, if any, toward democracy and therefore the enjoyment of these freedoms that might exist in these countries. It might be seen from another point of view that such an interference is the only way whereby citizens in these countries will be free.

The Survey has been subjected to extensive criticism either for its methods or for being ethnocentric. Thomas Quigley, for instance, stresses that: 'Mr Gastil says his definition of freedom would not be "extended rhetorically" as the expression "freedom from fear". But until he has shown some sensitivity to such fundamental freedoms as the right to self-determination, equality, health, education, work, and adequate standard of living, maintenance of one's culture, and protection from arbitrary arrest, detention, or torture, he is not qualified to speak for more than the tiny minority of which white, male Americans are today's paradigm' (1974, 39).

Is the Survey, then, a wholly invalid measure of the distribution of rights and freedoms on a cross-national basis? Less so in the 1990s, perhaps, than in earlier years. The checklist of items on which it is based has steadily expanded over the years, taking account of criticism and of the operation of the Survey itself. Later Surveys, as we have seen, include measures of national self-determination, equality, and freedom from torture and arbitrary arrest or torture. The Survey still takes no direct account of socio-economic circumstances in its measures but it has begun to report some relevant indices together with its political freedoms and civil liberties ratings. The Survey does, at least, provide a measure of the limited range of freedoms with which it deals; and its shortcomings have been steadily reduced. The rating scheme introduced in 1989 (a scale from two to 14) is a distinct improvement as compared with the free/not free dichotomy of earlier surveys (the 1990

Survey, without any explanation, reverted to the older classification). This rating was further refined by the new Survey's team in 1992. The search for a valid cross-national measure of rights and freedoms will clearly continue; in the meantime, the Comparative Survey of Freedom provides a lesson in the pitfalls that attend any exercise of this kind, together with a helpful starting point in the examination of Western political liberties and their global distribution.

Part Three: Conclusion

In the first part of this work a lengthy discussion focused on the definition and the content of human rights. It is a concept vigorously contested between East and West on the one hand, and developed and developing countries on the other. The clash between liberal and socialist ideas, and the emergence of many 'Third World' countries on the international political scene, strengthened such vigorous contestation. This made agreement on a widely acceptable definition of the concept very difficult, not to say impossible. The discussion, then, moved to consider the operationalisation of this concept by looking at some of the attempts to measure or conceptualise human rights on a cross-national basis. Non-governmental organisations such as Amnesty International and Freedom House, political scientists such as Dahl and Bollen, or international bodies such the UN Human Rights Committee, have been concerned with the issue of human rights and political democracy. Some of these have developed different criteria upon which they measure human rights and therefore rank countries. Others have just been concerned with monitoring the situation in countries around the world and helping governments improve their records.

The discussion that follows assesses the extent to which these exercises have successfully conceptualised the problem of human rights, and particularly whether the task itself, to compare human rights on a cross-national basis, is a feasible one. It seeks to evaluate the case studies, and asks whether they have been successful in resolving the problems relating to comparative political analysis on the conceptual, data and operational levels (Bahry, in Manheim and Rich, 1986). The interpretation of human rights, as discussed in the first part, has a long history, is influenced by various factors, and therefore varies between individuals, political scholars/researchers and regimes. Quantification of human rights, however, is a more recent exercise where different organisations and scholars took an interest in the subject, gathered information and engaged in systematic quantification and measurement which resulted in a ranking of countries. However, if 'the very variety of human rights', Horn argues, 'makes it difficult to fit them into a single structure balanced measurement' (1993, 180), how did the case studies undertaken in this work attempt to measure them? Thus, the discussion begins with an overall assessment and comparison between the different inquiries undertaken in this study. I shall particularly look at the definitions employed and their operationalisation through the approaches and the variables selected. This analysis should help to provide a better understanding of the strengths and weaknesses of each study as an attempt to measure human rights on a cross-national basis. Then, I shall discuss whether or not a comparative study of human rights, in the light of the different studies discussed earlier and the diversity of political systems, is a possible one. The discussion concludes with a number of recommendations for future research.

The case studies: a comparison

It has been suggested earlier that a clear-cut definition of the content of human rights has yet to be achieved. The United Nations, considered to be the authority on the subject, has steadily increased the items on its list of human rights. The 'third generation' of human rights, and particularly the right to development recognised as an inalienable human right in 1986, are the best example of this broadening of a concept that was originally conceived more narrowly. Nevertheless, the inquiries undertaken in this study have limited their scope in general to some aspects of the subject. The rights of solidarity, and economic, social and cultural rights, to some extent, have not really been taken seriously by the scholars and organisations involved with the issue of human rights.

Inadequate definitions and data

Inadequate definitions

One might suggest that international conventions, signed by the majority of countries, provide a strong base upon which human rights can be defined and measured. However, one must bear in mind the fact that a comprehensive list of human rights, based on United Nations documents, is extremely lengthy, which in turn makes coverage of every aspect a near impossible task. In the case studies undertaken, the choice of indices upon which measurements were based was necessarily an arbitrarily one. Indeed, apart from Charles Humana's second and third studies (1986 and 1992) and the work of the Human Rights Committee, the case studies suffer a kind of personal arbitrariness.

The Human Rights Committee's definition is based on the provisions of the International Covenant of Civil and Political Rights and its Optional Protocol. It applies these provisions to states which committed themselves to fulfil these obligations by ratifying this document. Humana's second and third studies (1986 and 1992) are based exclusively on the Universal Declaration and the two Covenants. This makes them more balanced since they are drawn from the main documents of human rights. His first study (1983), however, suffers from arbitrary selection since some of the aspects considered are not really supported by international instruments.

Amnesty International takes the view that covering every aspect of human rights would not lead to fruitful results, and as a result opted for a narrow definition. There are some advantages to this strategy; comparatively more accurate information is available on the chosen aspects. However, this narrow definition also has its shortcomings. Amnesty bases its annual reports on a few aspects of human rights that it has selected to give a picture of human rights in different countries in the world. There is no doubt about how significant are some of the issues with which Amnesty is concerned, such as 'prisoners of conscience', to the whole debate of human rights. Amnesty is the leading organisation on such an issue. However, this is just one among many. Thus, it is difficult to accept the contention that one is talking about the state of human rights in a given country when the aspects chosen for consideration are so few. To make generalisations on the basis of a few indices is not likely to lead a researcher to convincing conclusions.

Freedom House, Dahl and Bollen have exclusively reserved their definitions to political rights and civil liberties, and attempt to construct a ranking of countries upon these aspects. Perhaps the unbalanced dialogue on the issue of human rights and democracy has led to these different assumptions. The fact that most scholars and organisations involved with these issues are based in the West has meant that they have tended to look at matters on the basis of their own perceptions. The definitions adopted for the study of human rights and democracy confirm this claim. They are usually drawn from a range of civil and political rights, that are most treasured in the West. Thus, if one looks at the definitions employed on a cross-national basis, one sees that they are unsatisfactory or ethnocentric in many instances, representing what the scholar or the organisation thought to be the norm.

Inadequate data

Dahl's, Humana's and Freedom House's studies suffer from a lack of information and personal judgements. If one recalls the peculiar position of France (Dahl ranked it twice at points 6 and 11 on a 29 points scale), one sees that the actual strategy whereby such a ranking is achieved is doubtful, or that a better strategy could be developed. If it was not for Dahl's personal judgement, France would not have been moved upwards on the scale. The judgements themselves could have been harsher when dealing with a country with long traditions of democracy and respect for human rights. When the answers do not quite correspond to the prior knowledge of that country, its final ranking will be significantly lowered.

Humana's studies were divided according to the strategies followed. It was obvious that a number of countries were assessed through summary forms because of lack of information and data. However, even among the countries analysed under the questionnaires, the recorded data were doubtful in many cases. Freedom House also still cannot overcome this problem. It has been pointed out earlier that, while some countries have received the same scores, their final rankings have been different. Even within one country, the same score has meant different ranking from year to year. This suggests that the approach can be considered as the weakest point of measurement. There has been a selection of indices and a choice of the aspects one looks at against a set of criteria. In principle, whenever the results match, the final ranking of countries is the same. However, this has not been the case, particularly in Humana's and Freedom House's inquiries.

In addition, it seems that there has been an inconsistency on the part of Freedom House. Different indices have been added to the initial list; the strategy followed to obtain the final ranking has changed and those involved with the Survey have intervened repeatedly to re-evaluate the ranking position of certain countries.

Statistics can also be misleading if they are exclusively relied upon. It is appropriate if these facts are looked at within the context in which they occur. If the number of 'prisoners of conscience' Amnesty publishes is taken as the basis for a comparative study, then the interpretation of such a number is significant in attaining a clear picture. To say that there are 100,000 'prisoners of conscience' in countries A and B, it does not automatically follow that the two countries violate human rights to the same extent. The number ought to be looked at as a percentage of the total population. This number represents a high percentage of the population in countries such as Kuwait or Luxembourg, but can be insignificant in others like China or India. Thus, quantification can have different interpretations which make a general agreement difficult to reach.

In addition, the scarcity of data and its unreliability adds to the existing difficult issue of comparing human rights on a cross-national basis. It has always been claimed that the former communist countries had better records than liberal democracies in providing for economic and social rights. However, the collapse of communism in these countries and the unprecedented flow of information that followed about their domestic records suggest that these claims have little validity. Some of the human rights violations, denied for decades, have been confirmed by successive governments in these countries.

Approaches

Independence of variables

Such an arbitrary definition and selection of the indices have led to human rights being looked at separately from the environment in which they evolve and develop. The Human Rights Committee represents an exception in this area. It is perhaps worth stating again that such practices, either respecting or violating human rights, develop in accordance with the realities of a given society. They are influenced by the environment in which they occur. Amnesty annual reports provide facts and statistics about almost every country in the world without any reflection on what is happening in any particular one. The time-series statistics on the treatment of 'prisoners of conscience' by a particular government does not lead to satisfactory conclusions. Amnesty reports on the aspects on which it has particular interests. However, such aspects need to be explained in more detail. Why, for instance, has the number of 'prisoners of conscience' suddenly increased for one or two years in one particular country? There is no satisfactory explanation of this matter in its annual reports. The space reserved to every country is too small to enable a clearer picture to be established. This, in turn makes a comparison very difficult.

However, Amnesty does publish country reports. These are more informative, since the focus is just on the chosen country. More details are available and different explanations are provided which may influence the government's treatment of its citizens. These reports are still limited in number, do not cover every country and could be out of date after their publication because of the changes that the country in question may have witnessed.

Dahl and Bollen, similarly, have concentrated their efforts on civil and political rights and these factors are looked at with little reference to the circumstances in which they evolve. In this respect, it is perhaps appropriate to stress that, although Dahl did not take into account the conditions that favoured polyarchy in his measurement, he made a significant point by stressing them. Thus, polyarchy did not exist as such, but some conditions have to be met first for such a system to work properly. The conditions discussed by Dahl help the understanding of why some countries are more democratic than others. Conditions such as historical sequences or the level of economic development, for instance, play a significant role in favouring a democratic system (Dahl, 1971; Lipset, 1959). However, when Dahl proceeded to the measurement of polyarchy, his judgements were based only on the opportunities to participate and to oppose. In the total absence of the seven conditions that favour polyarchy in terms of Dahl's discussion, one can assume that a system is not democratic and therefore that opportunities to participate and to oppose are non-existent.

Both Charles Humana and Freedom House do not give satisfactory explanations as to why some countries and not others violate human rights.

They both develop their own criteria upon which they measure countries' performances and therefore construct a ranking. Nevertheless, they take these variables independently from what is happening in reality. Freedom House updates its Survey by highlighting gains and losses in freedom around the world. However, the explanation of these changes is very limited. The same thing could be said about the work of Charles Humana, especially his first study in 1983.

The UN Human Rights Committee, on the contrary, takes into consideration the circumstances of every state party to the Covenant whenever their reports are considered. This makes its work more significant towards improving their standards. The Committee does accept that some conditions may hamper the observance of human rights and may make it very difficult for some countries, especially in the 'Third World', to bring their laws into accordance with the provisions of the Covenant. Perhaps the best example of this effect is the right to derogation, under article 4 of the Covenant. The article stresses that the rights to be derogated from should be in accordance with the demands of the new situation and that the Committee should be notified of these measures. This, in turn, enables the Committee to take into account the circumstances of the country concerned and the environment in which the rights have evolved.

Ranking and non-ranking approaches

Although the main aim of all the studies undertaken is, among others, the improvement of human rights around the world, their approach is quite different. While the Human Rights Committee tries to help states party to the Covenant to enhance their human rights standards by providing assistance whenever needed, Amnesty publicises abuses and pressurises governments to treat their citizens fairly. Dahl, Bollen, Humana and Freedom House, at the other end of the spectrum, have engaged in a systematic comparison and ranking of countries on different scales. However, they differ in the ways whereby this ranking is achieved.

It seems that the approach undertaken by the Human Rights Committee, and the one taken by Amnesty to some extent, would be likely to achieve more useful results. Both of them do not engage in any sort of ranking. Amnesty puts different pressures on governments which, in many instances, succeeds in securing fair trials or freeing some 'prisoners of conscience'. However, in the long run, the practice in the country concerned seems to persist. The Committee's approach, on the other hand, is completely different. It is a body which works under the auspices of an international organisation of which almost every country is a member. It approaches governments from an angle on which they have agreed. It engages in friendly dialogues aimed at helping, not condemning, the practices of the state concerned. Although it is a long process, it has tended to achieve an overall improvement in the long run.

Any ranking of countries in terms of human rights and political democracy is bound to be controversial, and could be difficult to accept in many parts of the world. Controversies seem inevitable not only with regard to the indices chosen, but also regarding the strategies adopted, the information and the data gathered and the personal assumptions of those involved in the studies themselves.

Weighting

Bollen and Dahl do not engage in any kind of weighting in the measurement of political democracy. They deal with the different aspects independently to conclude whether the aspect in question is respected or not. Although it is relatively the most acceptable strategy whereby rights are considered equal, it is very difficult to come to any clear-cut conclusions on the boundaries of the indices they measure. Indices such as 'freedom of the press' to name just one, are very difficult to assess. Bollen assesses it on a nine-point scale based on a judgemental source, while the breakdown of this index in Dahl's study resulted in four categories. The point that needs to be stressed here is which countries received nine points on Bollen's scale and which countries had complete freedom of the press according to Dahl? By which means can we decide such a point? These questions are not aimed at directly comparing the two scales in these two separate studies, but to stress the need for clarification of when one category ends and another begin.

Both Humana (1986 and 1992) and Freedom House opted for a system of weighting in their final ranking of countries. This system of weighting is generally misleading and should be disregarded if these studies are to be considered more seriously. They have introduced such a system at a later stage: Humana in his second and third editions, and Freedom House in the late 1970s.

A system of weighting inevitably gives more importance to some rights than others. It can be understood, in principle, that some rights could be more valuable than others; nonetheless, the denial of the latter does not mean that they do not constitute a serious violation. That is what Humana did in his 1986 and 1992 studies, which influenced the ranking of some countries. However, what Freedom House has done seems to be more confusing. In the 1977 and the 1978 Surveys, the weight has changed from one dimension of freedom to another. This suggests that the system and the approach as a whole are at fault.

In any study where a system of weighting is employed, the results and the final ranking are open to question. Once again an arbitrary selection of the indices or dimensions to weight is left completely to the discretion of those involved with the studies. It biases not only the results but also the ranking of countries. It only takes a country to score maximum points on the weighted rights to see it ranks higher than those which did not.

Perhaps the most important point in the studies which engage in the measurement of human rights and democracy is the ranking of a peculiar country: South Africa. It is very difficult to accept the contention of Dahl, Bollen and Freedom House that South Africa, before the end of apartheid, was more democratic and freer than the majority of 'Third World' countries and some former communist countries. Humana, on the other hand, ranked it very low on his studies. Any study that considers South Africa to be more democratic that many other parts of the world is questionable, unless the application of the indices was to the whites only. In any country where 80 per cent of the adult population was not eligible to vote (people were denied the right to participate in elections, and indeed to oppose the government), it is very difficult to accept the suggestion that the country in question is democratic or free? South Africa was classified among the democratic countries in Dahl's and Bollen's studies. Freedom House, on the other hand, has always classified South Africa either in the 'partly free' or 'not free' categories. However, the former classification does not seem to be appropriate in some cases given its comparative nature.

Longitudinal assessment

Finally, the nature of the studies themselves is of paramount importance to any over time assessment or comparison of countries in terms of human rights and democracy. The studies carried out by Dahl and Bollen are significant, but are narrow in scope. The strategy they followed may perhaps be limited to some countries. The data, however, needs to be updated to take into account different changes that have taken place since the studies were published. Humana's studies are more recent, and enable the reader to make comparisons between the three enquiries and pinpoint the gains and losses in human rights in countries that need to be studied. However, these studies are limited in time and do not provide the reader with some information regarding the periods of time that a researcher wishes to cover.

However, the Human Rights Committee, Amnesty International and Freedom House offer more grounds upon which to carry out an over time comparison. Although the Committee discusses a state's report once in every five years, this practice however, enables any improvement in the field of human rights to be monitored. One is able to conclude, after considering different reports of a given state, whether the state in question has taken the necessary steps towards bringing its laws within the provisions of the Covenant. This, in turn, helps to conduct a comparison between a number of states to find out about their attitudes towards improving their human rights records.

Freedom House and Amnesty, however, offer a year-to-year picture of almost every country in the world. This makes an over time assessment more possible and easier to execute. In this respect, Freedom House is more successful and straightforward than Amnesty. The latter describes the situation in country A for year 1, then describes it for year 2, and so forth. It is left to the reader to conclude whether the state in question has improved or not over the years.

Having dealt with the different studies to monitor human rights and democracy, especially those which have engaged in measurement and ranking on a cross-national basis, the question that needs to be asked here is: is a comparative study of human rights on a cross-national basis possible? This will be dealt with in the following section.

Is a comparative study of human rights on a cross-national basis possible?

In the light of the case studies dealt with above and the diversity of political systems in the world, total comparability of human rights, at any rate, is very difficult if not impossible. A variety of problems may face a researcher if he is to engage in such an exercise.

Human rights, as already suggested earlier, mean different things to different people. It is very difficult to achieve a consensus on what a list of human rights should consist of. Although some might suggest that such a consensus was achieved and resulted in the Universal Declaration, it is not the case for various reasons. Firstly, the majority of 'Third World' countries did not participate in the drafting of this document. Secondly, many 'rights' have emerged since the adoption of this document in 1948. Third, and perhaps the most significant, within this consensus there were priorities of rights championed by different governments. This makes a comparative study of human rights on a cross-national basis, even on the basis of the Declaration, a very difficult exercise. In this connection one cannot avoid asking these question: what is the basis upon which to conduct such a study? And what definition should be employed in the comparative study of human rights?

The most basic problem is of a conceptual nature. Concepts alien to particular societies are the source of the difficulties surrounding the process as a whole. In many instances, problems are viewed from one angle: the viewpoint from which the scholar sees the phenomenon in their own societies. What can be considered as a human right in a given country might not be automatically considered as such in a different country. This difference in perception, in turn, leads to a completely different understanding of what a violation is, and thus to an overall misplacing of countries' positions if a ranking is undertaken.

If a comparative study of human rights on a cross-national basis is conducted, measures are needed which refer to the same concept in the different countries studied. The use of civil and political rights, while reference is made to human rights, in a country such as Chad or China is simply difficult to accept. Concepts such as multi-party elections and freedom of associations, for instance, simply do not 'travel' very well (Sartori, 1971 and 1984), and restrict a researcher to study countries with multi-party systems, which hold election and guarantee freedom of associations. Such qualifications, as we have seen in the case studies, automatically eliminate more countries than they include. Furthermore, the difficulties in translations is an added burden, especially when there is no precise meaning for a concept in another language. Thus, the very idea itself may connote two different phenomena. In this respect, Professor Donoho argues that 'abstract rights may legitimately mean and require different things in diverse cultural settings. Each country's cultural and political heritage, as well as the vagaries of language itself, fundamentally shape the meaning of abstract rights, such as political participation, due process, and equal protection' (1991, 369).

The second fundamental problem concerns data and information. A comparison without data on the subject hardly makes sense. To conclude whether a given country abuses or respects human rights, or whether it ranks above or below another, data to support the arguments should be available. However, data concerning the state of human rights is generally scarce. Governments, especially in the 'Third World' and the former communist countries, are notorious for not co-operating with the specialised agencies. Their response is that human rights are being fully respected. Different Amnesty's reports and the reports by the Human Rights Committee, after the reforms in the former communist countries, suggest that efforts have been made to hide facts. So, there is a tendency to hide or falsify the facts concerning the ways whereby citizens are treated. Nobody knows the exact number of those imprisoned during the Cultural Revolution in China, for instance, or those tortured in Latin America during the reign of military government. What is reported in the press or by non-governmental organisations, at best, does not represent the actual situation and at worst, is based on mere guesses. What makes the situation even worse is that some countries are closed societies with virtually no contact with the outside world. Data concerning their GNP or level of literacy are hard to obtain, let alone those concerned with human rights.

Having established the fact that different perceptions of human rights may lead to a different understanding of what a violation is may pose a problem of a different nature. Although some data may be available on different countries, they may not represent a 'violation' in the country in which they occur. 'Even if data were available', Bahry points out, 'many countries use slightly different definitions in representing data, and thus their own publications may offer us information that is not entirely compared from one country to another' (in Manheim and Rich, 1986, 232). Amputation of an arm may not only be seen as a violation of human rights, but as a cruel and inhuman punishment in liberal democracies. However, it is not seen as such in some countries. Under Islamic law, for instance, amputation of an arm is the punishment for repeated theft. The point that needs to be stressed in this context is that, in principle, this penalty does not represent a violation of human rights in an Islamic society where the teaching of Islam is fully implemented. The practice is there and will remain. However, would data on such an aspect yield convincing results?

In addition to the concept and data difficulty, the scope of a study is more or less limited or imposed. The reports published by non-governmental organisations, for instance, are based on the information available to them. In the total absence of information on a particular country, the latter would not be included in the reports. In the early 1980s, for instance, Amnesty did not include Saudi Arabia in its annual reports. The work of the Human Rights Committee makes any comparison based exclusively on states party to the Covenant. Therefore, any attempt to measure human rights on a cross-national basis would automatically be based upon the information provided by these organisations. This does not only limit the choice of countries to be included in a comparative analysis of human rights, but does not provide over time data if a longitudinal assessment is sought.

Concepts and data are crucial, however, they are not the only problems towards total comparability of human rights. The diversity of political systems in today's world adds to these difficulties. This diversity consists not only in the type of political system and institutions, but on the level of economic development also.

Respect or abuses of human rights depends, to a great extent, on the form of the political system. A close look at what kind of a system prevails in a particular country suggests how citizens are treated. Military governments, for instance, are based on a heavy military apparatus and a coercive system ready to curtail every movement aimed at changing the situation. Yet, this system has frequently been a feature of many 'Third World' countries. Changes of governments in these countries scarcely follow a smooth path. Under such a system, it is difficult to argue about the observance of human rights. Power is assumed by a military junta and a division of powers of the traditional kind is not generally observed. Respect for human rights is based on, among other things, the independence of the judiciary and competitive elections to the executive and legislature, as well as a free and independent press to ensure freedom of expression. These are hardly met in the majority of 'Third World' countries and what remains of the communist states. The lack of institutions able to adapt to different situations adds to these difficulties. In such countries, it is difficult to anticipate respect for human rights on the same scale as in liberal democracies.

It is perhaps worth stressing that the ultimate goal would eventually be total respect for human rights, but such a process may take a long time. The fact that most 'Third World' countries are newly independent adds to these difficulties. The form of government they may choose, or might be imposed on them, may perhaps be better equipped, at the time, to deal with any problem than another form of government would be.

The level of economic development plays a significant role in enhancing observance of human rights. It is not only up to governments to grant such rights, but it is also up to the people to claim them. The pressures people put on their governments may have a significant impact on the changes in the ways whereby their governments treat them. However, for people to pressurise their governments, they must be aware of their rights. In this context, education and communications are vital for such an awareness. Many people are unaware of what their rights are. The level of illiteracy is very high in the majority of poor countries, and many rural areas are still out of reach of television or newspapers. In such an environment and under these circumstances, what would human rights mean to these people? At best, human rights to them would mean the enhancement of their living conditions.

The type of political system and the level of economic development play significant roles in determining the attitudes of governments towards their citizens. The way in which they respond to pressures by their citizens could be ascribed to the institutions being able to adapt to different situations. However, there is a limit to what institutions in the 'Third World' can cope with and adapt to. If demands and pressures exceed what these institutions can cope with, the result is the use of violence as a way to respond to such pressures. It is only against this background that human rights should be examined on a cross-national basis. The level attained by liberal democracies is ascribed to a process which has evolved over centuries. Such a process is, to some extent, taking place in the rest of the world.

Is the cross-national comparison of human rights, then, wholly invalid since it raises problematic questions and should the idea be abandoned entirely? Not necessarily is the answer since a narrow approach can be taken. Such an approach will not give a general picture of every country undertaken in the comparison. However, it suggests that, at least in principle, some rights can fairly be compared on a cross-national basis without any serious allegations of bias. In this connection freedom of conscience can perhaps be the starting point for such a universal comparison. The freedom to practise any faith cannot be said to be a culturally biased concept, and it does not depend on how wealthy a country is, as with all social and economic rights. The collapse of many communist countries, which curtailed this right, is an added factor for such an argument.

What seems to be a better approach to the study is the 'segmented' one (Dogan and Pellasy, 1984, 101-5). In other words, the countries to be investigated have to be carefully selected before engaging in any kind of comparison. One way of conducting such an exercise is through 'a most-similar-systems design' (Bahry, 1986, 229; Daalder, in Keman, 1993, 49; Dogan and Pellasy, 1990, 132-43). This choice would avoid many of the difficulties discussed above. It also offers a basis upon which a large number, if not the total aspects of human rights can be compared. Liberal democracies, for instance, taken as a whole, can offer the basis upon which such an exercise can be carried out. This has been made more possible by the fact that many former communist countries have adhered to Western conception of human rights. The differences that have existed between them over the years have become less significant. This, is turn, has enlarged the scope of countries if any comparative study of this kind is to be carried out.

Another way of measuring human rights is through the use of the opposite strategy referred to as the 'most-different-design' (Bahry, 1986, 230; Daalder, 1993, 49; Dogan and Pellasy, 1990, 132-4). By selecting relatively different countries for a comparative study, conclusions can be reached which suggest shared characteristics of the countries studied. This might suggest that the differences that exist between countries are not the factors offering explanations to their differing attitudes, but other possible explanations may be revealed.

Recommendations for future research

The study of human rights has received unprecedented attention over the past two decades. More political scientists and different organisations have focused their attention on it and have tried to develop frameworks through which this issue can be examined. Yet, the conceptualisation of human rights on a cross-national basis is far from being adequate. The reliance on the quantification of human rights is, in itself, a doubtful strategy. The methodology whereby different percentages and ranking were achieved, at least in the case studies discussed above, is of questionable validity.

However, many of the difficulties encountered may be overcome, or at least reduced, in future work if fuller attention is given to the following:

(i) Whenever human rights are dealt with, they should be taken within the environment in which they are studied and the cultures of the actors involved in it. Scholars as well as organisations should not only limit themselves to 'what', but go further to ask 'why'. Questions on the state of human rights in Canada and Nicaragua, for instance, are significantly different from questions on the state of human rights in Nicaragua compared with Canada. If one takes just the 'what', the conclusion will be that Canada observes human rights better than Nicaragua and thus may offer arbitrary conclusions. However, if future work concentrates more on the 'why', it will not only identify the reasons behind such violations, if any, but will make the first steps towards an overall improvement. It is the view of the present author that the aim behind any comparative study of human rights is not only to identify which is 'good' and which is 'bad', a result of which aid may be granted or refused, but also to offer solutions to problems that may exist. Conclusions of this kind can only be achieved by looking for 'why'. Economic, military and political factors may be very significant in answering these questions.

(ii) A more balanced view of the issue of human rights should be sought. The dialogue on human rights is still unbalanced and concentrated overwhelmingly in the West. 'The scoring pattern,' Horn argues, '... suggests that socialist (pre-Glasnost) and less developed countries did not accept the idealised Western view of human rights and allotted them a lesser role in their systems, as compared perhaps with religious and political goals. This seems to support an ethnocentric view of human rights, rather than the assumption of a universally valid standard' (1993, 183). Different traditions, as discussed earlier, may have a significant impact on human rights and can be seen from different perspectives. The study of non-western societies by scholars based mainly in the West, without deep knowledge of the day-to-day needs of these people, leads, sometimes, to arbitrary judgements. More concern should be given to scholars from the 'Third World' to carry out studies on their own countries and others. The criteria they would use in measuring human rights may differ from those encountered in the studies undertaken hitherto. Dominguez cites a rather different alternative formulation presented by Argentina's Bariloche Institute. He states that 'The Bariloche group identified a number of needs without satisfaction of which human beings are in one way or another impaired to become ill. The needs, it is claimed, are universal. The Bariloche Institute's authors have argued that human-beings tend to satisfy needs along a hierarchical scale, though the hierarchy of needs may be different from the hierarchy of aspirations. This assumption of hierarchies led those authors to concentrate on four basic needs: food, health care, housing and education. The Bariloche Institute's work, therefore, stresses a set of values quite different from those emphasised by Freedom House' (1979, 32). The 'dialogue' would, undoubtedly improve the understanding of those involved with the issue of human rights in the different parts of the world. It may also uncover the peculiarities and priorities some countries may have. Thus, this global balance can be achieved through:

(a) The United Nations, not only by organising different study programmes, but through the establishment of research centres devoted to human rights. The 29th Graduate Study Programme (Geneva, July 8-25, 1991), for instance, attended by the present author, provides the best example for a more balanced discussion of the issue. It was a significant initiative whereby graduates from different parts of the world, with their differences in religions, traditions, cultures and levels of economic developments gathered to discuss current international issues. Human rights was on the agenda. It is the kind of opportunity where one finds out about the interests and priorities of others, the different issues that need to be looked at more closely and the obstacles that a country may have to overcome. At the same time, the United Nations Organisation lays down the principles and the international agreements it sought to implement.

(b) Apart from the United Nations, this balanced view may be achieved through different regional organisations. The works of the Arab League and the Organisation of African Unity, for instance, with their counterparts in Europe and America should be taken more seriously. Each of these organisations works within its region. As a result, their work is more closely linked to the problems and the understanding of the concept in the relevant cultural traditions of the regions.

(iii) The study of human rights and democracy ought to follow a more global approach. In other words, abuse of human rights should not be made the responsibility of the state concerned only, but should be taken on a more global level. This would give more weight to foreign domination as an index, and perhaps to a change in the way whereby some indices are judged. This suggests a change in the indices upon which scholars compare human rights and democracy on a cross-national basis.

Foreign domination was considered, in some inquiries dealt with previously, as an index which influences the level of enjoyment of freedom and democracy. Thus future work should be concerned not only with the country which violates human rights, but with others which are involved also. Every government violates human rights in one way or another. A global view of human rights would answer some of these questions. In the view of the present author, a government which violates human rights in Africa, for instance, is no more guilty than the government which supplies the equipment to do so. It is a difficult matter to establish since interests take priority over principles. Nonetheless, future work should not only be concerned with the violators, but with the suppliers also. It is easy to condemn torture in the 'Third World' and overlook the German, French and American equipment used in such violations.

By the same token, from a moral view point, it makes little, if any difference, if a human being is sentenced to death or left to starve. In future research, particular attention should be paid to different new indices which can be introduced in any scale for measuring human rights. The destruction of food stocks is perhaps a starting point in the development of such new criteria.

In addition to these, although many 'Third World' countries are still concerned with political rights and civil liberties, which are mostly in the West (iv) the study of human rights should move to cover more issues in liberal democracies. Issues such as women's rights, refugees, and the rights of indigenous people, such as those in Australia, are very much at the centre of human rights and are too significant to be left ignored. Finally, given the changes which have been taking place over the past decade, the greatest threat to mankind is the new challenges it faces. The time has come when the rights of (v) the 'third generation' should be considered more seriously by those involved in the issue of human rights. Future work should concentrate on this new set of rights and the best possible ways to generate respect for them, which may be the basis for an overall respect for human rights.

Bibliography

Addo, M. K. (1990) 'Are Human Rights passé in East-West Relations?', *Coexistence*, Vol. 27, No. 2, pp. 79-104.

Akinola, A. (1990) 'Manufacturing the two-party system in Nigeria', *Journal of Commonwealth and Comparative Politics,* Vol. 28, No. 3, pp. 309-27.

Akroun, M. (1989) 'Origines Islamiques des droits de l'homme', *Revue des Sciences Morales et Politiques*, Vol. 144, No. 1, pp. 25-37.

Alston, P. (1984) 'A Third generation of solidarity rights: development or abjuscation of international human rights law', *The Netherlands International Law Review*, Vol. 29, No. 3, pp. 307-322.

_____ (1984) 'Conjuring up New Human Rights. A proposal for equality control', *American Journal of International Law*, Vol. 78, No. 3, pp. 607-21.

Alston, P. and Quinn, G. (1987) 'The nature and scope of states parties' obligations under the ICESCR', *Human Rights Quarterly*, Vol. 9, No. 1, pp. 157-229.

Amnesty International, (1976a) *Amnesty International in Quotes* (London: Amnesty International).

_____ (1976b) *Amnesty International 76-1976. A chronology 76* (London: Amnesty International).

_____ (1976c) *The Republic of Nicaragua. An Amnesty International report including the findings of a mission to Nicaragua, 10-15 May, 1976* (London: Amnesty International).

_____ (1978) *Political Imprisonment in the People's Republic of China* (London: Amnesty International).

_____ (1979) *The death penalty (1979). A world Report* (London: Amnesty International).

_____ (1983) *Amnesty International Handbook*, 6th edition. (London: Amnesty International).

_____ (1984) *China: Violations of human rights. Prisoners of conscience and the death penalty in the People's Republic of China* (London: Amnesty International).

_____ (1988) *Journal of the British Section of Amnesty International* No. 33 June/July.

_____ *Amnesty International Report: 1978; 79; 80; 81; 82; 83; 84; 85; 86; 87; 88; 89; 90; 91; 92; 93; 94* (London: Amnesty International.)

Bandura, Y. (1986) 'The News From Geneva', *Moscow News Weekly*, No. 9.

Banks, A. S. and Textor, R. B. (1963), *A Cross-Polity Survey* (Cambridge MA: MIT).

Baranbas, R. (1991) 'Political Pluralism in Hungary: The 1990 Elections' *Soviet Studies*, Vol. 43, No. 1, pp. 76-89.

Barsh, R. L. (1991) 'The right to development as a human right: results of the global consultation', *Human Rights Quarterly*, Vol. 13, No. 2, pp. 322-28.

Beetham, D. ed. (1994) *Defining and Measuring Democracy* (London: Sage).

Beitz, C. (1978) 'Democracy in Developing Countries' in Gastil, R., *Freedom in the World. Political Rights and Civil Liberties 1978* (New York: Freedom House in co-operation with G. K. Hall).

Benn, D. (1992) *From Glasnost to Freedom of Expression. Russian openness and International relations* (New York: The Royal Institute of International Affairs).

Bobbio, N. (1987), *The Future of Democracy. A defense of the rules of the Game*. Translated by Roger Griffin. (Oxford: Polity Press).

Boguszak, M. et al (1990) 'Czechoslovakia Ready for Democracy', *The Washington Post*, 7 February.

_____ (1979) 'Political Development and the Timing of Development', *American Sociological Review*, Vol. 46 No. 4, pp. 572-87.

_____ (1980) 'Issues in the Comparative Measurement of political democracy', *American Sociological Review* Vol. 45, No. 3, pp. 370-90.

_____ (1986) 'Political Rights and Political Liberties in Nations. An Evaluation of Human Rights Measures, 1950 to 84,' *Human Rights Quarterly,* Vol. 8, No. 4, pp. 567-591.

_____ and Grandjean, B. (1981) 'The Dimension(s) of Democracy: Further issues in the measurement and effects of political democracy', *American Sociological Review*, Vol. 46, No. 4, pp. 651-59.

_____ and Jackman, R. (1985) 'Democracy and the size distribution of income', *American Sociological Review*, Vol. 50, No. 4, pp. 438-57.

Bouandel, Y. (1993) 'Quantitative approaches to the comparative study of human rights: The work of Charles Humana', *Coexistence*, Vol. 30, No. 2, pp. 145-64.

_____ (1993) *Human Rights and Comparative Politics* (Department of Politics: University of Glasgow Ph.D.).

_____ (1994) 'Charles Humana. An update', *Coexistence*, Vol. 31, No. 1, pp. 79-85.

_____ (1995) 'Human rights and East-West rapprochement: Towards global measurement of human rights', *Coexistence*, Vol. 32, No. 4, pp. 341-54.

_____ and White, S. (1993) 'Measuring Human Rights: The Comparative Survey of Freedom', *Politics*, Vol. 13, No. 1, pp. 17-21.

Brandt, W. (1980) *North-South: A Programme for Survival* (London: Pan Books).

Bretherton, C. and Ponton, G. (1996) *Global Politics. An Introduction* (Oxford: Blackwell).

Brownlie, I. ed. (1972) *Basic Documents In International Law,* 2nd edition (Oxford: Oxford University Press).

Bryman, A. and Cramer, D. (1992) *Quantitative Data Analysis for Social Scientists* (London: Routledge).

Cingranelli, D. A. ed. (1988) *Human Rights: Theory and Measurement* (London: Macmillan).

Claude, J. and Jabine, T. eds (1992) *Human Rights and Statistics: Getting the Record Straight* (Philadelphia: University of Pennsylvania Press).

Cohen, C. (1971) *Democracy* (New York: The Free Press).

Cohen, R. (1987) 'The People's Republic of China. The human rights exception', *Human Rights Quarterly*, Vol. 9, No. 4, pp. 447-542.

Cohen, S. (1982) 'Conditioning US security assistance on human rights practices', *American Journal of International Law*, Vol. 76, No. 2, pp. 246-79.

Connolly, W. (1983) *The Terms of Political Discourse* (Oxford: Martin Robertson).

Copper, J. F. et al (1985) *Human Rights in Post-Mao China* (Boulder: Westview).

Cranston, M. (1962) *Human Rights Today* (London: Ampersand).

_____ (1973)*What Are Human Rights?*(New York: Taplinger).

_____ (1956) *A Preface to Democratic Theory* (Chicago: The University of Chicago Press).

_____ (1971) *Polyarchy. Participation and Opposition* (New Haven: Yale University Press).

_____ (1980) 'The Moscow Discourse. Fundamental Rights in Democratic Order', *Government and Opposition,* Vol. 15, No. 1, pp. 3-30.

_____ (1982) *Dilemmas of Pluralist Democracy Autonomy vs. Control* (New Haven: Yale University Press).

_____ (1984) *Democracy and its Critics* (New Haven: Yale University Press).

Dallin, A. and Breslauer, G. W. (1970) *Political Terror in the Communist Systems* (Stanford/California: Stanford University Press).

De la Chappelle, P. (1967) *La Declaration Universelle des Droits de L'homme et le Catholoicisme* (Paris: Librairie Generale de Droit et de la Jurisprudence).

Decaux, E. (1980) 'La Mise en Vigueur du Pacte International Relatif aux Droit Civil et Politiques', *Revue Generale de Droit International Public,* Vol. 84, No. 1, pp. 487-534.

Del Prado, J. L. G. (1985) 'United Nations Conventions on Human Rights. The Practice of the Human Rights Committee and the Committee on the Elimination of Racial Discrimination in Dealing with Reporting Obligation of States Parties', *Human Rights Quarterly*, Vol. 7, No. 4, 486-99.

Denstein, Y. Human Rights in Israel. A talk at the Department of Law and Financial Studies, Glasgow University. Friday, Feb. 9, 1990.

Desmond, C. (1984) *Persecution East and West. Human Rights, Political Prisoners and Amnesty* (Hammondsworth: Penguin Books).

Dogan, M. and Pelassy, D. (1984) *How To Compare Nations? Strategies in comparative politics* (New Jersey: Chatham House).

Dominguez, J. I. (1979) *Enhancing Global Human Rights* (New York: McGraw-Hill).

Donnelly, J. (1981) 'Recent Trends in UN Human Rights activity: description and polemic', *International Organization,* Vol. 35, No. 4, pp. 633-55.

_____ (1982) 'Human Rights and Human Dignity: An Analytic Critique of Non-Western Conceptions of Human Rights', *American Political Science Review*, Vol. 76, No. 1, pp. 82-96.

_____ (1984) 'Cultural Relativism and Universal Human Rights', *Human Rights Quarterly*, Vol. 6, No. 4, pp. 400-19.

_____ (1985) *The Concept of Human Rights* (London: Croom Helm).

_____ (1989) *Universal Human Rights in Theory and Practice* (Ithaca: Cornell University Press).

_____ (1993) *International Human Rights* (Boulder: Westview).

Donnelly, J. and Howard, R. E. eds (1987) *International Handbook of Human Rights* (New York: Greenwood).

_____ (1988) 'Assessing National Human Rights: A Theoretical Framework', *Human Rights Quarterly*, Vol. 10, No. 2, pp. 214-248.

Donoho, D. (1991) 'Relativism Versus Universalism in Human Rights: The Search For Meaningful Standards', *Stanford Journal of International Law*, Vol. 27, No. 2, pp. 345-391.

Dowrick, F. (1979) *Human Rights. Problems, Perspectives and Texts* (Aldershot: Gower).

Doyal, L. and Gough, I. (1991) *A Theory of Human Needs* (London: Macmillan).

Edwards, R. R. et al (1986) *Human rights in Contemporary China* (New York: Columbia University Press).

Falk, R. (1979) 'Comparative Protection of Human Rights in Capitalist and Socialist and Third World Countries', *Universal Human Rights,* Vol. 1, No. 2, pp. 3-29.

Forsythe, D. P. ed. (1989a) *Human Rights and Development* (London: Macmillan).

_____ (1989b) *Human Rights and World Politics*, 2nd edition revised, (Lincoln: University of Nebraska Press).

_____ (1991) 'Human Rights in a Post-Cold War World', *The Fletcher Forum,* Summer pp. 55-63

_____ ed. (1994) *Human Rights in the New Europe. Problems and Progress* (Lincoln and London: University of Nebraska Press).

Freeden, M. (1991) *Rights* (Milton Keynes: Open University Press).

Freedom House, (1975) 'The Comparative Survey of Freedom', *Freedom at Issue,* Jan./Feb.

_____ (1976) 'The Comparative Survey of Freedom', *Freedom at Issue,* Jan./Feb.

_____ (1977) 'The Comparative Survey of Freedom', *Freedom at Issue*, Jan./Feb.

_____ (1986) 'The Comparative Survey of Freedom', *Freedom at Issue*, Jan./Feb.

_____ (1988) 'The Comparative Survey of Freedom', *Freedom at Issue,* Jan./Feb.

_____ (1989) 'The Comparative Survey of Freedom', *Freedom at Issue,* Jan./Feb.

_____ (1990a) *Freedom in the World. Political Rights and Civil Liberties 1989-90* (New York: Freedom House).

_____ (1990b) *Ethiopia: The politics of famine* (New York: Freedom House).

_____ (1990c) 'The Comparative Survey of Freedom', *Freedom at Issue,* Jan./Feb.

_____ (1992) 'The Comparative Survey of Freedom', *Freedom Review*, Jan/Feb.

_____ (1995) 'The Comparative Survey of Freedom', *Freedom Review*, Jan/Feb.

Garling, M. (1979) *The Human Right Handbook. A Guide to British and American international human rights organizations* (London: Macmillan).

Gastil, R. D. (1978) *Freedom in the World. Political Rights and Civil Liberties 1978* (New York: Freedom House in co-operation with G. K. Hall).

———————— (1979) *Freedom in the World. Political Rights and Civil Liberties 1979* (New York: Freedom House in co-operation with G. K. Hall).

———————— (1980) *Freedom in the World. Political Rights and Civil Liberties 1980* (New York: Freedom House).

———————— (1981) *Freedom in the World. Political Rights and Civil Liberties 1981* (New York: Greenwood).

———————— (1982) *Freedom in the World. Political Rights and Civil Liberties 1982* (New York: Greenwood).

———————— (1984) *Freedom in the World. Political Rights and Civil Liberties 1983-84* (New York: Greenwood).

———————— (1985) *Freedom in the World. Political Rights and Civil Liberties 1984-85* (New York: Greenwood).

———————— (1987) *Freedom in the World. Political Rights and Civil Liberties 1986-87* (New York: Greenwood).

Gewirth, A. (1982) *Human Rights. Essays on Justification and Application* (Chicago: The Chicago University Press).

Goldsmith, A. (1986) 'Democracy, political stability, and economic growth in developing countries. Some evidence on Olson's theory on distributional coalitions', *Comparative Political Studies*, Vol. 18 No. 4, pp. 517-31.

Goldsmith, R. J. (1986) 'The Limitations of using quantitative data in analysing human rights abuses', *Human Rights Quarterly*, Vol. 8, No. 4, pp. 607-27.

Gorbachev, M. (1985) *Perestroika, New Thinking for our Country and the World* (London: Collins).

Goulet, D. (1974) 'Freedom does not exist in a vacuum', *Worldview*, November.

Graham, K. (1986) *The Battle for Democracy. Conflicts, Consensus and the Individual* (Brighton: Harvester Wheatsheaf).

Green D. G. (1987) *The New Right. The Counter-Revolution in Political, Economic and Social Thought* (Brighton: Wheatsheaf).

Hadenius, A. (1992) *Democracy and Development* (Cambridge: Cambridge University Press).

Hartman, J. F. (1985) 'Working Paper for the Committee of Experts on the Article 4 Derogation Provision', *Human Rights Quarterly*, Vol. 7, No. 1, pp. 89-131.

Henkin, A. H. (1979) *Human Dignity. The Internationalization of Human Rights* (New York: Aspen Institute for Humanistic Studies).

Henkin, L. ed. (1981) *The International Bill of Rights. The Covenant on Civil and Political Rights* (New York: Columbia University Press).

Higgins, R. (1988) 'Encouraging Human Right', *L. S. E. Quarterly*, Autumn, Vol. 5, No. 2, pp. 92-103.

Hill, R. J. and Zielonka, J. eds (1990) *Restructuring Eastern Europe* (Aldershot, Hants: Elgar).

Horn, R. (1993) *Statistical Indicators for Economic and Social Sciences* (Cambridge: Cambridge University Press).

Howard R. E. and Donnelly J. (1985) 'Human Dignity, Human Rights, and Political Regimes', *American Political Science Review*, Vol. 80, No. 2, pp 185-199.

Howard, R. E. (1983) 'The Full-Belly Thesis. Should Economic Rights take Priority over Civil and Political Rights? Evidence From Sub-Saharan Africa', *Human Rights Quarterly*, Vol. 5, No. 4, pp. 467-90.

_____ (1984) 'Evaluating Human Rights in Africa: Some problems of implicit comparisons', *Human Rights Quarterly*, Vol. 6, No. 2, pp. 160-179.

Humana, C. (1983) *World Human Rights Guide* (London: Hutchinson).

_____ (1986) *World Human Rights Guide* (London: Pan Books).

_____ (1992) *World Human Rights Guide* (Oxford, Oxford University Press).

Inkeles, A. ed. (1991) *On Measuring Democracy* (Brunswick and London: Transaction).

Jhabvala, F. (1984) 'The Practice of the Covenant's Human Rights Committee, 1976-1982: Review of State Reports', *Human Rights Quarterly*, Vol. 6, No. 1, pp. 81-106.

_____ (1985) 'The Soviet-Bloc's View in the Implementation of the Human Rights Record', *Human Rights Quarterly*, Vol. 7, No. 4, pp. 461-91.

Joyce, J. A. (1978) *The New Politics of Human Rights* (London: Macmillan).

Juviler, P. et al, eds (1993) *Human Rights for the 21st Century: Foundations for Hope: A US-Post Soviet Dialogue* (Armonk, NY and London: M. E. Sharpe).

Kaplan, J. (1989) 'Les Origines Juives des droits de l'homme', *Revue des Sciences Morales et Politiques,* 144 (1), pp. 15-24.

Keman, H. ed. (1993) *Comparative Politics. New Directions in Theory and Methods* (Amsterdam: V U University Press).

Kozyrev, A. (1992) 'Russia and Human Rights', *Slavic Review*, Vol. 51, No. 2, pp. 281-93.

Kurian, G. T. (1984) *The New Book of World Rankings* (London: Facts on File Publications).

Lane, D. (1985) *State and Politics in the USSR* (Oxford: Basil Blackwell).

Leng, S. C. (1981) 'Criminal Justice in Post-Mao China: Some Preliminary observations', *China Quarterly*, No. 87, pp. 155-68.

Lentini, P. (1991) 'Reforming the Electoral System: the 1989 elections to the USSR Congress of People's Deputies', *Journal of Communist Studies*, Vol. 7, No. 1, pp. 69-94.

Lipset, M. (1959) *Political Man* (London: Heinemann).

Lizhi, F. (1992) 'China is a World Problem', *Index on Censorship*, Vol. 21, No. 8, pp. 1-9.

Macfarlane, L. J. (1985) *The Theory and Practice of Human Rights* (London: Maurice Temple Smith).

Macpherson, C. B. (1972) *The Real World of Democracy* (Oxford: Oxford University Press).

Manheim, J. and Rich, R. (1986) *Empirical Political Analysis* (London: Longman).

Marks, S. P. (1980) 'The Peace - Human Rights - Development Dialectic', *Bulletin of Peace Proposals*, 11 (4) pp. 339-47.

_____ (1981) 'Emerging Human Rights: A New Generation for the 1980s', *Rutgers Law Review*, Vol. 33, No. 2, pp. 435-52.

McDougal. M. S. et al, (1980) *Human Rights and World Public Order* (New Haven: Yale University Press).

McGolrick, D. (1991) *The Human Rights Committee. Its Role in the Development of the International Covenant of Civil and Political Rights* (Oxford: Clarendon).

Medina, Q. C. (1988) *The Battle of Human Rights, gross systematic violations and the inter-American system* (Dordrecht: Martinus Nijhoff).

Mehl, R. (1989) 'Les Origines Protestantes des droits de l'homme', *Revue des Sciences Morales et Politiques*, 144 (1) pp. 39-51.

Morsink, J. (1984) 'The Philosophy of the Universal Declaration', *Human Rights Quarterly*, Vol. 6, No. 2, pp. 309-34.

Mrazer, J. (1990) 'Human Rights: Their international standards and protection', *Coexistence*, Vol. 27, No. 4, pp. 301-335.

Nanda, V. P. et al, eds (1981) *Global Human Rights: public policies, comparative measures and NGO strategies* (Boulder: Westview).

Neubauer, D. (1967) 'Some Conditions of Democracy', *American Political Science Review,* Vol. 61, No. 1, pp. 1002-9.

Novosti Press Agency, (1986) *The Concern for Human Rights. Real and False* (Moscow: Publishing House).

————————————— (1987) *Human Rights in the Capitalist World* (Moscow: Publishing House).

O'Manique, J. (1990) 'Universal and Inalienable Rights: A search for foundation', *Human Rights Quarterly*, Vol. 12, No. 4, pp. 465-85.

Osmanczyk, E. J. (1985) *Encyclopaedia of the United Nations and International Agreements* (Philadelphia and London: Taylor and Francis).

Pearson, L. B. (1969) *Partners in Development. Report of the Commission on International Development* (London: Pall Mall).

Pollis, A. and Schwab, P. eds (1979) *Human Rights. Cultural and Ideological Perspectives* (New York: Praeger).

Powell Jr, G. B. (1976) 'American voter turnout in comparative perspective', *American Political Science Review*, Vol. 80, No. 1, pp. 17-44.

Power, J. (1981) *Amnesty International. The Human Rights Story* (Oxford: Pergamon).

Quigley, T. (1974) ''Miss Freedom' Awards Are, at Best, Irrelevant', *Worldview*, November.

Ramcharan, B. G. ed. (1979) *Human Rights: Thirty Years after the Universal Declaration* (The Hague: Martinus Nijhoff).

Raphael, D. D. ed. (1967) *Political Theory and The Rights of Man* (London: Macmillan).

Rustow, D. A. (1967) *A World of Nations: Problems of Political Modernization* (Washington, D. C.: Brookings).

Renteln, A. (1990) *International Human Rights: Universalism versus Relativism* (Newbury Park: Sage).

Robertson, A. H. and Merills, J. G. (1992) *Human Rights in the World*, 3rd edition (Manchester: Manchester University Press).

Rosenbaum, A. ed. (1980) *The Philosophy of Human Rights. International Perspectives* (London: Aldwych).

Rozier, J. (1989) 'Sources Catholiques des droits de l'homme', *Revue des Sciences Morales et Politiques*, 144 (1) pp. 53-66.

Sartori, G. (1971) 'Concept Misinformation in Comparative Politics', *American Political Science Review,* Vol. 54, No. 4, pp. 1033-53.

_____ ed. (1984) *Social Sciences Concepts* (Beverley Hills: Sage).

Shue, H. (1980) *Basic Rights* (Princeton: Princeton University Press).

Sobel, L. A. (1978) *Political Prisoners. A world report* (New York: Amnesty International Publication).

Stokel, M. et al, (1986) 'State Violations of Human Rights: Issues and Problems of Measurement', Human Rights Quarterly, Vol. 8, No. 4, pp. 592-606.

Szymanski, A. (1984) *Human Rights in the Soviet Union* (London: Zed Books).

Tokes, R. L. (1979) *Opposition in Eastern Europe* (London: Macmillan).

Trehub, A. (1988) 'Human rights in the Soviet Union: Recent developments', *Radio Free Europe, Radio Liberty Research Bulletin*, 32nd year no. 8 (3473), 24 February.

United Nations (1968) Yearbook of the United Nations 1966 (New York: United Nations).

_____ (1971) Yearbook of the United Nations 1968 (New York: United Nations).

_____ (1972) Yearbook of the United Nations 1969 (New York: United Nations).

_____ (1974) Yearbook of the United Nations 1971 (New York: United Nations).

_____ (1975) Yearbook of the United Nations 1972 (New York: United Nations).

_____ (1980) Yearbook of the United Nations 1977 (New York: United Nations).

_____ (1990) Yearbook of the United Nations 1986 (New York: United Nations).

_____ (1986) (CCPR/1) Yearbook of the Human Rights Committee 1977-1978. Vol. 1. Summary Records of the Meetings of the First to the Fifth Sessions. (New York: United Nations).

_____ (1986) (CCPR/1/Add. 1) Yearbook of the Human Rights Committee 1977-1978. Vol. 2. Documents of the First to Fifth Session including the Reports of the Committee to the General Assembly. (New York: United Nations).

_____ (1986) (CCPR/2) Yearbook of the Human Rights Committee 1979-1980. Vol. 2. Summary Records of the Meetings of the Sixth to the Tenth Sessions. (New York: United Nations, 1986).

_____ (1986) (CCPR/2/Add. 2) Yearbook of the Human Rights Committee 1979-1980. Vol. 2. Documents of the Sixth to the Tenth Sessions including the Reports of the Committee to the General assembly. (New York: United Nations).

_____ (1989) (CCPR/3) Yearbook of the Human Rights Committee 1981-1982. Vol. 1. Summary Records of the Eleventh to the Sixteenth Sessions. (New York: United Nations).

_____ (1989) (CCPR/3/Add. 3) Yearbook of the Human Rights Committee 1981-1982. Vol. 3. Documents of the Eleventh to the Sixteenth Sessions including the Reports of the Committee to the General Assembly. (New York: United Nations).

_____ CCPR/C/SR. 928. 31 October 1989.

_____ CCPR/C/SR. 930. 1 November 1989.

_____ CCPR/C/SR. 942. 10 November 1989.

_____ CCPR/C/SR. 944. 13 November 1989.

_____ CCPR/C/SR. 943. 27 November 1989.

_____ CCPR/C/SR. 931. 27 November 1989.

_____ CCPR/C/SR. 945. 30 November 1989.

_____ Rules Of Procedures of the Human Rights Committee CCPR/C/3/Rev. 2. 14 December 1989.

_____ (1983) Basic Facts About the United Nations (New York: Department of Public Information).

_____ (1988) Yearbook of the United Nations 1984 Volume 38. (New York: Department of Public Information).

Vanhanen, T. (1984) *The Emergence of Democracy* (Helsinki: The Finnish Society of Sciences and Letters).

Vargas, D. U. (1984) 'La Troisiemme Generation des Droits de L'homme.' *Academie de Droit International*, (1) pp. 359-375.

Vasak, K. (1979) 'A 30-Year Struggle. The sustained effort to give force of law to the Universal Declaration of Human Rights', *UNESCO Courier*, November, 28-31.

Vincent, R. J. ed.(1986a) *Human Rights in International Relations* (Cambridge: Cambridge University Press).

_____ ed. (1986b) *Foreign Policy and Human Rights* (Cambridge: Cambridge University Press, 1986).

Walker, T. (1986) *Nicaragua. The Land of Sandino*, 2nd edition (Boulder and London: Westview).

Weston, B. (1984) 'Human Rights', *Human Rights Quarterly*, Vol. 6, No. 2, pp. 257-83.

White, S. (1991a) 'The Soviet Elections of 1989: From Acclamations to Limited Choice', *Coexistence*, Vol. 28, No. 4, pp. 513-39.

_____ (1992) *Gorbachev and After* (Cambridge: Cambridge University Press).

_____ et al, (1993) *The Politics of Transition* (Cambridge: Cambridge University Press).

_____ et al, (1990) *Communist and Post-Communist Political System*, 3rd edition (London: Macmillan).

Wilson, D. (1979) *Tito's Yugoslavia* (Cambridge: Cambridge University Press).

List of interviews:

1) Professor R. Higgins. A member of the Human Rights Committee, and Professor of International Law at the London School of Economics and Political Science. April, 1991.

2) Marie Staunton, Director of the British Section of Amnesty International, London. February 1989.

3) Students from Saudi Arabia, Exeter University. March 1989.
4) John Pace, Chief. External Relations and Prevention, United Nations Office in Geneva. July 1991.
5) Dr Joseph Ryan, Director, the Comparative Survey of Freedom, Freedom House, New York. May 1995.

Index